American Studies

American Studies

A USER'S GUIDE

*Philip J. Deloria and
Alexander I. Olson*

UNIVERSITY OF CALIFORNIA PRESS

University of California Press, one of the most distinguished university presses in the United States, enriches lives around the world by advancing scholarship in the humanities, social sciences, and natural sciences. Its activities are supported by the UC Press Foundation and by philanthropic contributions from individuals and institutions. For more information, visit www.ucpress.edu.

University of California Press
Oakland, California

Library of Congress Cataloging-in-Publication Data

Names: Deloria, Philip Joseph, author. | Olson, Alexander I., 1979– author.
Title: American studies : a user's guide / Philip J. Deloria and Alexander I. Olson.
Description: Oakland, California : University of California Press, [2017] | Includes bibliographical references and index. | Identifiers: LCCN 2017007892 (print) | LCCN 2017013685 (ebook) | ISBN 9780520962699 (ebook) | ISBN 9780520296794 (cloth : alk. paper) | ISBN 9780520287730 (pbk. : alk. paper)
Subjects: LCSH: United States—Study and teaching. Classification: LCC E175.8 (ebook) | LCC E175.8 .D45 2017 (print) | DDC 973.007—dc23
LC record available at https://lccn.loc.gov/2017007892

Manufactured in the United States of America

26 25 24 23 22 21 20 19 18 17
10 9 8 7 6 5 4 3 2 1

In memory of Michael Lewis Goldberg

Nations reel and stagger on their way; they make hideous mistakes; they commit frightful wrongs; they do great and beautiful things. And shall we not best guide humanity by telling the truth about all of this, so far as the truth is ascertainable?

W. E. B. DU BOIS

Follow the money, and tell good stories.

CARLO ROTELLA

CONTENTS

Introduction

THE OBJECT OF AMERICAN STUDIES

AN INTRODUCTION SHOULD *INTRODUCE*, RIGHT? And we take that obligation seriously. The "we," in this case, is composed of Phil Deloria and Alex Olson, your guides through this adventure in the field of American Studies. Both of us teach it, study it, write it, and are—like you—students of the field itself. We're pleased to meet you. In what follows, we'd like to introduce you to this book, and to offer you a place from which to begin your work in American Studies. We'll start by proposing a working definition of American Studies, a field that resists definition at every turn. Then we'll summarize the rest of the book, offering a few thoughts on how you might or might not read it. And then we'll dive right in. Let's begin, though, with three quick notes on music, which we offer as helpful analogies—invitations to start thinking about this book, and about how one learns the complex thing that is American Studies.

Note One (Alex here): There's a bit of folklore that in the early days of rock and roll, when singles were released on 45s (so named because they played on a turntable at 45 revolutions per minute), you could learn a song by slowing the turntable down to 33 1/3 or even 16 rpm. A whole generation of musicians learned something about their craft by slowing down the records this way (figure 1). Today, of course, you can buy apps that slow down digital songs, allowing a guitar player to learn them note by note—and to do so with relative ease. One song that sounds fantastic at a slower speed is Dolly Parton's "Jolene." Check it out.

Note Two (Phil here): I have checked it out. It does indeed sound great—and the song itself is worth a critical close look. As a terrible songwriter in my own right, I've been teaching a short course on ... acoustic songwriting. I've designed it so that my students learn about what makes a good song, what

FIGURE I. Slowing down the records. Photograph by Anton Hooijdonk.

kinds of processes great songwriters use, and the basic necessities of music theory and literary technique. But really? One powerful motive for the class is to force *me* to think *systematically* about what goes into a good song, and maybe help me become a better writer. So the class writes in various forms (blues and ballads to begin, then more complex forms), and we break apart our favorite songs to see what makes them tick. Our goal is not to simply reproduce, in new flavors, the songs we like, but rather to move beyond those songs and to allow our own creativity to flourish. To that end, our final exercises include questioning or rejecting everything familiar, all the stuff we've just learned! We embrace dissonant harmonies (or no harmonies at all!), weird and shifting time signatures and beats, discordant melodies, anti-rhyming and inconsistent lyrical patterns, and challenging performance styles. It's crazy and it's fun, and while most of us will retreat into more familiar alt-folk-acoustic territory, that territory does in fact look different after we've learned the craft and then pushed the boundaries. And some of our writers stay on the edge and write interesting and challenging songs. It's all good.

Note Three (Alex again): I love the idea of practicing songwriting by riffing on what's already out there. The world of music is enormous, and your creative juices will flow very differently depending on whether you're listening to Mozart or Madonna, Ella Fitzgerald or Elliott Smith. But all of these draw on practices that take shape, more or less, as "rules." In some traditions, listeners have expectations that music will have a tonal center ("It's in the key of C"), and that a piece will (likely) begin and (almost certainly) end on that center. That's a "rule." But I put the "scare quotes" around the word "rule" because, as in most creative endeavors, rules are something to learn and, sometimes, something to challenge and transcend. A good song (like a good essay) will play by the rules enough to bring us into its world, even as it bends the rules in order to pique our interest—and maybe even to say something new and important.

You may be thinking, "I like music well enough, but what does this have to do with American Studies?" One of the ways human beings are wired to think—perhaps the oldest way—is through comparison and analogy. We find things that are like one another (mostly), and shift between those things, noting points of similarity and difference, and layering up a rich sense of both. Sometimes it's a bad habit. We humans tend to make sense of difficult questions by replacing them with similar but easier questions that we already understand. But it can also be very useful. You probably already know a lot about music—even if you've never had formal training—and by analogy we hope that you can convert some of that knowledge about music into new knowledge about American Studies. So what are the lessons you might consider?

First, the field of American Studies is almost as wide as that enormous field of music we just talked about. American Studies, as one of our colleagues has observed, is not defined by what it chooses to include, but by what it *refuses to exclude*—which is pretty much everything. There are writers who take very different stances on "the rules," from close adherence to constant rejection—and everything in between. For some, American Studies means something like classic literary criticism or cultural history. For others, it means pushing back against the very idea of "discipline." For some, it's closely grounded in the folk, mass, and popular culture of the United States. Others see the U.S. as an important—but not all-defining—pivot point in a global and transnational circuit of people, ideas, money, and goods. American Studies is in close dialogue with a number of adjacent fields—ethnic studies, queer studies, disability studies, environmental studies, and more. It has almost always been linked, in one way or another, to questions of politics and social justice, and it has encouraged a scholarship that emanates from pressing social issues, one that takes seriously the past and present of those issues. Scholars in American Studies often bring a particular passion and intensity to their work that has its roots in a desire to change the world—and thus, to change the social, political, and economic "rules" that have structured unevenness and inequality.

That's important to know, since this book is, in effect, about "the rules"—which is to say, the *methods* through which many writers have successfully approached American Studies—and some of its partner fields—in the past. It is tempting to treat the rules of an intellectual field like the laws of a police state: oppressive dictates that stifle creativity and should be questioned and perhaps undone. This temptation is especially strong when people criticize our work. But this is an example of an *unhelpful* analogy. The "rules" of an intellectual field are not laws but invitations to creativity. The "rules" of American Studies are more like the rules of a board game or bowling league; you can always create your own house rules, but it's still worth learning the more standardized rules if you want to play with people outside your immediate circle of friends. It seems to us that becoming familiar with some common rules can actually help American Studies (and allied) scholars in the work of understanding and explaining the nature of inequalities and dominations. So we want to be clear: we are not trying to dictate ironclad "rules"—because where's the fun in that?—but to *describe practices* that have proven helpful to many people thinking about American Studies, and that many scholars continue to use to great advantage. This book is an open invitation to think more about an open field—it's a user's guide, not an owner's manual.

On the other hand, it's important to know that this book is also not a textbook. It's written with examples, not exercises. We've tried to fit our digressions into a narrative, rather than boxing them off in a set of sidebars. A user's guide aims to split the difference between the "Do this! Learn this!" quality of a textbook and the open, welcoming spirit of American Studies scholarship. Other authors have tried to make sense of American Studies by, among other things, breaking it into a set of "paradigm dramas" (Gene Wise); surveying a range of "keywords" (Bruce Burgett and Glenn Hendler); assembling essay collections on emergent themes (Lucy Maddox); and explaining links to adjacent fields like queer studies and ethnic studies (Robyn Wiegman). We'll draw from all of these ways of thinking about the field, but a book like this will inevitably be a bit idiosyncratic, slanting more toward things we know and care about. Undoubtedly, you know and care about other things. Your opportunity lies in making connections between your interests and whatever insights you can take from the histories and methods that we discuss. If you should find yourself thinking that we're bossy textbook writers, please know that we are respectfully assuming you are quite capable of making your own decisions about how you do or do not use this book.

Second, *American Studies: A User's Guide* is meant to be something like that songwriting class. We want to summarize practices as a way of consolidating your American Studies knowledge and then allowing and encouraging creativity, both within the familiar structures and sometimes in *relation to* the structures themselves. We have found that in creative expression and scholarship alike, mastery of the "rules" is actually critical to pushing beyond them. You may wake up one day, start throwing paint on canvas, and claim to be an artist of abstraction—it happens!—but your work would have far more meaning, depth, and texture if you studied art history, learned to draw, acquired a sense of color theory, mastered techniques, and *then* stepped outside of them. Knowing "the rules" and questioning the rules are not mutually exclusive; in fact, those actions are tightly linked. One useful way to achieve the knowledge of practices is through structured study and examples, something like a class. We hope to provide that to you. Our own view is that it is possible to know a complicated field like American Studies through its past (that is, its history and historiography) and its methodology (that is, the ways in which it has practiced its craft past and present).

Third, it's important to us to play those 45s at 33 1/3, to *slow down the song* so that you can learn the notes. Too often, in our experience, American Studies classes offer up interesting work in the field without slowing down to really think through, note by note, how a project works. What kinds of sources did she use, and how did she interpret them? What's an archive and can I build one of my own? How did she make her argument fit so seamlessly into a narrative? What are the theoretical roots of the piece? How can I create a richly sourced, incisively argued, beautifully narrated, theoretically interesting piece of writing? What might look easy when we are reading an American Studies book or article turns out to be quite difficult when we are taking a stab at it ourselves. In this book, we hope to serve as *guides,* offering techniques and frameworks that can help you both produce your own work, and productively read the work of others.

THE OBJECT OF AMERICAN STUDIES

Before you can practice American Studies, you have to know what it is— which calls for a definition. But we need to tread carefully. When taken as gospel, definitions have a way of ending conversations instead of starting them. By contrast, in the tradition of philosophical pragmatism—which has heavily influenced our thinking—definitions are generated by practices rather than vice versa. When practices change in a field like American Studies, so do its definitions. With this in mind, let's start with a simple, provisional definition and then see how it checks out:

American Studies is an interdisciplinary practice that aims to understand the multiplicity of the social and cultural lives of people in—and in relation to—the United States, both past and present.

Like most definitions of complicated things, this one piles words and phrases together, each one chosen to evoke certain specific ideas and histories. Other people, interested in emphasizing other ideas, might well offer competing definitions. This one hardly closes the book on the possibilities. What it does offer is a provisional series of boundaries that help establish what it is you care about. Boundaries illuminate the "object" of American Studies—that is, the complicated "things" that we seek to understand through interpretation and analysis. So let's break the definition down into four of its most important constituent words: "interdisciplinary," "America / United States" (since these exist in relation to one another), "social," and "cultural." We'll take them in reverse order.

Culture

Our first lesson is upon us, before we can even catch our breath. Since definitions of words rely upon other words (and each new word of course carries its own definitions) we can immediately see that no definition of anything will ever be final. We can chase strings of words forever! This does not mean that words lack meaning. Rather, in coming to understand something, we weave our way through complex chains. One word leads us to another. Which leads us to another, and another . . . and so on through a network of meaning. You might think that this network just gets more and more confusing. But that's not quite right. Actually, it becomes better and richer with each new connection.

Let us give you an example (figure 2). This is Bella. You might start by noting that she's a dog. But what, exactly, *is* a dog? It is easy to slide down a slippery slope of biological attributes that seem to define a dog; for example: a dog is a mammal. But what is a mammal? Flip to the "M" pages of the dictionary. You'll find that a mammal is vertebrate; it has hair, three middle ear bones, a neocortex, and mammary glands. You can see the problem. To

FIGURE 2. Bella.

This is not a cigar. [handwritten annotation in left margin]

go down this road, you'll have to flip to "V" for vertebrate, "H" for hair, "N" for neocortex, and so on. Your sense of Bella will get deeper with every turn of the page—until it doesn't. Bella is a more complex creature who requires that you put down the dictionary and start thinking about *culture*.

We can start with those big eyes and floppy ears, which make Bella's image tantalizingly shareable online. We might assume people own dogs for companionship, but there's also the possibility that her image can help garner validation for one human (her owner) from other humans (her owner's friends) on social media. In that sense, the picture reflects a kind of contemporary fashion shoot, and it's changing what it means to be a "dog" as we speak. Instead of simply a pet and an owner, we're dealing with an image and its viewers. This shift has consequences beyond the realm of aesthetics. Many people find their companion animals through online clearinghouses, where pictures like these are posted with profiles unnervingly similar to dating websites. In this context, working dogs like German shepherds and pit bulls often lose out. They have long histories as companion animals, with a wide range of personalities, energy levels, and obsessions. But are they cute enough to generate likes on Instagram?

Of course, there is a danger that you might lose track of poor Bella in all this ruminating on the idea of a "cute dog." She has never heard of Facebook; she just wants to roll in the grass or play with a chew toy. But you are just as likely to find that your understanding of Bella has become richer and more complex. That's a good thing. More than a good thing, actually, because it also points us to the complexities of "culture." A rich sense of Bella is a *cultural* sense, one concerned with the concepts and practices we've imagined together as groups of human beings sharing common languages and histories. Our furry friends are part of this story, shaping how we relate to one another.

Perhaps no single word calls issues of language and meaning to our attention more thoroughly than "culture." There are scores of definitions from which to choose, but before we propose one, let us take a look at some of the elements we might want to consider:

- Culture can be described as a *form or pattern* that helps structure the thought and behavior of human beings in groups.

- Culture can also be described as a *practice*—the actual thinking and doing of people—that is rooted in a world of meanings.

- These practices and meanings have a *history*. That is, they have developed over time through human action, and they continue to develop. They also have a recognizable character, which circumscribes future human action. In other words, culture is about patterns and forms that guide actions and make them sensible to others.

- Culture operates across *multiple scales* of group cohesion. The larger the group of people, the more difficult the concept is to use. A large category—a national culture, for instance—is full of regional and local cultures, subcultures, sub-subcultures, microcultures, countercultures, alternative cultures, and more. These subcultures are rarely in harmony or alignment with one another.

- Culture is *public*. It cannot be limited to private fantasy, but must be shared. Our inner worlds certainly draw content from culture, but selfhood alone is not enough for calling something a cultural activity. Even at the smallest scale, relationships are a necessary ingredient.

- Culture is transmitted through human actions and human-created objects. Each act of transmission carries the past of culture forward into the future. It's historical. And yet, culture *changes*. Each transmission of culture—from one generation to the next, from one social group to another, from one person to another—also carries the possibility for the transformation of culture.

- In this way, culture is both the repository of familiar traditions that determine how we will face the future ("we do things this way, not that way!") *and* a constantly moving target that does not necessarily determine anything ("let's try something a little different this time, okay?"). Though it changes mostly through small tweaks and adjustments over time, there are plenty of instances in which cultures have been radically and rapidly remade.

- As the domain of meaning, culture can be usefully disaggregated from other human worlds: the economic world in which we exchange value; the political world in which we structure our collective governance; the legal world in which we establish laws for our conduct; the ethical world in which we decide upon right and wrong; the social world in which we interact with one another as people; the psychological world of our inner beings.

- At the same time, culture is inseparable from each of these worlds; they are, in turn, inseparable from one another. You cannot consider our economic or political behavior, for example, without thinking about culture. We split these things apart in order to analyze graspable pieces of the whole. Culture, then, is (among other things) a particular *analytical category* that we use to think about a particular aspect of human life—the one concerned with meanings.

As you can see, these elements have a tendency to circle around one another, exchanging different, overlapping meanings as we use different words: pattern, transmission, history, analysis. With this cluster of meanings buzzing about our heads, we can now venture a definition:

Culture is the word we use to describe the ways we think about (1) the transmission and transformation of meanings, (2) the practices that situate those meanings in the world, and (3) the full range of consequences surrounding those meanings: how they structure our senses of self, group, and world; how they both delimit and open up possibilities for being and becoming; how they cross social, political, and other kinds of boundaries; how they change through creative activity; and how they serve as sites of contest and consent.

And, thus, the first payoff: American Studies takes as one of its central objects the question of *culture*, particularly as it has been applied to the human beings inhabiting the place we call the United States of America. By framing "culture" not only as practices and meanings, but as the *analytical category* that we use to think about those things, we take our first step down the road to the question of methods and methodology, which is one goal of this book—to think through the question "how might one do American Studies?"

Social

Culture is a lived experience, an exercise in meaning conducted by human beings in relation to one another. That category—humans acting in relation to one another—we have given another name: "social." If not quite as complex as "culture," this term is nonetheless a slippery concept. It too has distinct elements worth naming.

- The word itself takes its root from the Latin word for "allies," which suggests that social relations are characterized by direct intent and an idea of mutual benefit. That's a start, but maybe it's a little too blunt.
- Others—Karl Marx, for instance—have argued that humans are simply born "social": we do not survive without some form of association and cooperation. Of course, such association and cooperation can take many different shapes and forms, including various levels of coercion.
- The sociologist Max Weber suggested if, in your interactions with others, you take into account the consequences of your actions, and of their actions, you are being "social."

These give us three distinct pictures of sociality, operating at three interlocking registers. First, there is a sense that we join with one another in social cohesion in order to advance our collective interests in relation to *other* groups of people. We become allies with one another in relation to "those other people," those "outsiders." In other words, we create a "we"—and that creation implies the simultaneous creation of one or more "theys." Second, there is the sense in which the term "social" might focus not only on insider / outsider dynamics, but on the mechanics through which we, as social creatures, interact with one another. And third, there is a sense in which the individual person experiences and participates in social interactions and social worlds. To be social is to act and imagine along overlapping vectors: "me," "us," "we," and "them."

Social worlds are tightly connected to cultural formations. Indeed, it has long been convenient—and often useful—to delineate cultures by mapping them onto social groups. You know the most prominent categories already: race, class, gender, sexuality, age, nation, religion, ability, and more. Your identity lies somewhere in the intersection of these categories. Paradoxically, these identities are seen as essential to one's nature—and able to be transgressed and questioned. The critic Michael Warner calls it a mistake to think of social relations in terms of "ascriptive belonging," or as something you *are* instead of something you *do*. This is because we join in the social world of "publics" (or in norm-busting "counterpublics") only through participation and attention. Identity is linked to discrete cultural expressions, some practiced by millions and others by small, clandestine communities. Indeed, culture is often the ground upon which social categories are questioned and transgressed. How much "white" "American" culture has its origins in African American social experience? Um . . . lots and lots! In the late 1940s, Richard Penniman, later known as the singer Little Richard, was active in Southern interracial drag culture as "Princess Lavonne, Freak of the World." When making the jump from queer counterpublic to mass popular musical culture a few years later, Little Richard brought with him practices and styles from the social world of drag—hidden in plain sight.

There are a nearly infinite number of social categories, limited only by the human imagination and our capacities for interaction. Some focus on choices and affinities: riot grrrls, evangelicals, hackers, hipsters, hunters. Others trade on spatial locations: Detroit, Appalachia, the Delta, Beverly Hills. But none of these are neutral. All work to construct the hierarchies and fault lines that divide people as well as bring them together. You can't understand the flows and fields and contests surrounding *culture* without understanding the ways cultures function in relation to social groups. Revolutionary social groups strive to produce revolutionary culture. Dominant social groups strive to impose their cultural norms and values on subordinate groups. Curiously, dominant groups *also* frequently admire and appropriate the cultural practices of the groups they oppress. By the same token, marginalized social groups often use mainstream cultural forms to critique domination, counter despair, and imagine dreams for the future. We don't think you can do American Studies without paying close attention to the ways human beings interact with one another. We'll have much more to say about these two categories—the "social" and the "cultural"—but for now, let's focus on one particular social boundary, imagined around the complicated idea of the *nation*.

America / United States

As a field, American Studies has taken on different names in different places. Some colleges and universities have programs in American Culture or American Civilization. Such names reflect the fact that understanding *culture* has been central to American Studies. Words like "civilization" reflect "culture" less overtly, but with no less force (of which more, later). The word that has not shifted in any of these examples is, of course, *American* (which turns out to be as complicated an idea as culture, and maybe even more contentious). It represents a third object of American Studies. People have tried to pin down *America* for more than four centuries; those writings and utterances have created distinct clusters of ideas, many of which continue to be used today, most evocatively in the words of politicians and leaders seeking to create a shared sense of national unity. You might ask, for example, how many of these seem familiar.

> What then is the American, this new man? ... He is an American, who, leaving behind him all his ancient prejudices and manners, receives new ones from the new mode of life he has embraced, the new government he obeys, and the new rank he holds.
> J. Hector St. John de Crèvecoeur, *Letters from an American Farmer* (1782)

> American social development has been continually beginning over again on the frontier. This perennial rebirth, this fluidity of American life, this expansion westward with its new opportunities, its continuous touch with the simplicity of primitive society, furnish the forces dominating American character.
> Frederick Jackson Turner, "The Significance of the Frontier in American History" (1893)

> It was not particular environments that determined the American character or created the American type, but the whole of the American environment— the sense of spaciousness, the invitation to mobility, the atmosphere of independence, the encouragement to enterprise and to optimism.
> Henry Steele Commager, *The American Mind: An Interpretation of American Thought and Character since the 1880s* (1950)

We could take each of these writings as key moments in a particularly *American* kind of studies, aimed at understanding the nature of cultural life in the United States. J. Hector St. John de Crèvecoeur wrote during the earliest years of the nation, and he emphasized not only the newness and potential of American government and culture, but the transformative quality of the New World itself. Diverse people would "melt" together to create a new people, or what he described as "this new man." A century later, Frederick Jackson Turner contemplated the end of the frontier, and argued that the experience of westward expansion explained something he called "American character." By the middle of the twentieth century, Henry Steele Commager and many American Studies scholars would be trying to describe the "American mind"—a unique configuration of history, culture, and shared identity.

Each of these writers thought that there was something special about America. Whether it was the influence of the New World environment, the presence of divine guidance, the development of new political institutions, or the equalizing possibility of economic opportunity, there was *something* in America's location, history, and possibility that made Americans different from other peoples. Figuring out the various *somethings* that made Americans *Americans* offered American Studies its earliest impetus, and it is one that takes us back to the eighteenth century. But these traditions hardly exhaust the ways writers have tried to make sense of America. Let's look at a few others.

One ever feels his twoness—an American, a Negro, two souls, two thoughts, two unreconciled strivings; two warring ideals in one dark body, whose strength alone keeps it from being torn asunder.
W.E.B. Du Bois, *The Souls of Black Folk* (1903)

I give my right hand to the Occidentals and my left to the Orientals, hoping that between them they will not utterly destroy the insignificant connecting link.
Sui Sin Far (Edith Maude Eaton), "Leaves from the Mental Portfolio of an Eurasian" (1909)

The status of the immigrant who came to America because he *willed to do so* and had an end in view, the status of the slave who was *forced to come,* and the status of the American native who was here, in their original form, all differ. It is one thing to say, "I came because I desired to rule," another thing to say, "I came because I was compelled to serve," and quite another thing to say, "I was here and this continent was mine."
Arthur C. Parker, "Problems of Race Assimilation in America" (1916)

The U.S.-Mexican border *es una herida abierta* [is an open wound] where the Third World grates against the first and bleeds. And before a scab forms it hemorrhages again, the lifeblood of two worlds merging to form a third country—a border culture. Borders are set up to define the places that are safe and unsafe, to distinguish *us* from *them*. A border is a dividing line, a narrow strip along a steep edge. A borderland is a vague and undetermined place created by the emotional residue of an unnatural boundary.
Gloria Anzaldúa, *Borderlands / La Frontera: The New Mestiza* (1987)

Yes, and this is how you are a citizen: Come on. Let it go. Move on.
Claudia Rankine, *Citizen: An American Lyric* (2014)

The United States was never simply a land in which white settlers labored to create new political institutions, social relations, and cultural meanings. It was also a land of unevenness and domination. We know these stories, too, and we know them *also* to be foundationally "American": the conquest of the continent, the terrors of the slave trade, the labor regimes that recruited and controlled immigrants, the oppressions of gender, class, race, and religion. W. E. B. Du Bois understood that the historical trauma of slavery would always be embedded within that thing called *America.* Arthur C. Parker insisted on the recognition of conquest and the aboriginal ownership—still contested—of the continent. Gloria Anzaldúa and Sui Sin Far wrote, like Du Bois, of the terrors of twoness, of borders that are gaping wounds, and people in danger of being torn apart. And Claudia Rankine reflects on how people of color are expected to simply ignore this trauma as a condition for full citizenship.

Anthropologists have labored long and hard to define "culture," and their definitions are everywhere. In this particular discussion—concerning America—there are fewer explicit definitions to guide us, and a number of divergent experiences. What we do have, however, are a series of powerful *assumptions,* often unquestioned, that have *seemed* to function as definitions. Many of these turn out to be dubious. Consider the following examples:

- Many people assume that "America" is the same thing as the nation-state called "the United States." But these are not the same thing. People of the *Americas* (that is, those across the Western Hemisphere) have rightly objected to this conflation of terms. So maybe we should talk about "United States Studies" rather than American Studies. Or, if we stick with "American Studies," perhaps we should expand our horizons to a broadly hemispheric, if not global, perspective?

- We often hear that the United States is *exceptional*—that its history and experience are not only *distinct* but *unique,* and that this radical distinction marks its superiority over other nations. This "American exceptionalism" has a long history in the United States. It turns out, under closer inspection, that the United States has many practices and processes in common with other countries. The claim to be exceptional and special is more *political* than historical. Indeed, politicians often compete to see who can affirm this idea most emphatically.

- There is an assumption that the United States as a *nation* maps coherently onto the *culture* of the people living within its boundaries. Culture, as we have seen, is too fluid a concept to be adequately contained by rigid

State vs Nation (togetherness of people)

political boundaries. When we speak of things such as "French culture," we might be referring to certain practices that *do* map—somewhat—onto the political unit that is France. But those things surely do not encompass *all* the makings and expressions of culture that take place in France—which is, by all measures, an increasingly diverse place struggling over the very meaning of "French culture."

- So we should once again remind ourselves that there is no single culture of the United States, no such thing as a distinct "American mind" or "American character." Rather, there are multiple *cultures*—each transforming, each overlapping, each struggling and fighting and sharing with one another. Some scholars have noted that cultural segregation is actually on the upswing, as the geographic mobility of a flexible labor market makes it easier to seek out like-minded friends and neighbors. The writer Bill Bishop has called this "the big sort."

- And we might go further: those multiple cultures do not exist simply within the territorial boundaries of the United States. From the very beginning, cultural practices have flowed across American borders from around the world. That fluidity has accelerated over time—demographically, politically, economically, and culturally—with a proliferation of free trade agreements and multinational treaty organizations. *Melting Pot.*

Whoa! America is vanishing before our very eyes! But let's not throw the baby out with the bathwater. It is a fact that the United States—existing as a nation-state—is *not* Canada, *not* Mexico, *not* France. Scholars have pointed out that the United States has developed a number of powerful homogenizing institutions—a single economy, a unified legal system, and a federal political structure, among others—that channel American worldviews in constricted ways. The familiar metaphor of the "melting pot" implies an endgame, a kind of final moment in which the varied streams of immigrants and natives eventually pour their lives into a thing called "America." But if we reject the exceptionalism of concepts like "the American mind," and note instead the porosity of the boundaries that define the United States itself, we might find ourselves with a different set of possibilities.

What if, for example, we imagine American Studies as a series of conversational layers? Its version of "America" might look something like this:

- As *a physical place* that is the United States, or perhaps the Western Hemisphere, with oceans and cities, mountains and rivers, borders and crossings that open out to other physical places around the world. People, objects, and "nature" flow in and out of this place. The consequences of this flow are varied: sometimes devastating, sometimes amazing, often both at once.

- As *a social world,* built around myriad relationships and categories of identity. These relations are often brutal, as the lines that define and distinguish people are not eradicated, but continually negotiated and changed.

Conur
- As *an institutional world,* full of structures that both generate multiplicity and constrain Americans' abilities to think outside of surprisingly narrow boundaries.

- As *a cultural field*—not simply the *product* of "many cultures" interacting but also an open ground of exchange and a space for the creation of "the new." Such a field cannot be adequately conceived outside of the worlds of educational, political, economic, and legal institutions.

- As *an imaginary,* a set of dreams and ideals that motivate people to believe, think, and act in certain ways.

In the beginning, the object of American Studies emerged out of the mutual relation between "American" (as in the United States) and "culture" (as in the expressions and sensibilities that seemed "American"). Raymond Williams once suggested a concept that may be useful to us here: the *structure of feeling,* which refers to shared cultural contents—feelings rather than thoughts—that are not fully emerged or understood in the world of "the official." Williams saw such structures as evolving into visible trajectories.[1] But perhaps it is most useful to recognize that *Americanness*—as often as it has been articulated—continues to exist in so many cases as a set of feelings, dissolved in the water, distributed in the air. Sometimes—in the pageantry of political conventions, for example—these feelings are highly staged and on display for all to see. As often, however, these structures of feeling are diffuse and uncertain, omnipresent, but not so easily made visible.

The relation between the official "United States" and the cultural "America" will inevitably take us to other categories of analysis. In American Studies, the United States is now seen in terms of its internal complexities and its transnational and international contexts—that is, its relations with people in other nations, and with forces and people that exist "in between" or outside of those other nations. And the possibility of a unique American "character" has given way to the complex relations among social groups and the ways these take shape not simply in terms of culture, but across a whole range of possibilities.

We have been wrestling with the big aims and goals of American Studies, but at the outset we promised to try to see how our definition matched up against the actual practice of the field. To do so, we need to make sense of the idea that American Studies is *interdisciplinary,* and to get there, we need to turn our attention toward the institutional structure of American colleges and universities, and in particular, to a moment in the last half of the nineteenth century, when universities and faculty members were consolidating themselves around *disciplines.*

Interdisciplinary

Disciplines are those bodies of knowledge through which we have organized and asked questions about our world. They are easily visualized as the units that structure most of our universities, which have departments of history, sociology, physics, biology, and the like. Why does this matter? Time for a quick historical detour.

In medieval times, when scholarship was the product of religious institutions in the West, scholars did their work in four areas of disciplinary study: theology, medicine, canon (or church) law, and the arts. Faculties of science and philosophy came into being in the seventeenth and eighteenth centuries as the Enlightenment pushed scholarship in a more secular direction. By the late nineteenth century, disciplines began to proliferate in number and in scope. It became apparent that there were interesting things to say, in a focused and specialized way, about law, politics, social relations, exchange, subsistence, aesthetic expression, communication, thought, and emotion. Indeed, the narrowing of inquiry into these discrete bundles allowed rapid acceleration in the making of knowledge itself. And so the disciplines of legal studies, political science, sociology and anthropology, economics, communications studies, psychology, art, and literature emerged within the framework of the university system.

We should pay attention to the actual word "discipline," for it too has multiple possibilities for meaning. Perhaps most important is the way that the word suggests a kind of regulation or ordering of knowledge that must be adhered to if one is allowed to claim membership in "a discipline." Not just anybody, in other words, can hang out a shingle announcing herself as a "historian" or "physicist." There are rules! Indeed, when you think about another meaning of the word—"discipline" as a form of punishment or consequence for some kind of transgression—you can see how the two definitions work

Curriculum

together. The creation of an intellectual "discipline" requires the "disciplin-ing" of the membership, so that everyone stays more or less in line. A new graduate student follows a rigorous course of study determined by an exclusive group of professional practitioners. She must pass an examination certifying her as possessed of the knowledge required by the discipline. And she must produce her own small subset of knowledge defined as part of the discipline and following the rules laid out by its professional practitioners.

It's all quite prescribed, isn't it? In the United States today, this sequence produces a PhD dissertation, which then, in theory, allows you to teach at the level of the university or college. The rules of the discipline—policed by journals, peer reviewers, professional associations, publishers, departments, hiring committees, and tenure requirements—determine what kinds of subjects we study and write about, what kinds of evidence we use, how we use that evidence, and what kinds of "truths" we try to prove. These rules keep disciplines distinct from one another, and often also reflect how disciplines jockey for status relative to one another.

But wait. Are disciplines really so contained? Consider boundary-crossing stuff like "the historical novel" (is it history or is it fiction?) or "environmental history" (is it history or is it biology?) or "culture and personality" (is it anthropology or is it psychology?). Disciplines are categories, but they have never been as autonomous and self-contained as scholars have imagined. People have always been trying to escape.

Think back to the last time you were *disciplined*—you may well remember feeling that you wanted to push back against the rules even more. The anti-disciplinary streak in the modern research university was obvious from the start, in terms of the number and variety of *subdisciplines* contained (barely!) by the disciplines. In fact, subdisciplines acted as central points of articulation with other disciplines. If you studied history, for example, you could imagine subdisciplines such as legal history, political history, social history, art history, or economic history. Each was linked to another discipline. Intellectual boundary-crossers are always looking for, and finding, like-minded souls, and as they do, they continually push the limits of disciplines.

Many scholars who think about disciplines have defined interdisciplinarity as the *mastery* of two or more fields, such that their methodologies blend together to form a new practice. A cross-disciplinary or interdisciplinary scholar retains a disciplinary legibility, then, even while creating a practice that aims to transcend it. Eventually, new practices are consolidated, new rules are written, and new structures are invented to support what becomes a new interdisciplinary field. We see this all the time in the contemporary university setting, with the creation of new fields such as neuroscience, biophysics, complex systems, informatics, and the like. We also saw it in the 1960s and 1970s, when inter-, multi-, cross-, and trans-disciplinary efforts sprang up everywhere. Scholars found it illuminating and exhilarating to "blur genres," as the anthropologist Clifford Geertz put it, to transgress the boundaries between disciplines and borrow the methods, sources, questions, and subjects of other fields to open up their minds and broaden their horizons. It was a liberating way of thinking well suited to that moment in time, and it has been with us ever since, accelerating as we've come to understand that if *knowledge* is often made through a narrowing of one's focus, *problems* are more likely to be solved by more expansive ways of thinking.

And thus, to the point: American Studies was one of the *first* interdisciplinary areas of inquiry, emerging in the 1930s out of crossings between history, literature, anthropology, and (it turns out) many other disciplines. In the years between then and whatever "now" you happen to occupy, many of the writers and thinkers who cared about American Studies worked hard to define it as a particular kind of interdisciplinary practice and to fill it with all kinds of methods, ideas, theories, and shared assumptions. Others, it is worth noting, resisted any and all efforts to define an "American Studies method." Many emphasized the idiosyncratic nature of the field, arguing that a writer in American Studies would devise his or her own method from a constellation of interdisciplinary possibilities. All of the strategies we'll pursue in this book have shared their history with the development of American Studies as an *interdisciplinary field.* As you can imagine, there have been agreements and disagreements, innovations and retrenchments, debates and discussions. It's no wonder, then, that we need an anchor point, a place from which to begin.

We have divided this book into three main sections: histories, methods, and writing. In the first section, you'll find three chapters narrating the past of American Studies. Its first chapter offers a brief explanation of how and why we think it important to grapple with American Studies historiography. The next chapter offers a series of "mixtapes"—great tunes that trace a broad, *text-based history* of the field of American Studies over more than two centuries. It surveys a range of writers, past and present, who have considered the cultures and meanings surrounding the United States and the idea of "America." The third chapter offers an *institutional history* of the field, exploring how the story changes when you shift from books and articles to seemingly dry organizational issues like budgets, course offerings, and conferences. Together, these chapters illuminate how American Studies has struggled with the concept of "method." We will explore the field's turns to popular culture, ethnic studies, transnationalism, and a range of emergent areas, often tightly linked to social movements and identities outside the academy.

In the second section, you will find four methodological "toolkits" that cover a wide set of possibilities for interpretation, analysis, contextualization, and theorizing, all of which we hope will be useful for readers across the full range of American Studies practices and interests. We'll begin, however, with a brief consideration of the very idea of "method" and "methodology." Since American Studies has reveled in questioning and experimenting with "method," it seems worthwhile to pause and consider exactly what we are talking about. What are we doing when we ask questions, solve problems, come to conclusions, and make knowledge?

The first toolkit (chapter 5: Texts) concerns *interpretation*—our direct confrontation with sources, texts, facts—and our immediate and close engagement with them. How do we make sense of a book or an object? Of a video or a piece of clothing or a game? A photo or a meme or a particular style? Interpretation is a building block for analysis—the weaving together of interpretations in order to advance a reasonable and logical claim—and it's important to understand some of the ways writers have thought about and practiced it.

The second toolkit (chapter 6: Archives) moves to the question of *curation*—the collection of a set of sources—a project archive—that assembles evidence for an analysis of shared cultural meanings. What does such an archive look like? How many texts do we need? How can our practice of interpretation help establish some of the criteria we will use to select those texts? How do we place archives in productive relation to one another?

In the third toolkit (chapter 7: Genres and Formations), we'll move to the register of *analysis,* where we'll engage multiple texts, seeking to make sense of the shared forms and genres made visible in our project archive. One of our goals in American Studies is not simply to name a cultural formation or ideology, but to show how it developed and how it has functioned. The first step toward that end is to work with individual texts that are bundled together through cultural, curatorial, and analytical logics. Having developed analyses of our project archive, we'll then turn to the world of context—the institutions, processes, circuits, and formations through which we produce, distribute, network, consume, and critique texts and archives.

A final toolkit (chapter 8: Power) takes us to the world of *theory,* the practice of generalizing conclusions at an abstract level that speaks to other times, places, and situations. In an American Studies context, this move to generalization will take us to questions concerning the unevenness and dominations that structure the politics of the nation and the world. We'll do a quick (and no doubt incomplete) tour of some of the theoretical traditions and concepts that have been important to American Studies over the last decades, assembling them around four key categories: subjectivity, identity, state, and market.

The closing section of the book—From Jotting It Down to Writing It Up—consists of two chapters that consider what doing American Studies looks like in practice. Chapter 9 offers thoughts on characteristic ways of structuring an American Studies argument as well as style and strategy. In chapter 10, Dispenser: A Case Study, we'll pull together all the strategies discussed earlier, using what might seem like the most quotidian, unpromising object imaginable.

You may be coming to American Studies from any number of places. You may be novice or veteran. We have tried to organize the book so that it can be useful to all. If you're just beginning with American Studies, it will probably be to your benefit to work through our historiographies. If you want to think about the ways we produce knowledge, it might be useful to start with questions of method. Conversely, if you are simply looking for some thoughts on social theory, you can skip ahead to the theoretical toolkit, and then backtrack if you'd like. If you're looking for an entertaining American Studies read, you might want to begin with the case study. Our role is simply to offer possibilities and suggestions that you can use, as you will, to structure your own exploration. Good luck!

PART ONE

Histories

ONE

History and Historiography

YOU MIGHT WONDER why we're taking a detour into history. After all, we're calling this book a "user's guide," but a user's guide is something you can pull out, looking for help, when you are trying to *do something* in the here and now. History, on the other hand, offers stories about things that have *already been done* in the past. Why, then, is an entire section of this book—this user's guide—devoted to the (seemingly arcane) history of American Studies? We have four interconnected reasons. Two of these we'll discuss quickly, the third we'll develop into an extended example of how to navigate and utilize past scholarship. We'll circle back to the fourth (and most controversial) reason at the end of the chapter.

First, and at the simplest level, nobody wants to reinvent the wheel. Knowing the history of your field reduces the risk of wasting time writing something that's already been written. This is harder than it looks. Even if you spent your entire life doing nothing but reading books in American Studies, you'd only have time to read a fraction of a percent of what has been published. As of 2017, the OCLC WorldCat catalog of university libraries listed 66,312 entries for the keyword "American Studies." Books with the exact title of *American Studies*—no subtitle—have been written by Tremaine McDowell (1948), Harry Stessel (1975), Mark Merlis (1994), Louis Menand (2002), and Jim Dow (2011), not to mention journals of that title published by the Midcontinent American Studies Association, the Council for International Exchange of Scholars, the Institute of Social Sciences in Beijing, the German Association for American Studies, Seoul National University, and the University of Warsaw. You do, of course, have to weed out things like *American Studies in Papyrology* (a monograph series published by the American Society of Papyrologists) that aren't really relevant to the field. But you're still left with a lot of texts. And weeding out false hits is not easy. One might imagine, for example, an ethnographic study of papyrologists who live in the United States but devote their lives to studying ancient texts from Europe, Africa, and the Middle East. Such a project would fall squarely within the boundaries of American Studies, and it might eventually lead you to *American Studies in Papyrology*.

This hypothetical is not as far-fetched as it sounds—some of the earliest college and university programs in American Studies offered classes in things like forestry and botany, in addition to anthropology, economics, sociology, history, literature, music, and more. Anything related to American culture was fair game. On the other hand, students do not have unlimited room in their schedules, which meant the field was shaped, from the start, by struggles over what—and how—students should read. Some believed the purpose of American Studies was to encourage appreciation for democracy, free enterprise, and, at the University of Wyoming, "the American way."[1] Others wanted to foster critical thinking about topics like nationalism, militarism, and capitalism, especially when the threat of nuclear annihilation seemed to be looming over American culture like a storm cloud. Over time, these differences morphed into struggles over whether students should focus on a small "canon" of American writers and artists (mostly white men, and many from a single decade—the 1850s), or whether offering classes in American Studies should mean building the curriculum around texts by and about women, immigrants, sailors, slaves, and other marginalized groups.

But we're getting ahead of ourselves. There is a second reason to linger on the past of American Studies, and it has to do with method. Scholars in all fields, when embarking on a research project, are expected to identify their method or methods. History matters here, too, because it offers models for how scholars in the past have gone about their work. Imagine, for example, that you are a junior scientist applying for grant money to study lung cancer. You'll need to be able to answer some basic questions about your methods: How will you conduct the research? Why is your lab the best place to carry it out? And, perhaps most important: How does your study relate to past efforts to understand the disease? It might seem obvious that such research is a worthy cause—nobody in their right mind would oppose curing cancer—but the organization giving you money needs to know if your proposed research is credible. One way that credibility is established is by demonstrating your familiarity with the methods and findings of previous studies. This step is not merely opportunistic and individual; careful articulations of method help to build trust for a body of scholarship as a whole.

A third reason: you need to be able to explain the significance—the "so what?"—of your work by connecting it to a larger conversation. Some of your explanation will revolve around understanding, explaining, and applying methods. But another way to establish the "so what?" of your work is to situate it in relation to the *historiography* or *genealogy* of your field. These might be unfamiliar terms, so let's linger on them for a moment. Historiography is based on the Greek roots "historia" (narrative, history) and "graphia" (writing). Genealogy is based on the Greek root "genos" (gene, offspring, race) together with the suffix "-logy" (study of), which comes from the Greek "logos" (word).

Historiography = "historia" (history) + "graphia" (writing)
= writing about history

Genealogy = "genos" (gene) + "-logy" (study of)
= the study of genetic origins

We will get to genealogy a little later, but let's start with historiography. Like "method" and "methodology," it is easy to get "history" and "historiography" mixed up. These are not synonyms. History, as James Harvey Robinson put it in 1912, is "the vague and comprehensive science of past human affairs." It includes everything that has happened in the past, all the way down to "this morning's newspaper."[2] Historiography, by contrast, refers to the study of what people have written *about* history.

In American Studies, historiography refers to the history of scholarship in the field of American Studies. But it is more than just a matter of surveying individual texts; the key is figuring out how they come together to create scholarly conversations, and how those conversations have changed over time. Paying attention to historiography can help you plan your research by establishing a road map of the places other scholars have gone—both to avoid getting lost in trivia, and to make sure you locate the most interesting questions and landmarks. We think that this particular reason for studying historiography is so important that we'd like to give you an extended example of how it works.

AN EXAMPLE: THE PLANTATION HOUSEHOLD

Imagine that you are about to start a project on plantation households in the U. S. South. How do you go about investigating the relevant historiography? An online search can be useful for getting a sense of the lay of the land, but—as we've seen—such searches are sometimes better for quantity than quality. The best approach might be to ask for suggestions from someone who has seriously studied this topic already. Historiographical curation is a *social* activity, even if it's not always recognized as such. What you're looking for are the most vibrant conversations about your topic, which is why an experienced guide is invaluable. You could also try to find a published bibliography on your topic, or search for book reviews in a database like JSTOR or Project MUSE. Yet another route is to find one well-respected book on your topic, and then check its introduction and footnotes for additional sources. Usually the introduction will explicitly refer to other sources that you can add to your list, which can help you start mapping out your topic's historiography.

Together, these methods should leave you with a short list of books to find at the library. We're going to focus on books for a couple of reasons. A book—as opposed to an article, blog, website, etc.—offers a *long-form* argument. Because of its length, a book is able to tackle a big and important "so what?" question, one that can only be answered through multiple subquestions and sub-subquestions. Done well, a book pulls together years of research into a coherent narrative whole that readers can digest within a few days. For this reason, the book remains the gold standard in American Studies research. We do not want to slight other forms—they all have important functions—but, despite predictions of its demise, a good book remains the goal for many American Studies scholars. For your topic, the initial list of books might look something like this:

Stephanie McCurry, *Masters of Small Worlds: Yeoman Households, Gender Relations, and the Political Culture of the Antebellum South Carolina Low Country* (New York: Oxford University Press, 1995)

Thavolia Glymph, *Out of the House of Bondage: The Transformation of the Plantation Household* (Cambridge: Cambridge University Press, 2008).

Annette Gordon-Reed, *The Hemingses of Monticello: An American Family* (New York: W. W. Norton, 2008).

Tiya Miles, *The House on Diamond Hill: A Cherokee Plantation Story* (Chapel Hill: University of North Carolina Press, 2010).

These books are what scholars call monographs, or studies of a single specialized subject as opposed to a broad survey like a textbook. To break that down:

Monograph = "mono" (one) + "graphia" (writing) = book about one thing

You might be thinking, "If these are all credible books on my topic, why should I read all four instead of just one of them?" Without a doubt, each of these books *is* extremely valuable on its own. But they are far from redundant, and in fact the areas where they differ can provide some of the best clues about how *your* voice might fit in. Think of it like joining a group of unfamiliar people at a party. It's almost always a good idea to listen and pay attention before trying to steer the conversation in a new direction. Is somebody in the middle of telling a story? Are they debating something? How do they know each other? Are they old friends or just getting to know one another? What is the atmosphere of the conversation? Similarly when working in American Studies, paying attention to historiography provides useful information that can help you decide whether and how to join a particular scholarly conversation.

Although there is no substitute for reading books, start to finish, you can start looking for clues right away, before even cracking open any of the books. Lay them out on the table side by side and examine the covers (figures 3–6). What do you notice? The first thing that might jump out at you is that each of the four covers depicts houses. But there are also some subtle differences between these images that offer clues about what you'll find in the books. For example, both Gordon-Reed and Miles depict specific identifiable houses: Monticello, former home of Thomas Jefferson, and a Cherokee plantation house in Georgia now called the Chief Vann House State Historic Site. Both homes are large, distant, and protected by trees in pastoral settings. By contrast, McCurry's cover depicts a ramshackle home with chipped paint and uneven siding superimposed on a map. This helps illustrate what is meant by the term "yeoman households." The pluralization of McCurry's title— "masters" of small "worlds"—also signals that the book is about a pattern of relations across multiple households in the region, rather than a specific one. By contrast the subtitles of both Gordon-Reed ("An American Family") and Miles ("A Cherokee Plantation Story") make it clear that they are utilizing a case study method. But covers can also deceive. As we read, we learn that the Diamond Hill plantation, with its large population of enslaved people, was in operation for many years before the Vann House was constructed, thereby complicating our first impressions.

Glymph's cover is even more ambiguous. The phrase "out of the house of bondage" alludes to Exodus, signaling that the book deals with the aftermath

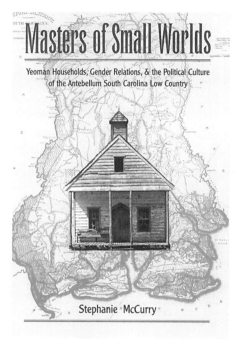

FIGURE 3. Image courtesy of Oxford University Press.

FIGURE 4. Image courtesy of Cambridge University Press.

of chattel slavery, but the subtitle does not point to a specific location, and instead hints at a focus on change over time ("transformation"). The cover art depicts a large house on the left alongside several outbuildings. The landscape is austere, with faint trees and an open field surrounding the row of structures. The crops in the foreground are easy to miss and divided from the field by a line that runs parallel to the forest in the background. As with the other covers, the sky is washed out, and all four books have roughly the same color scheme of earth tones—tan, pale blue, green, black, and a touch of brick red. Flipping over the book identifies the illustration as "Julianton Plantation, ca. 1800," in Georgia. Will this turn out to be a case study as well? It appears more likely that the image was chosen to create an atmosphere, or perhaps to suggest the multiplicity of living environments within the plantation household.

We haven't even started reading, and already we can surmise that the books represent different methods: case study, broad pattern, and transformation over time. Other clues can be found by flipping over to the blurbs of praise

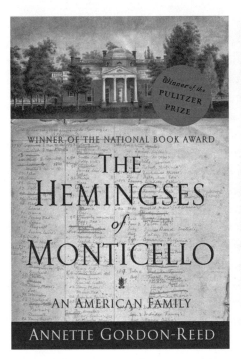

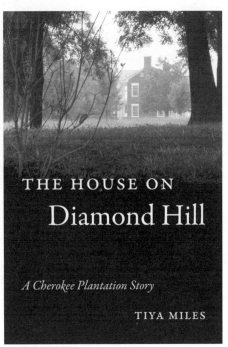

FIGURE 5. Image courtesy of
W. W. Norton.

FIGURE 6. Image courtesy of University of
North Carolina Press.

from reviewers on the back of the books. To start with *Out of the House of Bondage,* one calls it "a sweeping reinterpretation" that combines "the tools of an economic and social historian." Another blurb notes that it "demolishes the idea that some form of gender solidarity trumped race and class in plantation households." These can already get us thinking about the historiographical context. First, it suggests that Glymph is challenging books that portray white and black women as allies against patriarchal oppression. Second, it positions the book within economic and social history, suggesting a concern with structures rather than culture alone. Turning to *Masters of Small Worlds,* published thirteen years earlier, one reviewer asserts that it demonstrates "the centrality of gender as a category for understanding American political thought." A second blurb calls it "a pioneering beginning to the inclusion of gender in political history." By now you can make an educated guess, or hypothesis, that *Masters of Small Worlds* might be one of the books that Glymph challenges, with McCurry seemingly pointing to gender as the main avenue of power in plantation life, and Glymph seemingly pointing to race.

Let's see how this hypothesis plays out. Ultimately you would do this by reading both books, cover to cover. What you'd find is that McCurry and Glymph do offer differing interpretations of how power operated in plantation households, but close examination of their arguments, sources, and methods shows the conflict to be much more nuanced than a divide over whether gender or race is more important. As her subtitle suggests, McCurry is interested in the political culture of the antebellum South Carolina low country, and specifically the place of the yeomanry, or small-scale farmers, in

Men.

a region dominated by large planters. She argues that democratic bonds among white men, rich and poor, revolved around "the virtually unlimited right of an independent man to mastery over his own household and the property that lay within its boundaries" (6). Both marriage and slavery, McCurry argues, were based on this polyvalent metaphor of the family that was echoed in both religion and politics. Instead of creating solidarity between white mistresses and enslaved women, the equating of marriage and slavery was a rhetorical strategy that preachers and politicians used "to endow slavery with the legitimacy of the family" (214). Glymph, on the other hand, is less interested in cultural representations of the plantation household than the "flesh-and-blood practices" that made it, above all, a *workplace* where mistresses exerted brutal violence against domestic slaves. This experience of tyranny shaped the types of freedom sought out by black women after emancipation and, as a result, left its traces in the social life of the new postbellum household economy.

As it turns out, the conversation between McCurry and Glymph is not a conflict over which matters more—race or gender—but rather a discussion of how to think about *both* of these categories when you put them together. Glymph argues that historians have tended to reduce black women's stories to a sort of echo or imitation of white mistresses, thereby missing the texture of their historical experiences. McCurry stresses that overlapping layers of oppression can be found even in a metaphor as deceptively simple as the family. This concept of *intersectionality* has had a major influence on the field of American Studies in recent decades. In fact, one of the key articles on this concept, "It's All in the Family" (1998), by the sociologist Patricia Hill Collins, focused on the family as a place where categories such as race and gender intersect. Collins argues that such categories "mutually construct one another" and cannot be properly understood in isolation.

Other conversations between McCurry and Glymph emerge in the footnotes. This is where you can look to track down the evidence a scholar is using to support their arguments. There are two main kinds of sources: secondary and primary. Secondary sources are things like books and articles—anything written *about* a topic from a distance—whereas primary sources are forms of evidence that directly document the topic that a scholar is researching: letters, photographs, personal diaries, tax records, court filings, and more.

This distinction is blurred when studying historiography, since the secondary sources are themselves the objects of your study. Your goal is to figure out how a number of books are related, and organize them into *conversations,* not just fields. *Masters of Small Worlds,* for example, is hard to place in a single field: it won both the John Hope Franklin Prize for the outstanding book published in American Studies in 1995, but also the Charles Sydnor Prize from the Southern Historical Association. So is it American Studies? History? The very ambiguity of disciplinary categories is why we urge you to spend time in the footnotes of monographs and ask concrete questions such as: Who is this author in conversation with? How has she selected and organized her archives? What are her methods? What can I learn from the way she is using her sources? Can this book lead me to other books?

Both McCurry's and Glymph's footnotes reveal a wide range of primary sources. Glymph devotes particular attention to an archive that, as she explains in a lengthy footnote, is highly contested among historians: the former slave narratives recorded by the Works Progress Administration's Federal Writers' Project of the 1930s. This project provided work to unemployed—and mostly (but not exclusively) white—writers during the Great Depression. Its mission was to record life narratives from formerly enslaved African Americans, all of whom were elderly by the time of the project. Glymph notes that Walter Johnson's *Soul by Soul: Life in the Antebellum Slave Market* (1999) excludes these narratives because of the distorting effects of the power dynamic between white recorders and former slaves. Indeed, Catherine Stewart's *Long Past Slavery: Representing Race in the Federal Writers' Project* (2016) notes that some recorders were active United Daughters of the Confederacy members committed to romanticizing the antebellum South. Glymph herself quotes one woman who told her interviewer, "we old 'uns still knows dat we is got ter be perlite to you' white ladies" (13). But Glymph ultimately concludes that these WPA narratives are useful sources, since the "rumblings of renewed freedom" in the 1930s may have encouraged interviewees to speak out, even in a context shaped by ongoing violence. Crucially, it is important to consider Glymph's decision as an act of scholarly judgment. As Ramzi Fawaz notes, "There is an intuitive element to this part of research, where we have to go on hunches, trust our instincts, *and* provide evidence of why those hunches make sense."[3]

The footnotes in both books also identify certain secondary sources as important. For example, Elizabeth Fox-Genovese's *Within the Plantation Household: Black and White Women of the Old South* (1988) is credited by both authors for identifying the "plantation household" as an important object of study, with McCurry also pointing to Steven Hahn, *The Roots of Southern Populism: Yeoman Farmers and the Transformation of the Georgia Upcountry, 1850–1890* (1983) as influential in this regard. Glymph repeatedly cites Deborah Gray White's *Ar'n't I a Woman?: Female Slaves in the Plantation South* (1985) and Jacqueline Jones's *Labor of Love, Labor of Sorrow: Black Women, Work, and the Family, from Slavery to the Present* (1985), while pushing back against the concept of gender solidarity across the color line introduced in Anne Firor Scott's *The Southern Lady: From Pedestal to Politics, 1830–1930* (1970). Several of these authors appear in the acknowledgments section: another key place to look, for it reveals the personal networks (often a history of face-to-face conversations, mentorship, and mutual reading) that propelled these books forward. Notably, Glymph mentions McCurry as somebody who was supportive of her work, and she singles out a scholar named Darlene Clark Hine as particularly influential. Both authors thank Fox-Genovese, further underscoring the importance of *Within the Plantation Household* to their work.

Let's pause for a moment and take stock. We haven't even gotten to two of our original four texts—*The House on Diamond Hill* and *The Hemingses of Monticello*—and already our web of historiography is growing. What we see here is not simply a bookshelf, but the makings of a conversation (figure 7). We can start organizing them in a number of different ways, using clues such as what McCurry, Glymph, Gordon-Reed, and Miles say about them. In a bibliography they might be organized alphabetically, but we can also start thinking about overarching discursive "clusters" beyond your research topic, such as Southern history, political history, cultural history, and women's history. Each one contains a number of historiographical conversations, and each might frame any one of these books in terms of the cluster's own concerns and conversations.

You could also organize these books around questions. Indeed, one of the great benefits of reading historiography is that it helps you figure out what to ask as you embark on your own research:

FIGURE 7. Photograph by Alexander Olson.

Did patriarchy produce solidarity between mistresses and enslaved women, or was their relationship organized around racial violence?

Was the plantation household a "private" or "public" space?

How did emancipation change the plantation household economy? What did freedom mean from the perspective of formerly enslaved women?

These questions bring us to the other key term of this chapter: *genealogy.* If historiography involves mapping scholarly *conversations,* genealogy is more about intellectual *influences.* It is also more holistic: a book's genealogical roots might include a wide range of people, texts, and institutions.

One way to think about "genealogy" is through the more colloquial use of the term as family history. In fact, Annette Gordon-Reed's *The Hemingses of Monticello* is about genealogy in both of these senses. It tells the story of the family of Sally Hemings, a woman enslaved by Thomas Jefferson who bore several children with him—a fact that some historians continue to deny, even after DNA testing in 1999 added further corroboration to documentary and oral history sources. These older sources include the autobiographical narrative of Sally Hemings's son, Madison Hemings, published in 1873, as well as circumstantial evidence regarding the timing of Jefferson's visits to Monticello. Also relevant are semi-fictional texts like William Wells Brown's *Clotel, or the President's Daughter* (1853), the first novel by an African American writer. Unlike white historians, Brown took the stories about Thomas Jefferson and Sally Hemings seriously. Gordon-Reed argues that the generations of white historians who dismissed such stories as rumor were reenacting "the world of master and slave in the pages of history" (85). Her explanation of the legal context of slavery in Virginia draws on texts like Edmund Morgan's *American Slavery, American Freedom: The Ordeal of Colonial Virginia* (1975), which has influenced the study of colonial American history for three decades with its provocative argument that slavery provided not only material support but also the social and cultural scaffolding for U.S. independence.

Mapping the historiographical and genealogical influences on Gordon-Reed's work opens the door to different kinds of questions, difficult ones focused on historiographical choices:

Why were historians so eager, for so long, to ignore the evidence that Thomas Jefferson had children with Sally Hemings?

How do scholars decide whether a story is credible? How have these criteria changed over time, and why?

These questions start to reveal some of the rewards of paying attention to historiography and genealogy. Mapping scholarly conversations does not simply mean finding texts that you agree with, but also accounting for texts that have later been discredited. The reasons why some stories get told and others get ignored involve complicated relationships between ideas and institutions that historiographical analysis can help illuminate.

In fact, the effort to shed light on Sally Hemings's story was part of a larger institutional struggle that accompanied the establishment of African American Studies and Women's Studies programs in the 1970s and 1980s—a movement that reshaped American Studies as well. In a 2007 article, Deborah Gray White described the practical challenges that she faced to publish her groundbreaking book, *Ar'n't I a Woman?: Female Slaves in the Plantation South* (1985), noting that "it was an uphill struggle to research, write, and get it published." She explained that although the WPA narratives were invaluable for her study of enslaved black women's lives, "I was repeatedly scolded for using them, for they were assumed to be invalid, in part because they were produced by African Americans, and thus were biased."[4] Crucially, the supposed bias that White's critics emphasized was very different from the bias that received scrutiny from Glymph, Stewart, and Johnson. Instead of questioning the credibility of the *recorders* involved with the WPA project, the critics of White's book in the 1980s doubted the credibility of *the former slaves themselves*—on the baldly racist assumption that they would exaggerate the hardships of slavery. Stepping back, this institutional context is a major reason why, for many decades, historians devoted so much more attention to the so-called founding fathers like George Washington and John Adams. Deborah Gray White and her peers were part of a movement to study the history of American culture "from the bottom up." Other contributions to this movement included Lawrence Levine's *Black Culture and Black Consciousness: Afro-American Folk Thought from Slavery to Freedom* (1977), which took seriously a range of sources from the black oral tradition such as jokes and songs. It also spurred the efforts of scholars like James Scott, Stephanie Camp, and Robin D. G. Kelley to develop methods for reading primary sources "against the grain" to find evidence of the voices of the marginalized, or what Scott called "hidden transcripts" and Kelley called "infrapolitics."

The problem of historical narration brings us to the final book from our original list of four, Tiya Miles's *The House on Diamond Hill*. Miles tells the story of the many lives—"American Indians, enslaved people of African descent, and Euro-American missionaries, craftsmen, and laborers" (3)—that came together on the plantation operated by the wealthy Cherokee landowner James Vann and his family before removal. Today the house is preserved as the Chief Vann House State Historic Site. The book's method combines archival research with what is called *participant observation*, or getting to know a group through direct interaction. For Miles, this meant attending events at the Vann House like a "Candlelight Christmas Evening" and getting to know the rangers who operate it. Part of the impetus for her book was the observation that (as with many other Southern plantation homes open to tourists) the interpretive materials at the Vann House did not acknowledge the enslaved men and women who worked there. At these sites, black chattel slavery is "the elephant in the plantation parlor" that, in Miles's telling, "mars the purity of mint julep moments, undoes the pleasure of white-only leisure, and justifies the wreckage of a bloody Civil War" (11–12).

As a study of a Cherokee plantation that has become a site of heritage tourism, *The House on Diamond Hill* not only engages scholarship on the history of black chattel slavery, but also connects us to adjacent conversations in fields such as Native American Studies. On the question, for example, of whether the Africans who were enslaved by Cherokees became "Indianized," *The House on Diamond Hill* differs from Miles's own first book, *Ties That Bind: The Story of an Afro-Cherokee Family in Slavery and Freedom*

(2005), which tells the story of a Cherokee farmer named Shoe Boots and his slave and partner Doll. Since Diamond Hill was much larger—and enslaved far more people—than most other Cherokee plantations, its enslaved people formed a semi-autonomous community. Miles notes that "the black community on Diamond Hill was composed of a diversity of people and family groupings, each with distinct experiences and backgrounds" (88). These included newly arrived Africans as well as slaves who had grown up speaking the Cherokee language, resulting in a cultural and social network that, Miles argues, is impossible to understand through a monolithic lens.

Miles stretches our historiographical mapping in other ways as well. In *Ties That Bind,* she identifies Toni Morrison's novel *Beloved* (1987) as a major influence on her approach to writing and scholarship. Miles explains that *Beloved*'s "enduring ability to mediate between our present selves and shrouded pasts, has echoed in my thoughts throughout the process of writing this book and thus has left an imprint on the story that I tell" (xxvi). This homage brings to mind the acknowledgments section of Glymph's *Out of the House of Bondage,* which offers thanks "to John Coltrane, Nina Simone, Leadbelly, and Oleta Adams for knowing and reminding me of what it would take to get this done" (xi). Such sources of intellectual inspiration—novels and music—complicate our historiographical and genealogical analysis in interesting and productive ways. They remind us of the affective dimensions of our work. It's not simply that we offer our readers an answer to the question, "so what?" It's that we undertake a project because *we,* as individuals, find reasons to care. We use research and writing to explore our own passions, which often have deep links to literature, art, music, and other forms of emotional experience. In fact, Miles followed the publication of *The House on Diamond Hill* with a fictional story of her own, *Cherokee Rose: A Novel of Gardens and Ghosts* (2015), which imagines a new ending for the intersectional histories she uncovered at Diamond Hill. Our interests and values, in other words, can go hand in hand with historiographical engagement: it's not a matter of picking one or the other.

At this point, our web of historiography has grown significantly. Let's recap what we have in the form of a bibliographical table (box 1). If you are a graduate student in American Studies, this is roughly the process that you can use to help build a list of books for your comprehensive exams. Indeed, "A Plantation Household Bibliography" offers a pretty good interdisciplinary mix of sources on plantation culture in the U.S. South, with monographs,

BOX 1. A PLANTATION HOUSEHOLD BIBLIOGRAPHY

Brown, William Wells, *Clotel, or the President's Daughter: A Narrative of Slave Life in the United States* (London: Partridge & Oakey, 1853).

Camp, Stephanie, *Closer to Freedom: Enslaved Women and Everyday Resistance in the Plantation South* (Chapel Hill: University of North Carolina Press, 2004).

Collins, Patricia Hill, "It's All in the Family: Intersections of Gender, Race, and Nation," *Hypatia* 13, no. 3 (Summer 1998): 62–82.

Fox-Genovese, Elizabeth, *Within the Plantation Household: Black and White Women of the Old South* (Chapel Hill: University of North Carolina Press, 1988).

Glymph, Thavolia, *Out of the House of Bondage: The Transformation of the Plantation Household* (Cambridge: Cambridge University Press, 2008).

Gordon-Reed, Annette, *Thomas Jefferson and Sally Hemings: An American Controversy* (Charlottesville: University Press of Virginia, 1997).

———, *The Hemingses of Monticello: An American Family* (New York: W.W. Norton, 2008).

Hahn, Steven, *The Roots of Southern Populism: Yeoman Farmers and the Transformation of the Georgia Upcountry, 1850–1890* (New York: Oxford University Press, 1983).

Hemings, Madison, "Life among the Lowly, No. 1" *Pike County Republican* (Ohio), March 13, 1873.

Johnson, Walter, *Soul by Soul: Life Inside the Antebellum Slave Market* (Cambridge, MA: Harvard University Press, 1999).

Jones, Jacqueline, *Labor of Love, Labor of Sorrow: Black Women, Work, and the Family from Slavery to the Present* (New York: Basic Books, 1985).

Kelley, Robin D.G., *Race Rebels: Culture, Politics, and the Black Working Class* (New York: Free Press, 1994).

Levine, Lawrence, *Black Culture and Black Consciousness: Afro-American Folk Thought from Slavery to Freedom* (New York: Oxford University Press, 1977)

McCurry, Stephanie, *Masters of Small Worlds: Yeoman Households, Gender Relations, and the Political Culture of the Antebellum South Carolina Low Country* (New York: Oxford University Press, 1995).

Miles, Tiya, *Ties That Bind: The Story of an Afro-Cherokee Family in Slavery and Freedom* (Berkeley: University of California Press, 2005).

———, *The House on Diamond Hill: A Cherokee Plantation Story* (Chapel Hill: University of North Carolina Press, 2010).

———, *Cherokee Rose: A Novel of Gardens and Ghosts* (Winston-Salem, NC: John F. Blair, 2015).

Morgan, Edmund, *American Slavery, American Freedom: The Ordeal of Colonial Virginia* (New York: W.W. Norton, 1975).

Morrison, Toni, *Beloved: A Novel* (New York: Alfred A. Knopf, 1987).

Scott, Anne Firor, *The Southern Lady: From Pedestal to Politics, 1830–1930* (Chicago: University of Chicago Press, 1970).

Scott, James, *Domination and the Arts of Resistance: Hidden Transcripts* (New Haven, CT: Yale University Press, 1990).

Stewart, Catherine, *Long Past Slavery: Representing Race in the Federal Writers' Project* (Chapel Hill: University of North Carolina, 2016).

White, Deborah Gray, *Ar'n't I a Woman?: Female Slaves in the Plantation South* (New York: W. W. Norton, 1985).

novels, cultural theory, and primary sources like Madison Hemings's 1873 narrative. There is a blend of depth and breadth, with more than one book by Tiya Miles and Annette Gordon-Reed, and a range of social, cultural, and economic approaches. But even for the narrow topic of plantation households, and even with the same four books as a starting point, this list is only one of the many possible directions that you could have taken this exercise.

Ultimately, historiography and genealogy are ways to find questions, not answers: What roads should we follow into the past? Where should we look to find the origins of the ideas we study? These things matter, for a good project *requires* a good question, and a good question cannot exist without a historiographical context. Genealogy pushes even further by organizing these contexts into narratives and origin stories. We are not the first to offer genealogies for the field of American Studies. Over the years, many writers have attempted such stories, and we'll give it a shot in the two chapters that follow.

In a field defined by multiplicity—with a long tradition of resisting and rejecting definitions—writing genealogies can be treacherous. Inevitably things get left out of the narrative, and as we noted in the Introduction, American Studies is suspicious of anything that smacks of exclusion. But this brings us to the fourth and final reason why this book opens with the history of American Studies. Quite simply, we believe that many of the classic origin stories of the field get things wrong. And this merits taking another look. For example, the origins of American Studies are often linked to the disciplines of history and literature, but if you go back and consult American Studies bibliographies from the early years of the field, you'll find a shocking range of sources, including *American Journal of Psychiatry* and *Bulletin of the Atomic*

Scientists.[5] Today, American Studies is often seen through the lens of its primary national academic organization—the American Studies Association—but when you look at the history of the organization it seems, well . . . generally disorganized. Perhaps most importantly, American Studies is often framed as complicit in U.S. global hegemony after World War II, but the reality is much more complex.

In the two chapters that follow, we approach these issues from two distinct modes of intellectual history: scholarship and institutions. The first tracks the story of American Studies through historiographical "mixtapes" of interesting and important works. The second outlines a few of the institutions—curricula, programs, journals, organizations, and more—that helped materialize the field as a concrete thing. We believe that attention to the past helps defamiliarize—or make strange—the assumptions of the present moment. In other words, we believe that understanding the history of American Studies in all its multiplicity might lead us to new and better kinds of writing in the future.

TWO

Four American Studies Mixtapes

- Mixtapes are like Archives, but its more essential.
- Mixtapes = Eras?. Relics of some old way of thinking.

AT FIRST GLANCE, the most daunting thing about historiography seems to be finding the time and energy for reading such a large number of books. But even the most herculean effort can only get you through a fraction of what's been published in a given field. In the end, time is limited—nobody lives forever—so we all make choices about what we're going to read and, just as importantly, what we're *not* going to read. Different contexts require different choices. Some might pack Jacques Derrida's *Of Grammatology* for beach reading (where you can learn about "the unheard difference between the appearing and the appearance")—but most of us are more likely to grab a magazine or fun novel. In American Studies, the challenge is particularly acute because there are so many *choices*. You can choose books and articles in history, anthropology, economics, women's studies, ethnic studies, and more—not to mention novels, poems, comics, and movies—all while staying within the field of American Studies.

Ironically, the result is that reading *practices* in American Studies can be like listening to a Top 40 radio station, where everyone flocks to the latest release from a small number of "superstars" in the field. Keywords and new concepts are introduced, voraciously consumed, and then left lonely (and perhaps underdeveloped) as they are displaced by another cycle of new ideas. There's an element of fashion to American Studies, one that invites both enthusiastic engagement and distanced skepticism. We're not suggesting that you turn your back on the latest work; we're just saying that there's so much more out there, especially older stuff, that's easy to overlook.

This chapter makes the case for learning about the history of American Studies through a more organized approach to reading. Specifically, we suggest deciding what to read is not all that different from making a playlist of

FIGURE 8. With e-book devices, your historiographical mixtapes can be this compact, too.

music. Curating a mixtape is not just about finding songs that work well together, but also about setting up contrasts and juxtapositions to keep the listener engaged. A mixtape samples freely and fearlessly, since it's not intended to be a commercial release. And not every mixtape has the same structure. Some might have a steady progression of songs based on a single artist, place, or feeling, whereas others are all about tensions and dissonance, with the listener getting exposed to a variety of tempos, keys, and even genres that play off one another. But either way, the mixtape can't go on forever; you need to make choices about what to include and what to cut. For this chapter, think of us like two music nerds at the college radio station, always trying to get you to check out little-known songs that might change your world. Sometimes our suggestions might turn out to be clunkers, but other times you may find music that inspires mixtapes of your own (figure 8).

This approach is actually a throwback to what Joseph Jones of the University of Texas proposed in 1957, in a comment from the floor during a panel discussion on American Studies curriculum development. He thought it "wonderful" that universities were starting to offer creative new courses in American Studies. And yet, he added:

> [T]he basic thing is books. Now I've thought for a long time that if I were to design an ideal program in American Civilization I would say to the student

at the outset, you must, before you enter upon this study, provide yourself with a basic reference library of some ten or twelve books. You are to possess these and live with them and ask questions about them and get criticism about them and then build on this core a personal library of a lot of other books.[1]

He emphasized that this was not a canon-building approach, clarifying that "I don't care which books" were included on a given list, as long the student owned them, lived with them, marked them up, and learned to criticize them. If the distinctive thing about American Studies is the flexibility to create one's own archive (or "library"), Jones wanted to prevent students from getting overwhelmed by options and, as a result, missing out on the benefits of historiographical engagement. In short, he wanted students to start their course of study by putting together a manageable list of ten to twelve books, and then building from there.

So let's try it. We will start with ten books that are closely associated with the early years of American Studies, but which are rarely read anymore, start to finish, by students of the field. Instead, people tend to learn about them secondhand from some of the popular genealogies that have been written about American Studies. We'll call this the "Old School American Studies

Mixtape" (box 2). Following Jones's suggestion, our premise is that the "mixtape," or library, only has room for precisely ten "songs," or books.

What is the value in reading older books like this? One of the most challenging things about working in an interdisciplinary field like American Studies is there are so many possible directions to take your work. The whirlwind of inter-, trans-, and even anti-disciplinary options can be intoxicating. But although it is tempting to immediately specialize in a tightly focused area of personal interest and investment, the slow work of historiography and genealogy is not just a disciplinary rite of passage. It is also a connective exercise that can draw your attention to unfinished conversations among writers in the past, or what the historian Richard White once called "a storehouse of the possibilities of being human."[2] Now, conversations in American Studies *have* changed—and will continue to change as we move into the future. As Carl Becker poignantly observed in 1935, "In the history of history a myth is a once valid but now discarded version of the human story, as our now valid versions will in due course be relegated to the category of discarded myths."[3] We are not urging you to resist these changes. Rather, we see the process of making sense of this flux as a great way to position yourself not simply within the present or immediate future, but within a *broadened* understanding of the past that can serve you well.

Though they ultimately come together under the category of American Studies, the "Old School" texts represent several distinct currents within the early years of the field. Like rivers eroding rock, these currents helped shape the intellectual landscapes of American Studies today. In this chapter, we take four of these texts—Matthiessen's *American Renaissance*, Parrington's *Main Currents in American Thought*, Mead's *And Keep Your Powder Dry*, and Smith's *Virgin Land*—and build mixtapes around them. On a continental map, think of them as the Hudson, the Mississippi, the Colorado, and the Columbia, each creating a basin into which work might flow, and across which ideas and goods might be transported. Each stream creates distinct landscapes that are, at the same time, all part of the same topography. According to literary scholar Robert Spiller, American Studies in this era was characterized, above all, by methodological multiplicity. He attributed this curious state to a crossing-over of disciplinary currents that seemed to happen all at once in the 1930s:

> The general historians were soon aware of sources of fresh and dynamic thought among their colleagues in economics, political science, and sociology, whereas the literary historians found their interest in environmental causa-

tion echoed among the historians of painting, sculpture, architecture, and the minor and "useful" arts. Both groups found the philosophers turning from the classical forms of their subject to pragmatism and experimentalism and from traditional histories of pure philosophy to a type of intellectual history which was firmly anchored to the time, the place, the group, and the thinker.[4]

From a historiographical perspective, the most challenging thing about mapping these currents is that it can sometimes feel like you need training in a dozen different fields just to figure out what people are talking about. To grasp Spiller's point in the passage above, it helps to know economics, political science, sociology, philosophy, and even sculpture. Today such a list might be expanded to include disability studies, ethnic studies, gender studies, and more. Instead of getting overwhelmed, however, think of it like a dance party: at first glance it might seem like chaos, but there's also an order to things, a series of unspoken rules.

From a distance, it might seem like our mixtape is unified by time—we ourselves are calling it "old school," after all. This also makes it easy to dismiss these books as outdated. But the history of American Studies isn't simply linear; many of the ideas in these texts remain alive in the present, if we take the time to engage with them. With this in mind, we have curated ten spin-off mixtapes, one for each of the books. These will comprise the soundtrack for our dance party. Let's call it the Great American Studies Dance Party! Although, as we noted, we only have room to discuss four of them in depth, the rest of the mixtapes are in a bonus section at the end of this chapter.

The American Problems Mixtape (Vernon Parrington)

The Early America Mixtape (Perry Miller)

The Mixtape of Mixtapes (Caroline Ware)

The Vernacular Mixtape (F. O. Matthiessen)

The Anthropological Mixtape (Margaret Mead)

The Theory 101 Mixtape (Kenneth Burke)

The American Education Mixtape (Tremaine McDowell)

The American Spaces Mixtape (Henry Nash Smith)

The Models of Method Mixtape #1 (David Potter)

The Models of Method Mixtape #2 (Leo Marx)

We made our choices with an eye toward illuminating both the central themes and the productive tensions within each current, and how these

BOX 3. THE VERNACULAR MIXTAPE

1. W.E.B. Du Bois, *The Souls of Black Folk: Essays and Sketches* (1903).
2. Van Wyck Brooks, *America's Coming-of-Age* (1915).
3. Constance Rourke, *American Humor: A Study of the National Character* (1931).
4. John Dos Passos, *U.S.A.* (1938).
5. F.O. Matthiessen, *American Renaissance: Art and Expression in the Age of Emerson and Whitman* (1941).
6. C.L.R. James, *Notes on American Civilization* (1950). Unpublished until 1993.
7. Ralph Ellison, *Shadow and Act* (1964).
8. Janice Radway, *Reading the Romance: Women, Patriarchy, and Popular Literature* (1984).
9. Miriam Hansen, *Babel and Babylon: Spectatorship in American Silent Film* (1991).
10. Michael Denning, *Noise Uprising: The Audiopolitics of a World Musical Revolution* (2015).

intersected in the rise of American Studies. We don't think that these ten are exhaustive, and so we encourage you to add, subtract, remix, and rearrange as you build your own mixtapes. And with that, let's dive in.

We will start off with a bold claim: the vernacular current is actually the most important strand in American Studies (box 3). All of the other mixtapes are just variations on a theme. Now you might be thinking, "Wait, what? I thought you just explained how American Studies is all about multiplicity, and now you're saying that this current is more important than all the others. That doesn't make sense!" And you know, that's actually a good point. We'll concede it. But just watch: this current will keep showing up again and again. Attention to the vernacular is one of those unspoken "rules" that can help make sense of the "chaos" of the party.

So what do we mean by *vernacular?* The Merriam-Webster dictionary offers a couple of different meanings:

The language of ordinary speech rather than formal writing.

The common style of a particular time, place, or group.

Using a language or dialect native to a region or country rather than a literary, cultured, or foreign language.

Right off the bat, we run into some problems. First, what counts as the "ordinary speech" of a place as diverse as the United States, let alone the rest of the Americas? Second, why do most of the titles on our playlist seem to focus on literature, music, or visual culture, when the definition seems to imply that vernacular refers to the *spoken* word? Third, what is meant by *common*? We'll take that third question first, and turn again to Merriam-Webster, which offers the following definitions for "common":

> Belonging to or shared by two or more individuals or things or by all members of a group.
>
> Widespread or general.
>
> Occurring or appearing frequently: not rare.

These are each very different meanings. The first speaks to shared property, or what some call the "commons"—the pool of resources that are shared by humanity. The second speaks more to popular practices or preferences, in the way you might make a friend by figuring out what you have in "common" with one another. The third specifies "not rare"—a meaning that is often attached to notions of monetary or cultural value. In commercial markets, something "common" is usually not worth as much as something rare. Drawing on these thoughts, we might then summarize:

The vernacular involves a recognition—but also rejection—of hierarchies of high and low culture, formal and informal speech and writing. It does so in favor of an investigation of the ordinary, shared, common expression of the everyday lives of non-elites. It is therefore difficult to locate in canonical work or elite archives.

The vernacular current of American Studies pushed, above all, for opening up the archive, or widening the range of cultural artifacts that could be considered worthy of scholarly analysis. If your university offers classes in comics or anime, it is partly because of the kinds of scholarship we've included on this mixtape. In the early twentieth century, this interest in "the common" was a fairly radical stance, especially in literary studies. In 1869, the critic Matthew Arnold had defined "culture" as "the best which has been thought and said." The task of the literary scholar, in his view, was to identify and explain those few transcendent great books, or great works of art, that could offer an intellectual bulwark against anarchy. In practice, this meant that students in literature classes in the United States read a small number of books written by (as critics would later describe them) dead white men from Europe, work placed decisively at the *top* of a hierarchy of high and low culture. The growing frustration with this status quo led a number of scholars to examine new sources in hopes of identifying an American idiom, or pattern of speech, in "common" art and literature. *But Higher-Culture,*

The organizing text around which we built this mixtape was F. O. Matthiessen's *American Renaissance: Art and Expression in the Age of Emerson and Whitman* (1941). From today's perspective, Matthiessen's focus on a small number of authors working in a limited period of American history (1850–55) would seem to smack of Arnold's call for studying "the best which has been thought and said." Indeed, the four main sections of *American Renaissance* ("From Emerson to Thoreau," "Hawthorne," "Melville," and "Whitman") are organized around five dead white men and don't even use first names, instead assuming that the reader is already familiar with these writers. But it must be remembered that Matthiessen was writing in a moment when few literature classes assigned *any* books written by Americans. As critic Jonathan Arac has argued of *American Renaissance:* "More than any other single factor it enabled hundreds of Ph.D.s in English to specialize in the American literature of the nineteenth century."[5]

Despite first impressions to the contrary, Matthiessen did *not* simply zero in on a few "great books" and treat them as timeless, transcendent classics. Instead, he treated these texts as entry points into the wider cultural world of their moment. Tellingly, his epigraph at the front of the book was a quote from Shakespeare that is identified as "marked by Melville in his copy of *King Lear.*" In other words, Matthiessen was signaling that he wasn't just interested in what Herman Melville *wrote,* but also in what, how, and why he *read.* Putting these questions together, Matthiessen identified abstract myths like "the common man" as a sort of literary time signature for the early 1850s. He wrote, for example, that Nathaniel Hawthorne was driven by a "habit of looking for emblems everywhere" that got him stuck, in one story, with "an array of symbolical potions, symbolical spiders, symbolical footsteps," but no ability "to find exactly what they symbolized."[6] Rather than making a case for Hawthorne's transcendent greatness, Matthiessen argued that Hawthorne's work was inextricable from the particular cultural context in which he lived and wrote. Dozens of scholars followed Matthiessen in their choice of American Renaissance topics, including Henry Nash Smith, Leo Marx, and C. L. R. James, who wrote an entire monograph on Melville. Their work was inspired by this relatively new and exciting vision of the nineteenth century in which vernacular culture mattered.

Book ask. One Thing.

But *whose* vernacular culture was to be considered common? Our Vernacular mixtape starts conceptually with Matthiessen. But chronologically, it begins four decades earlier with W. E. B. Du Bois's *The Souls of Black Folk* (1903), which famously and powerfully argued that "the problem of the Twentieth Century is the problem of the color-line." Du Bois recognized what Matthiessen and his colleagues often failed to see: that not all cultural artifacts could be reducible to a "common" expression of American culture. Some vernacular idioms in the United States were developed in explicit opposition to the nation, its deep inequalities, and its habits of social domination. These idioms were "common" (everyday), but not necessarily held *in common* (widely shared). Du Bois's book offered an interdisciplinary history of vernacular black culture that anticipated the future by looking to a black past. Each chapter opens with a bar of musical notes from black spirituals as an epigraph, signaling the book's expansive vernacular archive.

That black archive, as we know, shaped a significant amount of "common" (*both* everyday *and* widely shared) "American" expression in music, art, literature, and vernacular culture. Du Bois built his interpretation of that culture through an analysis of structural racism in the United States, introducing the central idea of "double-consciousness": one could be both black and American, neither of which could be reduced to the other. For Du Bois, the American vernacular cannot be understood through the erasure of difference ("we are all Americans"), but rather through African Americans acting as "co-worker[s] in the kingdom of culture" and refusing to whitewash the past—or to allow white Americans to do so.[8] In its critical attention to racism, *The Souls of Black Folk* stood uneasily alongside other vernacular-focused texts like Van Wyck Brooks's *America's Coming-of-Age* (1915), D. H. Lawrence's *Studies in Classic American Literature* (1923), Mary Austin's *American Rhythm* (1923), and William Carlos Williams's *In the American Grain* (1925), all of which articulated vernacular American culture primarily in contrast with Europe, ignoring the many faults and fissures within the United States. Brooks, for example, might have echoed Du Bois in calling for a "usable past" that could shape a future, but he failed to recognize how racial divisions complicated any unified description of American culture.

Du Bois was far from the only writer to complicate the American vernacular. In the 1930s, this current of scholarship was swept up in what Michael Denning has called "the laboring of American culture."[9] The push to expand the archive in yet another direction—toward class difference—was driven by leftist intellectuals, many of them folklorists, who wanted to raise working-class consciousness through the documentation of popular or folk culture. The field was heavily influenced by writers like John Dos Passos. In his *U.S.A.* trilogy of the 1930s, Dos Passos refigured "America" as "U.S.A.," a capitalist landscape populated with dissident readers willing to protest against "historybooks" (one word) in the margins. As he put it:

> U.S.A. is a slice of a continent. U.S.A. is a group of holding companies, some aggregations of trade unions, a set of laws bound in calf, a radio network, a chain of moving picture theatres, a column of stockquotations rubbed out and written in by a Western Union boy on a blackboard, a public-library full of old newspapers and dogeared historybooks with protests scrawled on the margins in pencil.[10]

Such work represented a sharp leftward turn in American intellectual life, with a particular focus on the folk arts and cultures of workers. Even Matthiessen himself resisted the canonization of the nineteenth-century American writers he wrote about, believing that "the folk art of an industrialized society, like that of Chaplin or Disney, must spring from new sources and new techniques of its own."[11]

By the late 1940s, the Red Scare in the United States made it difficult for many leftist scholars to continue publishing. One such intellectual, the Trinidadian writer C.L.R. James, could not find a publisher for his landmark manuscript, *Notes on American Civilization* (1950), which was posthumously published in 1993 under the abbreviated title *American Civilization*. James located the great challenge of the twentieth century in the mechanization of industrial production. He was concerned that responses to the ensuing unemployment crisis would be characterized not by political engagement, but by escapism in the form of celebrity worship—with stars constituting "the real aristocracy of the country."[12] James's critique was echoed by Ralph Ellison in *Shadow and Act* (1964), which noted (with Du Bois) that the study of "American culture" was often simply code for "what whites consider highest." Although in Europe, he argued, "it was the fascists who made the manipulation of myth and symbol a vital part of their political technology," social science had played a similar role in the United States by contributing a scientific veneer to policies that were fundamentally about reinforcing inequality.[13]

These writers were engaged in an important conversation: if "the vernacular" offered a way out of both "high culture" snobbishness *and* Eurocentric literary studies—if it captured something particularly "American"—then how should it be conceived? How should it understand the relation between "folk" processes that traveled from person to person and "mass culture" production that passed through the industrial structures that now mediated cultural life? How should the vernacular engage social differences such as class and race? The categories of race, class, gender, and sexuality (among others) function as analytical tools within the social sciences. But for James, Ellison, Du Bois, and many writers in American Studies down to the present, the categories also work as interdisciplinary, intersectional connectors. One cannot adequately understand a particular gender or racial formation, for example, without seeing it in action in economics, law, political science, and psychology, in addition to tracing its historical past and observing the ways it creates and is created through the common, meaning-making work of culture.

If those categories limn certain kinds of social inequalities, they also shape vernacular cultures that press back. Earlier we mentioned the "commons." This idea refers to common property or a pool of resources shared by humanity—the metaphorical equivalent of a common pasture or woodlot in a small village. The critics Fred Moten and Stefano Harney have taken this meaning a step further in their analysis of what they call the "undercommons" (still a commons, but one largely hidden from view), a place where dissident intellectuals ("refugees, fugitives, renegades, and castaways," as Moten and Harney put it) could share ideas and collaborate.[14] We might view many vernacular expressions as belonging to such a space: the crafting of blues cultures, borderlands cultures, resilient traditional cultures, immigrant enclaves, new emergent creative practices, and more. We might also see the undercommons functioning in opposition to persistent cultural hierarchies—shaped even by those scholars, like Matthiessen, who sought to undo older hierarchies.

As a radical scholar persecuted for his views, C. L. R. James was one of the many "fugitive" writers who participated in the "undercommons" that snaked through the interstices of the university and of American intellectual life. James crafted his words in a discursive space largely hidden from view, for social science was not the only place where a polite veneer covered over policies that perpetuated inequality. Unlike Matthiessen, who enjoyed the institutional support of a faculty position at Harvard University, intellectuals like James had to find alternative ways of supporting their writing and activism. Scholars interested in many other forms of social difference—gender and sexuality, for instance—have likewise often been forced to find creative, clandestine strategies for redrawing the boundaries of "vernacular" culture. These scholarly interlocutors needed not only conversation partners, but a paycheck, which in turn meant working to change institutions to make room, out in the open, for ideas originating in the undercommons.

Perhaps the core challenge of the vernacular current of American Studies is how to make sense of the nearly infinite range of artifacts that might comprise one's archive. One approach has been to emphasize practices of consumption, as exemplified by Janice Radway's *Reading the Romance* (1984), which utilized ethnographic methods such as interviews to explain why romance novels are so popular, or Miriam Hansen's *Babel and Babylon* (1994), which explored the practices of spectatorship that turned the silent film theater into an alternative public sphere for urban immigrants. More recent examples include Michael Denning's *Noise Uprising* (2015), which identifies a powerful current of musical styles from 1925 to the early 1930s that connected port cities such as Havana, New Orleans, Rio de Janeiro, Cairo, Johannesburg, and Buenos Aires through obscure underground recordings. These records were written off as "noise"— the soundtrack of the undercommons—and thereby slipped the notice of colonial officials and academic scholars alike, even as they helped build a web of transnational working-class dissent. For Radway, Hansen, and Denning, the turn toward processes of production, distribution, and reception—toward culture as an industry—is a response to the realization that books with limited archives like *American Renaissance* can only glimpse a fraction of the cultural artifacts that have been lost to history in what the critic Franco Moretti calls the "slaughterhouse of literature."[15] This is one major reason why the vernacular current might also be considered a project of *recovery* of lost textual goods, from Du Bois's fragments of traditional slave music in *The Souls of Black Folk* to more recent texts like Denning's *Noise Uprising*. The Vernacular mixtape is *really* a mix! But it is exactly the choppy waters of this current that have kept it intellectually relevant to this day, even as some of the other "mixtapes" discussed below have lost some of their vitality.

The core innovation of the vernacular current of American Studies was to open the archive to a wider range of sources. It was fueled by scholars who looked to literature to find the voice of the people. The American Problems mixtape, on the other hand, represents a strand of scholarship that more directly addressed social and political issues (box 4). Today, programs in American Studies often tend to function as platforms for social justice activism. Skeptics have criticized this trend as a new development, but in fact it represents the continuity of a much older ideological orientation. One of the earliest degree-granting programs in the field—the American Problems major at Sweet Briar College in Virginia, launched in 1930—made "no effort to

BOX 4. THE AMERICAN PROBLEMS MIXTAPE

1. Charlotte Perkins Gilman, *Women and Economics: A Study of the Economic Relation between Men and Women as a Factor in Social Evolution* (1898).
2. Thorstein Veblen, *The Theory of the Leisure Class: An Economic Study in the Evolution of Institutions* (1899).
3. Ida Tarbell, *The History of the Standard Oil Company* (1904).
4. J. Allen Smith, *The Spirit of American Government: A Study of the Constitution, Its Origin, Influence and Relation to Democracy* (1907).
5. Jane Addams, *Twenty Years at Hull-House* (1910).
6. James Harvey Robinson, *The New History: Essays Illustrating the Modern Historical Outlook* (1912).
7. Charles Beard, *An Economic Interpretation of the Constitution of the United States* (1913).
8. Walter Lippmann, *Public Opinion* (1922).
9. John Dewey, *The Public and Its Problems* (1927).
10. Vernon Parrington, *Main Currents in American Thought: An Interpretation of American Literature from the Beginnings to 1920* (1927–1930).

include America's contributions to art, architecture, and literature."[16] Instead, it brought together requirements from history, economics, sociology, and philosophy. The Sweet Briar course catalogue explained: "Many problems facing America today result from the reciprocal play of forces which can be understood only by the study of their interrelations."[17] Thus the curriculum started with courses that introduced students to various social problems, and then progressed to another set of courses on "economic, social, and political thought" that would give them the tools for addressing those problems.

It is no coincidence that this program was launched in 1930, the same year that Vernon Parrington published the final volume of *Main Currents in American Thought*. This book was part of a widespread push to make intellectual life more relevant to the social problems facing the United States and the world. We have placed Parrington as the final track on this mixtape, but needless to say, it is not the only option; you could easily *start* with Parrington and trace, in Russ Castronovo and Susan Gillman's words, "the study of American problems" up to the present.[18] However, we have chosen to limit this mixtape to a narrow slice of time in order to illustrate a *synchronic* (which means emphasizing multiplicity within a single moment) rather than *dia-*

chronic (which means emphasizing change over time) approach to historiography. By avoiding a list spanning centuries, this mixtape has the benefit of situating Parrington's work within the specific context of the early twentieth century, which allows us to explore, in greater depth, how scholarship from a range of fields became intertwined in a single historical period. At the end of this chapter, we have included two "remixes" of this library—one from the twenty-first century and the other from the antebellum period—to illustrate a longer perspective. But for our purposes, a tight chronological focus allows us to read Parrington alongside some of his friends and colleagues—his most immediate influences. The mixtape also omits his detractors, including proponents of close reading who believed that literature had to be separated from history; these critics were interested in the text, the whole text, and nothing but the text (we'll say more about close reading in chapter 5). This textual focus did not sit well with Parrington and his friends, who were interested in understanding literature in the context of history, economics, sociology, and above all politics.

Main Currents in American Thought took over fifteen years to complete, from 1913 to 1930, and clocked in at a hefty 1,335 pages. Its extraordinary breadth masked a single-minded focus on showing that American literary history was, in the end, an echo of economic and sociological forces. Parrington explained this model with a gardening metaphor: if literature was a flower—and if most other literary scholars styled themselves "connoisseurs of fragile and elusive beauty"—he was interested in the soil. By focusing on things like money and property, Parrington recognized that he was "an upstart intruder in the haunts of gentlemen." In 1913, when he started work on the project, the study of literature was dominated by philologists and humanists. Philologists were essentially historians of grammar who traced the origins of language into the distant past. Humanists were interested in aesthetic qualities—Matthew Arnold's "best which has been thought and said"—but they failed, in Parrington's view, to appreciate that ideas are "weapons hammered out on the anvil of human needs." Instead of casting literature as something apart from the messy world of politics and commerce, Parrington argued that American culture was structured by economic forces every step of the way. In an article written in 1917 but published posthumously (it was deemed too controversial at the time), Parrington explained: "Literature is the fair flower of culture, but underneath culture are the deeper strata of philosophy, theology, law, statecraft—of ideology and institutionalism—resting finally upon the subsoil of economics. We may begin as critics but we end as historians."[19] This method required Parrington to engage with history, economics, and political science rather than sticking to literary studies (although he started there!), and it is a major reason why he is so commonly associated with the founding of interdisciplinary American Studies.

Parrington's reputation in American Studies has been heavily shaped by the scholar Gene Wise, who concluded in an influential historiographical essay in 1979 that "Parrington is a representative figure for this pre-institutional stage of American Studies because he did it almost all *alone*."[20] However, the assertion that Parrington was working in a vacuum could not be further from the truth. Although the image of a creative genius overturning conventional wisdom was alluring—and has continued to offer one of the most powerful narratives for American Studies scholarship—it erased a whole cohort of writers who shared Parrington's aversion to antiquarianism and his passion for making ideas relevant to a wider public. These compatriots included Parrington's close friends at the University of Washington, sociologist J. Allen Smith, historian Edward McMahon, and economist Theresa McMahon. It also included several better-known writers and activists around the country, including Charlotte Perkins Gilman, Charles and Mary Beard, John Dewey, Jane Addams, Thorstein Veblen, and Upton Sinclair. In varying degrees, these men and women were all affiliated with the progressive movement, which emerged between 1890 and 1915 as a reaction to the excesses of the Gilded Age, when extreme disparities in wealth and power led many to believe that democracy had been sold to the highest bidders. In tandem with other social movements, particularly organized labor and liberal feminism, progressives sought a series of structural reforms to many aspects of social, political, and economic life in the United States, including anti-monopoly legislation, the eight-hour workday, railroad regulations, the income tax, child labor laws, women's suffrage, and the direct election of senators.

Notably, several of these reforms required constitutional amendments. It was during this period that pro-business legal doctrines like corporate personhood (the idea that businesses have civil rights like due process) achieved their modern forms. As progressive legislative measures were repeatedly struck down as unconstitutional, intellectuals began to suggest that the Constitution itself might be the root of the problem. The result was a flurry of revisionist research that deeply influenced Parrington, including J. Allen Smith's *The Spirit of American Government* (1907) and Charles Beard's *An Economic Interpretation of the Constitution of the United States* (1913). In a tribute to Smith after his death, Parrington credited his colleague with opening his eyes to "the essentially undemocratic nature of the federal constitution," which was designed to check, rather than encourage, democratic impulses.[21] Smith and Beard argued that few had recognized this core structural problem smack in the middle of American political life (with the exception of nineteenth-century abolitionists like Frederick Douglass, Lucy Stone, and William Lloyd Garrison) because it operated in a clandestine fashion as "a covert but effective veto on important legislation" (in Smith's words) or a tool "to break the force of majority rule" (in Beard's words).[22] Parrington's innovation was to carry this interpretation into the literary and cultural domain. In his reading, American literary history was the story of a collision between genteel intellectuals, who sought to establish an undemocratic and aristocratic high culture, and writers like Walt Whitman, whom he called "the poet and prophet of a democracy that the America of the Gilded Age was daily betraying."[23]

Parrington, Beard, and Smith were part of a larger wave of scholarship that blurred disciplinary boundaries in response to the social problems of the Gilded Age. This movement was driven by "self-appointed men and women of letters, deviant professors, independent scholars, public intellectuals, and wide-ranging journalists and poets."[24] William James, for example, traversed the fields of psychology and religion in articulating the philosophy of pragmatism, and Charlotte Perkins Gilman blurred economics and sociology to call for greater economic independence for women. Among Parrington's main influences was James Harvey Robinson's *The New History* (1912), which, as one historiographer put it, "belligerently proposed to make history not only more all-embracing but also more relevant to the interests of contemporary democracy."[25] Robinson argued that historians should look beyond the traditional domains of politics and war to include studies of literature, culture, and everyday life. This vision of a more expansive field of historical inquiry paralleled Veblen's *The Theory of the Leisure Class* (1899), which pushed economists to consider "social life as it could be observed among actual, living human beings in a changing society."[26] Veblen heaped scorn on economic theories that obscured the hedonistic realities of conspicuous consumption and social inequality: a dissonance readily apparent in tabloids and gossip columns, which gleefully covered the exploits of the rich and famous.

Indeed, journalism was fertile ground for scholars seeking to wake the academy from its slumber and engage with the problems of public life. Between 1880 and 1895, for example, the journalist and poet José Martí agitated for Cuban independence while reporting from the United States on topics that included Coney Island amusement park, the Haymarket bombing in Chicago, and a lynching of Italians in New Orleans. He published these pieces in periodicals across Latin America as well as his own newspaper, *Patria,* in New York City. But Martí was not alone in placing journalism at the center of democratic activism in this period. The so-called "muckrakers," or reporters who exposed corruption during the Gilded Age, were central to moving the progressive agenda forward. Some of the most influential voices in this movement were photographers like Lewis Hine and Jacob Riis, who drew attention to child labor conditions and urban poverty, and writers like Ida Tarbell, who helped break up the Standard Oil Company with her 1904 serialized expose in *McClure's* magazine. Likewise Upton Sinclair sparked public outrage toward the Chicago meatpacking industry with his novel *The Jungle* (1906), and went on to run for political office in California.

But could journalism reliably spur democratic action? The question raised doubts among many writers during this period, who began to see the press as vulnerable to the same corruption befalling other institutions. During the Gilded Age, the Associated Press became a potential vehicle for stock manipulation through its control of information.[27] In *Public Opinion* (1922), Walter Lippmann took this particular line of critique from economics into culture, arguing that failures of democracy were not simply rooted in false information, but could also be explained through the psychology of news consumption. It was indisputable, in his view, that "under certain conditions men respond as powerfully to fictions as they do to realities, and that in many cases they help to create the very fictions to which they respond."[28] It was an American Studies kind of claim focused on meaning and its consequences in relation to the United States. The system, as he saw it, was rigged in terms of economic interests, with a cultural apparatus of fiction and misinformation that prevented effective democratic governance. His resignation to the necessity of supposedly disinterested technocrats to handle specialized policy decisions was echoed by several other progressives.

Lippmann's technocratic view of democracy was challenged by figures like Jane Addams and John Dewey, who advocated for participatory democracy through engagement in, and with, local communities. Addams was the founder of Hull House in Chicago, a "settlement house" where college-educated women lived and offered free classes for newly arrived immigrants in the surrounding community. Dewey recognized the significance of Addams's work as an example of democratic hope. In *The Public and Its Problems* (1927),

Dewey granted Lippmann's critique of the ability of individual citizens to gain a full and complete picture of all the major issues of the day, but he attributed this to the inescapable conditions of modernity. Contrary to Parrington, Beard, and Smith, who attributed the defects of the Constitution to class interests, Dewey pointed to broader technological and cultural changes. The "imagination of the founders," as he put it, was unable to fathom how the railroad, telegraph, and other technologies would transform the public sphere. But this did not mean that democracy was doomed, since examples like Hull House illustrated how citizenship could be rooted in the community through "participation in family life, industry, scientific and artistic associations."[29]

In these debates, we hope you will recognize continuities and resonances with arguments still being made today. The problems of technology, community, citizenship, and democratic action have not gone away. Parrington's approach was well suited to frankly political texts like Sinclair's *The Jungle,* Tarbell's *The History of the Standard Oil Company,* or Edward Bellamy's *Looking Backward* (1888), but was less effective for analyzing the complexities of literature that lacked a clear political message. This is one major reason why *Main Currents* must be placed alongside other strands of scholarship that converged in the development of American Studies. To this day, there is a productive tension between the field's political orientation, its methods, and its objects of study. Political commitments continue to set the agenda of American Studies as a movement, but the careful analysis of texts remains a bedrock of scholarship in the field.

In fact, Parrington offers a good illustration of some of the pitfalls of present-day American Studies, which sometimes shares his tendency to jump straight to theory instead of taking the time to carefully analyze sources and contexts. Put another way, Parrington's summary of method—"we may begin as critics but we end as historians"—was right on point, except he tended to leapfrog the part about beginning as critics. This meant that Parrington's method of reducing literature to economics could become a bludgeon that he applied "to his villains, the conservatives, but not to his heroes, the liberals."[30] In his eagerness to connect texts to a broader political agenda, Parrington sometimes lacked what Richard Hofstadter called "a certain delicacy of touch" necessary to illuminate a wider spectrum of ideas.[31]

For scholars seeking a more open-ended approach to the study of culture in the 1930s, the field of anthropology seemed to fit the bill perfectly (box 5).

BOX 5. THE ANTHROPOLOGICAL MIXTAPE

1. J. Hector St. John de Crèvecoeur, *Letters from an American Farmer* (1782).
2. Alexis de Tocqueville, *Democracy in America* (1835–1840).
3. Harriet Martineau, *How to Observe Morals and Manners* (1838).
4. Yone Noguchi, *The American Diary of a Japanese Girl* (1901).
5. Robert Lynd and Helen Lynd, *Middletown: A Study in American Culture* (1929).
6. Ruth Benedict, *Patterns of Culture* (1934).
7. Gertrude Stein, *The Geographical History of America: or, The Relation of Human Nature to the Human Mind* (1936).
8. Margaret Mead, *And Keep Your Powder Dry: An Anthropologist Looks at America* (1942).
9. Hortense Powdermaker, *Hollywood, the Dream Factory: An Anthropologist Looks at the Movie-Makers* (1950).
10. Kathryn Marie Dudley, *Debt and Dispossession: Farm Loss in America's Heartland* (2000).

Parrington's method began with a hypothesis—"literature is a product of economics"—and then sought to confirm or disconfirm it with evidence. Anthropology suggested the opposite: it began with observation and description before moving to analysis. It rested on a simple and sincere approach to understanding the culture of a place: putting aside books, traveling the country, and talking to people. In American Studies, anthropology's search for culture as "a total way of life" was often blended with psychology (particularly in the case of the "culture and personality" movement) and translated into the concept of "national character." This vogue for social science was extraordinarily widespread, influencing even Perry Miller's dense archival history of Puritan thought, *The New England Mind: The Seventeenth Century* (1939), which used "Anthropology" and "Psychology" as the titles for two of the four "books" of the volume.

Margaret Mead's bestseller, *And Keep Your Powder Dry: An Anthropologist Looks at America* (1942), was the most visible example of this strand of work in the early years of American Studies. Originally a specialist on communities in the South Pacific, Mead turned her attention to the United States as a result of the war effort in the 1940s. She emphasized that anthropology could be synthesized with psychology to reveal the "national character" of a given coun-

Influences from Freud? Jung?

try. In so doing, Mead adopted the theoretical framework of Ruth Benedict's *Patterns of Culture* (1934), which defined cultures as unique aggregates of what might be seen as individual personality traits. Prior to the twentieth century, the field of anthropology almost exclusively examined indigenous groups, which were portrayed as unchanging and therefore inappropriate for historical research (which focused on change over time). By the twentieth century, however, anthropologists like Benedict and Mead rejected the idea of hierarchies among cultures and argued that their methods could be used to understand *any* group identity, including American national identity.

But there's such a wide spectrum of "persons" within American culture

Mead's book was part of a flurry of projects that explored American culture through anthropological observations of representative places, including Robert Lynd and Helen Lynd's *Middletown: A Study in American Culture* (1929) and Hortense Powdermaker's *Hollywood, the Dream Factory: An Anthropologist Looks at the Movie-Makers* (1950). Texts such as *Middletown* were rooted in the desire to find what Sarah Igo has called "an American community so perfectly average that the views of its citizens mirror those of the national population."[32] Even Powdermaker's work on Hollywood saw its social life as a key for tapping into broad cultural norms that the movies simultaneously shaped and reflected. According to Igo, texts such as *Middletown* reached well beyond the academy to the realms of advertising and politics. This impulse—to locate and explicate the "averaged American"—was reflected in everything from Gallup opinion polling (first launched in 1935) to the reports on human sexuality published by Alfred Kinsey in 1948 and 1953.

But rather than mapping Mead's immediate influences, as we did with Parrington, this section's mixtape traces a much longer current that contextualizes the relatively brief ascendancy (1930s–50s) of anthropological American Studies. The effort to understand national character through direct observation has been a source of contention for over two centuries, with anthropology (the discipline) primarily contributing a more organized set of methods. In other words, unlike our American Problems mixtape, this collection of texts employs a *diachronic* (change over time) as opposed to *synchronic* (multiplicity within a single moment) approach to historiography. One challenge with the diachronic approach is that there is never a perfect starting point. This mixtape, for example, starts with Crèvecoeur's *Letters from an American Farmer* (1782), but we could go even further back to the *Jesuit Relations* produced by French missionaries in the seventeenth century. In this longer time horizon, we can pick from hundreds of North American travel narratives written by visitors who toured the United States and Canada and published analyses of the American character upon their return.

The best known of these texts was Alexis de Tocqueville's *Democracy in America,* published in two volumes in 1835 and 1840, based on a trip taken by the French writer in 1831–32. Tocqueville focused on the shift from aristocracy to democracy as it was playing out in the United States, which was a question of some relevance in France in the aftermath of the July Revolution. As it happened, Tocqueville's journey coincided with the rise of Jacksonian democracy and its creed of (white male) egalitarianism. This gave him insight into a pivotal moment, but it did not uniquely position him to glimpse the past and future. Even though many of Tocqueville's generalizations about the American people are still cited today, several of his observations were, as one historian puts it, "simply wrong," particularly insofar as he overestimated the "equality of conditions" enjoyed by Americans.[3] For example, Tocqueville relegated slavery and Indian removal to a chapter that functioned largely as a postscript, since it cut against his overall theory of democracy.

Other texts were less successful at disguising the writer's personal feelings toward the United States. Many British writers, in particular, used their work to score political points under the guise of observation. These included Basil Hall's *Travels in North America* (1829)—which mocked Americans for their "constant habit of praising themselves, their institutions, and their country"[34] and Fanny Trollope's *Domestic Manners of the Americans* (1832), which parlayed her unhappy experiences living in Cincinnati into a scathing bestseller. The most notorious travel narrative in this period was *American Notes for General Circulation* by Charles Dickens, published in 1842. Unlike most other visitors, Dickens was already a celebrity by the time he arrived, and his narrative is full of encounters with people who knew that he would be writing a book about his travels. He took note of what appeared to be a widespread concern for how such books were written, including one man who was "exceedingly anxious to expound at great length" on how "books of travel in American should be written by Englishmen."[35]

Although Dickens saw the willingness of people to meddle in his method as an example of typical American social ineptitude, other British writers, most notably Harriet Martineau, were also wrestling with the same problems of methodology. Shortly after completing her own travel narrative, *Society in America* (1837), Martineau published a user's guide of sorts, *How to Observe Morals and Manners* (1838), which argued that travel writers were "as much in need of intellectual preparation as any other student" owing to the risk of anecdotal error. She added, "The travelling arrangements of the English seem designed to cut them off from companionship with the people they go to see; and they preclude the possibility of studying morals and manners in a way which is perfectly ludicrous to persons of a more social temperament and habits."[36] Indeed, the itineraries reflected in these texts followed strikingly repetitive avenues. Seemingly mandatory stops for travel writers included Niagara Falls, Washington, DC, and the Eastern State Penitentiary in Philadelphia, along with opening accounts of the Atlantic voyage, which usually foreshadowed the author's views on the United States. For Martineau, the generic character of these narratives was making it difficult for writers to notice the full range of objects and people in front of them. As she put it, "Everything that [the travel writer] looks upon will instruct him, from an aqueduct to a punch-bowl, from a penitentiary to an aviary, from the apparatus of a university to the furniture of an alehouse."[37] Despite writing in 1838, Martineau's user's guide, and particularly her openness to a radically expanded approach to selecting sources, bears striking resemblance to the arguments put forth by the vernacular strand of American Studies nearly a century later.

Perhaps the clearest example of the degree to which the travel narrative had become generic (or in other words, had become a *genre*) was its vulnerability to parodies such as Mark Twain's *The Innocents Abroad* (1869), which followed the misadventures of an American "pleasure excursion" through multiple ports around the Mediterranean and Black Sea. The novel was written as a series of dispatches for the *Daily Alta California,* which paid for Twain's passage on the steamship tour. In the novel, Twain ruthlessly mocked the notion that one can discern national character through travel and observation. If anything, he suggested that such narratives tell you more about the tourist than the places being toured. For example, Twain's fellow passengers were disappointed whenever they came across examples of cultural hybridity: "We wanted something thoroughly and uncompromisingly foreign—foreign from top to bottom—foreign from centre to circumference—foreign inside and outside and all around— nothing to remind us of any other people or any other land under the sun."[38] The clash between expectations and reality proved an endless source of humor for Twain, who concluded that "the gentle reader will never, never know what a consummate ass he can become, until he goes abroad."[39]

Other spoofs were even more cutting. In 1901, Japanese writer Yone Noguchi published *The American Diary of a Japanese Girl* under the pen name Miss Morning Glory. Through its mimicry of the genre of travel writing, Noguchi's book convinced many readers that it was an actual diary of travels through California, Chicago, and New York. In so doing, Noguchi's gender-bending exercise served to mock how American readers would expect Japanese women to write about the United States. The book's form carried as much of the weight as its content, with entries like, "Let me learn the beauty of American freedom, starting with my hair!"[40] Miss Morning Glory becomes a sort of refracting lens for ironically channeling its readers' expectations.

Both Twain and Noguchi help underscore the pitfalls of the anthropological strand of American Studies. According to Margaret Mead, ethnography was not a method that intellectuals could simply dabble in; it required specialized training. "If the observer is untrained," she wrote, "he gives more data about his own cultural position than about the other upon which he is reporting."[41] Yet several of her contemporaries continued to find rich new avenues of writing in the less rigorous tradition of Tocqueville and Dickens, including those well outside the social sciences such as Gertrude Stein (who went on a 191-day American tour in which her method was to "talk and look and listen" to the people around her) and John Steinbeck (who, in *Travels with Charley: In Search of America* [1962], recounted a cross-country road trip with his dog, Charley, at the height of the Cold War). And so we might name at least three strands in the anthropological past of American Studies: a genial assumption that observation of people and places might yield insights into a vague concept of "national character"; a more rigorous ethnographic impulse that sought to systematize knowledge about a social group, even one as large and ambiguous as "the nation"; and a self-reflexive skepticism toward both the method and the results—even as writers continued to engage it.

In recent years, introspection about anthropology's fetishization of alterity and aversion to hybridity produced what might be called an "autobiographical turn," with anthropologists increasingly studying the very communities with which they identify. Among the many examples in American Studies include Kathryn Marie Dudley's *Debt and Dispossession: Farm Loss in America's Heartland* (2000) and Audra Simpson's *Mohawk Interruptus: Political Life across the Borders of Settler States* (2014). Dudley, for example, links her interest in the loss of family farms to her own childhood memories from western Minnesota. She notes:

> Without family ties to the area, it would have been difficult, if not impossible, to conduct the in-depth interviews upon which this book is based. The frank discussion of family and farm finances is not easy under any circumstances, but it can be especially hard to talk about such matters with an outsider, particularly when a painful loss is involved.[42]

The autobiographical turn is not without its problems. If the journalist Bill Bishop is correct that Americans are increasingly sorting themselves into homogenous ideological enclaves, it creates a greater urgency for ethnographies that reach across divisions to make sense of social movements that might otherwise blindside the academy. An exemplary text in this regard is Katherine Cramer's *The Politics of Resentment: Rural Consciousness in Wisconsin and the Rise of Scott Walker* (2016), which is based on dozens of interviews with residents of rural Wisconsin who felt alienated from the university and other state institutions. In such works, one can see the full flavor of an anthropological or ethnographic approach, which engages people, demands self-reflection and situatedness, and seeks to understand affinity groups, communities, publics, and counterpublics, without leaping to generalizations about American culture as a whole.

The impulse to generalize is perhaps the main reason why few of the texts from our Old School American Studies mixtape are still read today. But even so, few books in the historiography of American Studies have come in for as much criticism as Henry Nash Smith's *Virgin Land: The American West as Symbol and Myth* (1950) (box 6). Today the most common critique focuses on the word "virgin" in the title, which implies that the American West was a region empty of people and waiting to be "penetrated" by civilization. Smith himself later admitted that the book failed to adequately address the complicated histories of the Indian nations of the region. *Virgin Land* also became shorthand for the myriad failings of what Bruce Kuklick termed the "myth and symbol" school of American Studies.[43] But such critiques largely miss the main point of Smith's work. Far from simply homogenizing American culture, Smith was interested in making sense of how American culture was shaped by *regional* discourses and how, exactly, to distinguish between parts and wholes.

Today, Smith is often read as a conservative presence in the intellectual history of American Studies. But as early as the 1920s, Smith had already built a network of left-leaning scholars interested in studying regional folklore as a form of radical critique. He began his graduate studies in American Civilization at Harvard only after getting fired by Southern Methodist University for publishing a story by William Faulkner that the university considered profane. In a manifesto on "Culture" published in *Southwest Review* in 1928, Smith attacked the conservative cultural institutions of Dallas as "citadels of sweetness and light" that represented a "superficial striving" for European culture. He argued that the people of Dallas were failing to recognize their culture as "a queer milieu patched together from the shreds

Spaces = Cultures, communities
"borders".

of the musical ideas of New York song-writers, the artistic and ethical conceptions of California moving-picture producers, the mechanical triumphs of Detroit automotive engineers, the journalism of national syndicate-writers, and the skill of professional athletes."[44] Smith went on to make the case for a more clear-eyed approach to the study of regionalism that would account for modernity instead of simply resisting it.

In utilizing sources like dime novels, Smith was heavily influenced by writers like Constance Rourke and Benjamin Botkin, who were part of a larger movement to treat folklore as a valid subject of academic study. Rourke's *American Humor* (1931), for example, traced the role of three archetypal characters in American folk culture: the Yankee, the backwoodsman, and the blackface minstrel. She had little interest in Puritanism, which she saw as a relic of New England's past that had masqueraded as the basis of a universal American national culture for too long. Botkin had a similar impatience with those who treated New England as a substitute for the nation as a whole. As editor of the regionalist journal *Folk-Say,* Botkin curated dozens of anthologies of folklore from around the country, including a collection of urban legends called *Sidewalks of America* (1954). In his 1946 article, "Paul Bunyan Was OK in His Time," Botkin argued that archetypes such as

Smith and Rourke's backwoodsman had modern analogues in the labor movement, where tall tales about heroic work on assembly lines had spread much like Bunyan's story in an earlier generation. This can be seen in the physical comedy of texts ranging from Charlie Chaplin's film *Modern Times* (1936) to an iconic scene from the 1950s television series *I Love Lucy,* when Lucy and Ethel are overwhelmed by a speeding conveyor belt in a candy factory.

It is no surprise that the trope of heroic work exemplified by Paul Bunyan made its way into slapstick comedy. Whether on vaudeville, film, or television, slapstick was a genre that did not require English language skills to understand, and as such was popular among the polyglot communities of immigrant workers in cities. Moreover, as migration to cities reshaped the United States, the transposition of rural folkways onto industrial settings became a major theme of regionalist writing. Botkin noted that the 1930s had witnessed the first concerted effort to "round up this new urban and industrial lore, from taxi drivers, sandhogs, iron workers, plasterers, needle trade workers, shoe workers, hospital workers, stage hands, longshoremen, seamen, marine telegraph operators, Pullman porters and the like."[45] From Buster Keaton to Lucille Ball, comedians used the factory as a rich source of satire that tapped into the shared experience of regional and transnational migration.

Ideas of space and place were central to the development of vernacular cultures. As Susan Scott Parrish notes in *The Flood Year 1927* (2017), the experience of inhabiting a region of extreme environmental distress during the Great Mississippi Flood generated a parallel flood of literary and musical production. Parrish argues that songs like Bessie Smith's "Backwater Blues" (1927) made the flood legible to publics beyond the flood zone in ways that newspapers could only partially accomplish. This interconnectedness of culture and place scrambles the boundaries between the four mixtapes in this chapter. Folklorists like Rourke and Botkin might fit most comfortably within the Vernacular mixtape, but they grounded their work in raw material gathered from specific regions. To take one example, George Chauncey's *Gay New York* (1994) could easily be placed in *any* of the four mixtapes that we've just created. Chauncey combines meticulous documentary research with ethnographic interviews of more than seventy men who helped decode the networks, vocabularies, and rituals—in other words, the *vernacular*—that structured the particular gay world of New York City, and helped lay the groundwork for political activism at Stonewall and beyond. This convergence should underscore the point that historiographical inquiry is not about reading individual texts in a vacuum, but rather seeing how they interact with other texts to form a larger conversation.

Change
the context and
background

Indeed, the same text can take on different meanings simply by putting it on a different mixtape. A good example is Richard Wright's *12 Million Black Voices* (1941), which used both narrative and photography to depict the Great Migration of African Americans from the Jim Crow South to the northern cities in the early twentieth century. The images in the first half of the book include graphic examples of racial violence of the rural South, but as Wright follows hopeful black workers to cities like Chicago and Detroit, the reader encounters a world still structured by racism and poverty, with black migrants facing hostility from police, landlords, employers, and fellow workers. In so doing, Wright's book can be situated within a muckraking tradition reaching back to Jacob Riis's *How the Other Half Lives* (1890). Like Wright, Riis used vivid images of urban poverty to try to mobilize readers to take action in response to a social problem that they might otherwise ignore, which could justify moving both texts to the American Problems mixtape. Indeed, the underlying message of Wright's text in some sense *undermines* a regionalist approach by demonstrating how structures of racism followed workers from place to place, across regions. In other words, *12 Million Black Voices* serves as an indictment of the illusion that racism was a Southern problem, instead casting it as central to American democracy. These choices about how to combine and recombine texts are at the heart of historiographical analysis.

Recognizing the challenges of a strictly regional frame, scholars have developed a rich vocabulary for mapping American culture in spatial terms. Such concepts include *diaspora,* which allows scholars to understand culture as a set of practices—exchanging letters, reading newspapers—rather than a form of belonging rooted in place. Others have utilized the term *borderlands* to describe interstitial regions characterized by cultural and linguistic hybridity. In American Indian studies, by contrast, *removal* often seems a more accurate description of diasporic movement, and rootedness in space a still powerful concept. In recognition of such complexity, terms like *frontier* have largely disappeared from scholarship on the territorial expansion of the United States. The historian Pekka Hämäläinen has gone so far as to describe the Comanche as an *empire* that dominated the Southern plains as late as the nineteenth century, absorbing immigrants from Spanish territory, other Indian nations, and the United States. Other terms have taken on renewed importance. From an urban studies perspective, Benjamin Looker has argued for the symbolic centrality of the term *neighborhood* to the experience of space in the twentieth century—a "concrete, graspable microcosm" that structured declension narratives of urban blight as well as more optimistic visions of the democratic vitality of city life.

This problem of scale—local, regional, national, and global—is underscored by the two remaining examples on our mixtape: Gloria Anzaldúa's *Borderlands / La Frontera: The New Mestiza* (1987) and Lissa Wadewitz's *The Nature of Borders* (2015). Despite the fantasies of erasure at the heart of settler colonialism in Texas, Anzaldúa drew attention to the hybrid cultural identities that had been forged along borders both seen and unseen—geographic, spiritual, political, and linguistic. What came to matter in Anzaldúa's analysis was a new space, the borderlands, shaped and defined by two national spaces. This was a particular location—not exactly a region—that captured histories and pains at the very heart of the American experience. *The Nature of Borders* offers a distinctive echo of this argument. Wadewitz casts the maritime border between British Columbia and Washington State as a fiction that generated new practices. For example, some fishermen in the early twentieth century—the so-called "pirates of the Salish Sea"—would raid the corporate industrial traps that were threatening their livelihoods and escape across the border to evade capture and sell their stolen catch.[46] The salmon, of course, were impossible to contain within international borders without disrupting their migratory routes, which meant any efforts toward conservation demanded new mechanisms of transnational cooperation. In short, writers like Anzaldúa and Wadewitz argue that looking beyond borders can demystify the power structures—race, gender, language, and especially national identity—that masquerade as universals in monolithic representations of American culture.

FURTHER READING: MIXING AND REMIXING

DAMN.

These four mixtapes are only the tip of the iceberg of American Studies historiography. They form *heuristic* categories—that is, shortcuts that are adequate for the time being, things to get you thinking. They require elaboration, healthy skepticism, and continued thought. Through them, however, you can see themes that have come to matter greatly to many practitioners of American Studies. From the Vernacular mixtape, you can see a growing tradition of resistance to high-culture prescriptions of canonical writing, with scholars searching for ways to discover, organize, and use vernacular, or "common," cultural texts. The American Problems mixtape suggests a long-standing engagement with the social issues facing real people and groups. The Anthropological mixtape emphasizes methods of observation and conversation that demand self-reflection and systematic caution on the part of the investigator. It illustrates shifts over time, as scholars moved from large claims about "the American character" to more realistic efforts to understand smaller social bodies. The American Spaces mixtape reveals that one of the most important efforts to problematize such national character interpretations came from regionalists who rejected New England as a model for the nation, and turned instead to folk cultures. A spatial orientation has proven powerful and productive as scholars have sought to place terms such as local, regional, national, borderlands, transnational, and global in analytical relation to one another.

Changes to the perception of "the American experience"

But even within the four categories we chose, a strong case can be made that all forty books should be swapped out for different choices. With this in mind, we've created several other mixes—each strictly limited to ten texts—that you might find useful for further reading. Inevitably, this means important texts have been left out, but we hope these omissions will get you thinking about how you would make your own American Studies mixtapes. Historiography can be combined and recombined in a million different ways, each offering a different pathway into past scholarship.

The six mixtapes that follow are based on the remaining texts from the Old School American Studies mixtape that we didn't have room to discuss in depth (boxes 7–12). The Early America mixtape underscores the field's contributions to interdisciplinary understandings of early American history. The Mixtape of Mixtapes includes some of the field's most important anthologies, and the Theory 101 mixtape offers an eclectic collection of texts that illustrate the intersections of American Studies with various branches of cultural theory. The American Education mixtape contextualizes American Studies within a broad history of education. This is followed by two Models of Method lists—one by Phil and one by Alex—with some of our favorite examples of American Studies scholarship. Both of these mixtapes are curated with an eye toward methodological range and rigor.

At the end of this section, we have included alternate versions—or remixes—of the four libraries that we already discussed in this chapter. For ease of reference, we have also included the original lists (boxes 13–21). As you can see, any of the four original mixtapes (Vernacular, American Problems, Anthropological, and American Spaces) could have been arranged around ten entirely different books. But even then, we still are only scratching the surface. You could easily create a third version (or a fourth, or a fifth . . .) out of any of these mixes—and in fact we encourage you to try it!

BOX 7. THE EARLY AMERICA MIXTAPE

1. Perry Miller, *The New England Mind: The Seventeenth Century* (1939).
2. Edmund Morgan, *American Slavery, American Freedom: The Ordeal of Colonial Virginia* (1975).
3. Laurel Thatcher Ulrich, *A Midwife's Tale: The Life of Martha Ballard, Based on Her Diary, 1785–1812* (1990).
4. Ira Berlin, *Many Thousands Gone: The First Two Centuries of Slavery in North America* (1998).
5. Peter Linebaugh and Marcus Rediker, *The Many-Headed Hydra: Sailors, Slaves, Commoners, and the Hidden History of the Revolutionary Atlantic* (2000).
6. Allan Greer, *Mohawk Saint: Catherine Tekakwitha and the Jesuits* (2005).
7. Louise Pubols, *The Father of All: The de la Guerra Family, Power, and Patriarchy in Mexican California* (2009).
8. Jean O'Brien, *Firsting and Lasting: Writing Indians Out of Existence in New England* (2010).
9. Michael Witgen, *An Infinity of Nations: How the Native New World Shaped Early North America* (2012).
10. Jennifer Roberts, *Transporting Visions: The Movement of Images in Early America* (2014).

BOX 8. THE MIXTAPE OF MIXTAPES

1. Caroline Ware, ed., *The Cultural Approach to History* (1940).
2. Mary Turpie and Joseph Kwait, eds., *Studies in American Culture: Dominant Ideas and Images* (1960).
3. Marshall Fishwick, ed., *American Studies in Transition* (1964).
4. Lucy Maddox, ed., *Locating American Studies: The Evolution of a Discipline* (1998).
5. John Carlos Rowe, ed., *Post-Nationalist American Studies* (2000).
6. Charles Hale, ed., *Engaging Contradictions: Theory, Politics, and Methods of Activist Scholarship* (2008).
7. Greil Marcus and Werner Sollors, eds., *A New Literary History of America* (2009).
8. Bruce Burgett and Glenn Hendler, eds., *Keywords for American Cultural Studies*, Second Edition (2014).
9. Yuan Shu and Donald Pease, eds., *American Studies as Transnational Practice: Turning toward the Transpacific* (2015).
10. Brooke Blower and Mark Philip Bradley, eds., *The Familiar Made Strange: American Icons and Artifacts after the Transnational Turn* (2015).

BOX 9. THE THEORY 101 MIXTAPE

1. Kenneth Burke, *A Grammar of Motives* (1945).
2. Clifford Geertz, *The Interpretation of Cultures: Selected Essays* (1973).
3. Joan Wallach Scott, *Gender and the Politics of History* (1988).
4. W.J.T. Mitchell, *Picture Theory: Essays on Verbal and Visual Representation* (1994).
5. Michael Warner, *Publics and Counterpublics* (2003).
6. Kandice Chuh, *Imagine Otherwise: On Asian Americanist Critique* (2003).
7. David Harvey, *A Brief History of Neoliberalism* (2005).
8. Jane Bennett, *Vibrant Matter: A Political Ecology of Things* (2010).
9. Susan Archer Mann, *Doing Feminist Theory: From Modernity to Postmodernity* (2012).
10. Patricia Hill Collins and Sirma Bilge, *Intersectionality* (2016).

BOX 10. THE AMERICAN EDUCATION MIXTAPE

1. Alexander Meiklejohn, *What Does America Mean?* (1935).
2. Tremaine McDowell, *American Studies* (1948).
3. David Wallace Adams, *Education for Extinction: American Indians and the Boarding School Experience, 1875–1928* (1995).
4. Mary Kelley, *Learning to Stand and Speak: Women, Education, and Public Life in America's Republic* (2006).
5. Nicholas Longo, *Why Community Matters: Connecting Education with Civic Life* (2007).
6. Rodolfo Acuña, *The Making of Chicana/o Studies: In the Trenches of Academe* (2011).
7. Martha Biondi, *The Black Revolution on Campus* (2012).
8. Roderick Ferguson, *The Reorder of Things: The University and Its Pedagogies of Minority Difference* (2012).
9. Ruben Flores, *Backroads Pragmatists: Mexico's Melting Pot and Civil Rights in the United States* (2014).
10. Rebecca Onion, *Innocent Experiments: Childhood and the Culture of Popular Science in the United States* (2016).

BOX 11. THE MODELS OF METHOD MIXTAPE #1 (PHIL'S CHOICES)

1. David Potter, *People of Plenty: Economic Abundance and the American Character* (1954).
2. Grady Clay, *Close-Up: How to Read the American City* (1973).
3. John Stilgoe, *Common Landscape of America, 1580 to 1845* (1982).
4. Greil Marcus, *Lipstick Traces: A Secret History of the Twentieth Century* (1989).
5. Carlo Rotella, *Good with Their Hands: Boxers, Bluesmen, and Other Characters from the Rust Belt* (2002).
6. Christina Klein, *Cold War Orientalism: Asia in the Middlebrow Imagination, 1945–1961* (2003).
7. Julie Sze, *Noxious New York: The Racial Politics of Urban Health and Environmental Justice* (2007).
8. Matt Cohen, *The Networked Wilderness: Communicating in Early New England* (2010).
9. Suzanne Smith, *To Serve the Living: Funeral Directors and the African American Way of Death* (2010).
10. Kim TallBear, *Native American DNA: Tribal Belonging and the False Promise of Genetic Science* (2013).

BOX 12. THE MODELS OF METHOD MIXTAPE #2 (ALEX'S CHOICES)

1. Leo Marx, *The Machine in the Garden: Technology and the Pastoral Ideal in America* (1964).
2. Paul Johnson, *A Shopkeeper's Millennium: Society and Revivals in Rochester, New York, 1815–1837* (1978).
3. Stephanie Coontz, *The Way We Never Were: American Families and the Nostalgia Trap* (1992).
4. Anne Fadiman, *The Spirit Catches You and You Fall Down: A Hmong Child, Her American Doctors, and the Collision of Two Cultures* (1997).
5. Susan Glenn, *Female Spectacle: The Theatrical Roots of Modern Feminism* (2000).
6. Barbara Ransby, *Ella Baker and the Black Freedom Movement: A Radical Democratic Vision* (2003).
7. Laura Kipnis, *Against Love: A Polemic* (2003).
8. Ira Katznelson, *When Affirmative Action Was White: An Untold History of Racial Inequality in Twentieth-Century America* (2005).
9. Mel Chen, *Animacies: Biopolitics, Racial Mattering, and Queer Affect* (2012).
10. Elizabeth Armstrong and Laura Hamilton, *Paying for the Party: How College Maintains Inequality* (2013).

BOX 13. ORIGINAL #1: THE VERNACULAR MIXTAPE

1. W.E.B. Du Bois, *The Souls of Black Folk: Essays and Sketches* (1903).
2. Van Wyck Brooks, *America's Coming-of-Age* (1915).
3. Constance Rourke, *American Humor: A Study of the National Character* (1931).
4. John Dos Passos, *U.S.A.* (1938).
5. F.O. Matthiessen, *American Renaissance: Art and Expression in the Age of Emerson and Whitman* (1941).
6. C.L.R. James, *Notes on American Civilization* (1950). Unpublished until 1993.
7. Ralph Ellison, *Shadow and Act* (1964).
8. Janice Radway, *Reading the Romance: Women, Patriarchy, and Popular Literature* (1984).
9. Miriam Hansen, *Babel and Babylon: Spectatorship in American Silent Film* (1991).
10. Michael Denning, *Noise Uprising: The Audiopolitics of a World Musical Revolution* (2015).

BOX 14. VERNACULAR REMIX: AGAINST THE GRAIN

1. Vine Deloria, Jr., *Custer Died for Your Sins: An Indian Manifesto* (1969).
2. Lawrence Levine, *Black Culture and Black Consciousness: Afro-American Folk Thought from Slavery to Freedom* (1977).
3. Gloria Anzaldúa and Cherríe Moraga, eds., *This Bridge Called My Back: Writings by Radical Women of Color* (1981).
4. Robin D.G. Kelley, *Race Rebels: Culture, Politics, and the Black Working Class* (1994).
5. Nan Enstad, *Ladies of Labor, Girls of Adventure: Working Women, Popular Culture, and Labor Politics at the Turn of the Twentieth Century* (1999).
6. James W. Cook, *The Arts of Deception: Playing with Fraud in the Age of Barnum* (2001).
7. Rob King, *The Fun Factory: The Keystone Film Company and the Emergence of Mass Culture* (2009).
8. Robin Bernstein, *Racial Innocence: Performing American Childhood from Slavery to Civil Rights* (2011).
9. Raúl Coronado, *A World Not to Come: A History of Latino Writing and Print Culture* (2013).
10. Ramzi Fawaz, *The New Mutants: Superheroes and the Radical Imagination of American Comics* (2016).

**BOX 15. ORIGINAL #2: THE AMERICAN PROBLEMS
MIXTAPES**

1. Charlotte Perkins Gilman, *Women and Economics: A Study of the Economic Relation between Men and Women as a Factor in Social Evolution* (1898).
2. Thorstein Veblen, *The Theory of the Leisure Class: An Economic Study in the Evolution of Institutions* (1899).
3. Ida Tarbell, *The History of the Standard Oil Company* (1904).
4. J. Allen Smith, *The Spirit of American Government: A Study of the Constitution, Its Origin, Influence and Relation to Democracy* (1907).
5. Jane Addams, *Twenty Years at Hull-House* (1910).
6. James Harvey Robinson, *The New History: Essays Illustrating the Modern Historical Outlook* (1912).
7. Charles Beard, *An Economic Interpretation of the Constitution of the United States* (1913).
8. Walter Lippmann, *Public Opinion* (1922).
9. John Dewey, *The Public and Its Problems* (1927).
10. Vernon Parrington, *Main Currents in American Thought: An Interpretation of American Literature from the Beginnings to 1920* (1927–1930).

BOX 16. AMERICAN PROBLEMS REMIX: THE NEW GILDED AGE

1. David Shipler, *The Working Poor: Invisible in America* (2004).
2. Ruth Wilson Gilmore, *Golden Gulag: Prisons, Surplus, Crisis, and Opposition in Globalizing California* (2007).
3. Moustafa Bayoumi, *How Does It Feel to Be a Problem?: Being Young and Arab in America* (2008).
4. Russ Castronovo and Susan Gillman, eds., *States of Emergency: The Object of American Studies* (2009).
5. Bethany Moreton, *To Serve God and Wal-Mart: The Making of Christian Free Enterprise* (2009).
6. Michelle Alexander, *The New Jim Crow: Mass Incarceration in the Age of Colorblindness* (2010).
7. Jodi Melamed, *Represent and Destroy: Rationalizing Violence in the New Racial Capitalism* (2011).
8. Robert Sampson, *The Great American City: Chicago and the Enduring Neighborhood Effect* (2012).
9. Thomas Piketty, *Capital in the Twenty-First Century* (2014).
10. Keeanga-Yamahtta Taylor, *From #BlackLivesMatter to Black Liberation* (2016).

BOX 17. AMERICAN PROBLEMS REMIX:
ANTEBELLUM PROBLEMS

1. David Walker, *Appeal in Four Articles; Together with a Preamble, To the Coloured Citizens of the World, but in Particular, and Very Expressly, to Those of the United States of America* (1829).
2. William Lloyd Garrison, "Address at Park Street Church, Boston" (1829).
3. William Apess, *Eulogy on King Philip: As Pronounced at the Odeon, in Federal Street, Boston* (1836).
4. Margaret Fuller, *Woman in the Nineteenth Century* (1845).
5. Harriet Beecher Stowe, *Uncle Tom's Cabin; or, Life among the Lowly* (1852).
6. Henry David Thoreau, *Walden; or, Life in the Woods* (1854).
7. Frederick Douglass, *My Bondage and My Freedom* (1855).
8. Herman Melville, "The Paradise of Bachelors and the Tartarus of Maids" (1855).
9. Harriett Jacobs, *Incidents in the Life of a Slave Girl* (1861).
10. Rebecca Harding, "Life in the Iron Mills" (1861).

BOX 18. ORIGINAL #3: THE ANTHROPOLOGICAL MIXTAPE

1. J. Hector St. John de Crèvecoeur, *Letters from an American Farmer* (1782).
2. Alexis de Tocqueville, *Democracy in America* (1835–1840).
3. Harriet Martineau, *How to Observe Morals and Manners* (1838).
4. Yone Noguchi, *The American Diary of a Japanese Girl* (1901).
5. Robert Lynd and Helen Lynd, *Middletown: A Study in American Culture* (1929).
6. Ruth Benedict, *Patterns of Culture* (1934).
7. Gertrude Stein, *The Geographical History of America: or, The Relation of Human Nature to the Human Mind* (1936).
8. Margaret Mead, *And Keep Your Powder Dry: An Anthropologist Looks at America* (1942).
9. Hortense Powdermaker, *Hollywood, the Dream Factory: An Anthropologist Looks at the Movie-Makers* (1950).
10. Kathryn Marie Dudley, *Debt and Dispossession: Farm Loss in America's Heartland* (2000).

BOX 19. ANTHROPOLOGICAL REMIX: NOTES ON TRAVEL

1. James Fenimore Cooper, *Notions of the Americans: Picked Up by a Travelling Bachelor* (1828).
2. Frances Trollope, *Domestic Manners of the Americans* (1832).
3. Charles Dickens, *American Notes for General Circulation* (1842).
4. Mark Twain, *The Innocents Abroad, or, the New Pilgrims' Progress* (1869).
5. John Steinbeck, *Travels with Charley: In Search of America* (1962).
6. Jean Baudrillard, *America* (1986).
7. Mary Louise Pratt, *Imperial Eyes: Travel Writing and Transculturation* (1992).
8. Lucy Lippard, *The Lure of the Local: Senses of Place in a Multicentered Society* (1997).
9. Roxanne Euben, *Journeys to the Other Shore: Muslim and Western Travelers in Search of Knowledge* (2008).
10. Michelle Commander, *Afro-Atlantic Flight: Speculative Returns and the Black Fantastic* (2017).

BOX 20. ORIGINAL #4: THE AMERICAN SPACES MIXTAPE

1. Jacob Riis, *How the Other Half Lives: Studies among the Tenements of New York* (1890).
2. Richard Wright, *12 Million Black Voices: A Folk History of the Negro in the United States* (1941).
3. Henry Nash Smith, *Virgin Land: The American West as Symbol and Myth* (1950).
4. Benjamin Botkin, *Sidewalks of America: Folklore, Legends, Sagas, Traditions, Customs, Songs, Stories, and Sayings of City Folk* (1954).
5. Gloria Anzaldúa, *Borderlands / La Frontera: The New Mestiza* (1987).
6. George Chauncey, *Gay New York: Gender, Urban Culture, and the Making of the Gay Male World, 1890–1940* (1994).
7. Pekka Hämäläinen, *The Comanche Empire* (2008).
8. Lissa Wadewitz, *The Nature of Borders: Salmon, Boundaries, and Bandits on the Salish Sea* (2012).
9. Benjamin Looker, *A Nation of Neighborhoods: Imagining Cities, Communities, and Democracy in Postwar America* (2015).
10. Susan Scott Parrish, *The Flood Year 1927: A Cultural History* (2017).

BOX 21. AMERICAN SPACES REMIX:
TRANSNATIONAL SPACES

1. Paul Gilroy, *The Black Atlantic: Modernity and Double Consciousness* (1993).
2. Uta Poiger, *Jazz, Rock, and Rebels: Cold War Politics and American Culture in a Divided Germany* (2000).
3. Matthew Frye Jacobson, *Barbarian Virtues: The United States Encounters Foreign Peoples at Home and Abroad, 1876–1917* (2000).
4. Melani McAlister, *Epic Encounters: Culture, Media, and U.S. Interests in the Middle East since 1945* (2001).
5. Amy Kaplan, *The Anarchy of Empire in the Making of U.S. Culture* (2002).
6. Brent Edwards, *The Practice of Diaspora: Literature, Translation, and the Rise of Black Internationalism* (2003).
7. Mae Ngai, *Impossible Subjects: Illegal Aliens and the Making of Modern America* (2004).
8. Natalia Molina, *How Race Is Made in America: Immigration, Citizenship, and the Historical Power of Racial Scripts* (2014).
9. Lisa Lowe, *The Intimacies of Four Continents* (2015).
10. Julia Mickenberg, *American Girls in Red Russia: Chasing the Soviet Dream* (2017).

THREE

An Institutional History of American Studies

(OR, WHAT'S THE MATTER WITH MIXTAPES?)

> This idea of American Studies, whether disciplinary or inter-disciplinary, is an attempt to see that people aren't just philoso-phers, they are also baseball fans and they go on motor trips and things like that, and unless you approach things in terms of put-ting together as well as isolating I can't see that you're going to arrive at knowledge.
>
> LOUIS RUBIN, JR., 1957

SO NOW YOU HAVE A STACK OF BOOKS, or mixtapes. Maybe you've created a new mixtape with a different set of readings. Maybe you've read them already, or plan to read them. Either way, the exercise in our previous chapter echoes the long American tradition of *autodidactic* learning—the idea that people might not need a formal education, since everything you need to know can be found in a library, or online . . . or in, say, a user's guide. Indeed, there is an entire DIY-industrial complex of how-to manuals and self-help books meant to serve the ideal of independent learning. The list of things you can learn on your own seems endless.

In practice, things are never so simple. There's mediation involved in most skills. There's also practice, and correction, and apprenticeship, and context. Say that you're reading this very book—*American Studies: A User's Guide*—in the context of an American Studies class or curriculum. If so, your experi-ence is being mediated by a bunch of things out of our control, like require-ments, grades, assignments, and discussions. If not, take a moment to think about how you found us. Was it by word of mouth? Did Amazon's algorithm suggest this book based on your browsing habits? Regardless of how you found us (and don't get us wrong, we're glad you're here!), there had to be some sort of *institutional* or *technological* checkpoint to facilitate the process of distribution, or else you'd never know this book exists.

When it comes to the music that we put on mixtapes, things get even more complicated. Someone growing up in the 1970s might have had a record collection, which by the 1980s became cassettes, followed by CDs in the 1990s and mp3s in the early 2000s—unless you're into industrial noise, in which case you still prefer cassettes. Today's music streaming services are just technologically supercharged versions of these libraries. Approaching historiography through a collection of books (as we did in the previous chapter) sidesteps the issue of technology and institutional connections to the wider world. You can listen to the Beatles in *any* of these formats. "Strawberry Fields Forever" stays "Strawberry Fields Forever," forever. But when you emphasize music over its medium, you lose other, often-important aspects to the story. For example, the physical scratching of vinyl records at house parties was critical to the sound of hip hop in the Bronx in the 1970s. You don't want that fact to slip through the cracks.

The context in which music and books are made, distributed, and enjoyed matters. We can't ignore concerts and publicity, for example, or the trappings of celebrity. The documentary *Searching for Sugar Man* (2012) introduced many listeners for the first time to the music of Sixto Rodriguez, who lived in obscurity in Detroit for decades without realizing that bootlegged copies of his music had made him a legend in South Africa. After the film, sales of his debut album, *Cold Fact* (1970), soared in the United States—over forty years after its original release. Today its songs are being plucked out of context and included on mixtapes. And it's great music! But without the documentary, it would mostly be forgotten.

Why does the medium or the context matter? The problem with approaching intellectual history as a series of mixtapes is that it risks obscuring the institutional settings in which the books were written, published, and taught. Once we direct our attention to things like undergraduate degree majors, departmental budgets, and academic conferences, a whole new history of American Studies emerges from the shadows. It is a history filled with conflict, compromises, and roads not taken—departments that collapsed through lack of funding, ideas that went out of fashion, scholars who died young, and maneuvering over the role of American Studies in national and international politics. These conflicts over money and attention might seem dull. In the aftermath of World War II, however, there was no escaping the renewed importance of American Studies both at home and abroad. It had become, in the words of University of Oslo professor Sigmund Skard, "an important wheel in the complicated machinery of international cultural relations."[1]

This chapter will explore how American Studies became a discipline, and not just a loosely connected series of books; how it took on institutional shape, how some of these institutions have shaped the field, and to what degree. We will focus in particular on the many ways that scholars in American Studies have tried to connect their work to the world beyond the classroom. One notorious example was a class called "Coastermania" offered by Ray Browne at Bowling Green State University in 1978. To many outsiders, the fact that students could receive college credit for riding roller coasters seemed like an example of the "dumbing down" of higher education. It met at Cedar Point amusement park, and, according to the *Pittsburgh Post-Gazette,* it involved a series of guest lectures by sociologists, architects, art historians, and engineers.[2] The course was very much a product of a particular historiographical moment, coinciding with the release of John Kasson's path-breaking book on Coney Island, *Amusing the Million* (1978). But while lectures and readings gave students a theoretical scaffolding, Browne asked them to connect those ideas to the experience of the wind in their hair, the exhilaration of a sudden drop, the screaming of the other passengers, and the relief of stepping off the ride afterwards (figure 9). Now, it's true that many of the students had probably already experienced the roller coasters at Cedar Point. But put it all together—books, lectures, experience, interpretation, and reflection—and students came away with a whole new way of looking at American culture. This kind of course was possible at BGSU, which featured an American Studies program deeply invested in popular culture. That university's institutional character, in other words, enabled a particular kind of American Studies teaching (and research) to take place.

"A PLEASANT ACADEMIC SMORGASBORD" OR "THE DISCIPLINE OF CONSCIOUS CHOICE"?

The vocabulary used to describe American Studies is controversial. Some call it a *field* to emphasize abstract ideas over their institutional manifestations; others prefer the term *movement* to emphasize its embrace of social activism. A case can also be made for terms like *discourse* or *formation* to underscore the relationship of knowledge production to power. We use all these terms

FIGURE 9. Riding the roller coaster.

throughout this user's guide. But our contention, as we noted earlier, is that American Studies is, in fact, an academic *discipline*. According to Roy Harvey Pearce, writing in 1957, American Studies would only become a discipline when it arrived at "a formalized method of knowing and expressing the knowledge of a given subject-matter." He added, crucially, that the form of a discipline, "to be valid and authentic, must reflect the form of its subject-matter." In other words, a discipline created to overcome "hyperspecialization" in the study of culture could not itself become too specialized. What it demanded, rather, was "a disciplined way of looking" that would somehow remain flexible and inclusive.[3]

In the 1950s, the most common approach to solving this puzzle was curricular, with a tendency toward the individual and idiosyncratic. Music, for example, was rarely offered unless there happened to be "an enthusiast of jazz or folk music" already on the faculty.[4] Instead of adopting a uniform or standardized method, many American Studies programs used distribution requirements that allowed students to pick and choose techniques from a range of affiliated departments. In the University of Minnesota's American Studies program, students were tested on "their practical working knowledge of methodologies" acquired through coursework and asked to explain "their relation to American Studies." Because each student's course of study involved a different combination of electives, no two exams would be the same. The purpose of such flexibility, according to Minnesota's program director Tremaine McDowell, was to protect the unique role of American Studies as an experimental crossroads. As he put it, Minnesota's program "was undertaken as an experiment in education, not experimental merely in its initiation but continuingly and permanently experimental—fluid, flexible, and open to frequent revision in its procedures."[5]

Although McDowell's vision sounded promising, American Studies quickly developed a reputation for catering "to the dilettantes among the students."[6] In 1954, *Mademoiselle* cast American Studies as "a pleasant academic smorgasbord" in which students could learn about "anything from cowboy yarns to sermons to Emily Dickinson's private papers."[7] One photograph in the feature story depicted McDowell casually smoking a cigarette while screening a film, and Perry Miller was described as "Harvard's zesty apologist for the Puritans."[8] A later profile in *People Magazine* attributed the popularity of the University of Michigan's American Culture program to the broad scope of its curriculum and openness to "all fields of scholarly endeavor."[9] If, originally, American Studies had been "introduced without fanfare, almost casually, as a strictly local experiment in interdisciplinary teaching and research," this wave of popular attention did little to deter what Alan Trachtenberg called the field's "casualness toward methodology."[10] Meanwhile, some faculty feared (with good reason) that methodological consolidation would become a game of musical chairs—with their own methods left without a place to sit. Better to remain "a pleasant academic smorgasbord" than to "discipline" the field. It turns out that anti-disciplinarity—an important current in contemporary American Studies—has a long history.

To understand how American Studies got to this point of methodological anxiety, it is worth taking a quick trip through the history of higher education in the United States. In the early 1800s, universities served only a tiny fraction of the American population—mostly white, male, and Protestant. The humanities, for the most part, emphasized Greek and Roman classics and sought to produce virtuous, civic-minded leaders who could protect American democracy from corruption. It was not until after the Civil War that universities came to be seen more as engines of progress that could fuel economic growth through specialized knowledge, especially in the sciences. This change was heralded by a significant expansion of access to higher education. In 1862, the Morrill Land-Grant Act offered federal support to the states for establishing or expanding public universities, as long as they offered courses in "agriculture and the mechanic arts." Designed to serve the children of farmers and industrial workers, the Morrill Act not only increased the raw numbers of Americans who attended college but also oriented these institutions toward the vocational needs of citizens. The University of Wisconsin, for example, cast itself as "the university that reaches anybody, anytime, anyhow."[11] This diversification—both in demographics and purpose—made the old model of classical education obsolete. Academic life was instead carved up into an array of distinct disciplines, each staking claim to its own unique domain of knowledge through things like national professional organizations. Consider the compressed time frame in which the following groups were founded:

Modern Language Association	1883
American Historical Association	1884
American Economic Association	1885
American Psychological Association	1892
American Philosophical Association	1900
American Political Science Association	1903
American Sociological Association	1905

In 1919, the American Council of Learned Societies, or ACLS, was founded as an umbrella for groups like these. To this day, practically all American universities offer undergraduate academic majors in each of the distinct disciplines listed above.

The earliest rumblings of American Studies emerged around this same time. Primarily it reflected a nagging concern that something important had been lost when higher education in the United States moved away from older models that taught citizenship and civic virtue. Between 1875 and 1950, a trickle of classes and faculty positions grew into a full-fledged movement. Was that movement fundamentally conservative, nostalgic for the classical education of the early nineteenth century? Not really. At every step of the way, American Studies proved to be a magnet for scholars unhappy with what Henry Nash Smith called "academicism," or the detachment of scholarship from public life.[12] It resisted the disciplining of higher education, but did so not by resurrecting an elite past, but by embracing the vernacular, the public, and new ideals of citizenship. It developed its own (inter)disciplinary structures. By the 1950s, the nascent field had acquired an academic journal (*American Quarterly*), a national professional organization (the American Studies Association, or ASA), and numerous degree programs. It was resisted by faculty who were "jealously devoted to their own disciplines," but it also found a great deal of public support due to its emphasis on democratic education, particularly after the twin catastrophes of the Great Depression and World War II.[13] In 1958, the ASA was admitted into the ACLS alongside its older peers.

From the perspective of thirty thousand feet, this story certainly seems to describe the founding of a discipline. Things get murkier, however, when we zoom in on the details. There, you'll find a chaotic, interdisciplinary hodge-podge. As late as 1957, one leader in the field characterized American Studies as "little more than window-dressing" in "a rather large number of schools."[14] Even the issue of naming remained unsettled, as illustrated by the following sampling of degree programs appearing in one 1957 survey.[15]

American Studies
American Civilization
American Culture
American Thought and Civilization
American Ideals and Institutions
American Literary and Cultural History
American History and Literature

To make sense of this confusion, we might slow down and examine what, exactly, was taking place in the various American Studies classes and programs being established at universities around the world. As Warren French of Kansas State University noted in a 1964 anthology, *American Studies in Transition,* "It has been said that a student does not really need teachers and classes at all; by ransacking the library, he can learn for himself all that there is to be known. What is less frequently pointed out about such rugged individualism is the kind of narrow, anti-social creature those few who ever manage thus to educate themselves are likely to become." What was really needed, French continued, was not a free-form radical autodidacticism, but rather, "some kind of seasoned guide"—and this is precisely what American Studies programs sought to offer, in institutional form.[16] We've come back around to our point of departure: when considering American Studies historiography, we would make a grave mistake to focus exclusively on published writings without taking time to see how those books and ideas were actually produced and used in time and place. To find the discipline and the definition, in other words, we need to learn to recognize the practice.

During the surge in cultural nationalism that accompanied World War I, it became a truism that American literature was underrepresented in the university curriculum, and many saw this absence as a national embarrassment. In 1916, the University of Chicago scholar Percy Boynton marveled "how it was possible for the educated American to know so little about the best of American literature."[17] Another writer echoed this point in 1919: "Everywhere the story is the same; our own authors are neglected for the minute study of foreign writers."[18] In 1928, despite a decade of hand-wringing over the matter, the Iowa writer Ferner Nuhn complained that "the number of courses in American literature actually offered in American colleges remains insignificantly small."[19]

This lacuna has become central to conventional histories of American Studies, most notably through the scholarship in the "vernacular" current that we examined in the previous chapter. A very different story begins to emerge, however, when we look at more prosaic documents like syllabi and course catalogues. From this perspective, American literature was not nearly as marginal to the college curriculum as writers like Nuhn implied. In 1926, the American Literature Group of the Modern Language Association found "large voluntary enrollment" in American literature courses in "nearly all" of 150 departments that it surveyed.[20] Indeed, as far back as the 1870s, some universities began to express interest in an interdisciplinary approach, even though the term "American Studies" would not appear for another half century.

In 1875, Moses Coit Tyler offered a class at the University of Michigan exploring American literature from a historical perspective. According to students who attended Tyler's classes at Michigan, "it was hard sometimes to determine whether the subject they had just heard lectured upon was history or literature."[21] Similar courses were offered at Wisconsin (1883) and Mount Holyoke (1887). According to Gaynor Pearson, Tyler "insisted" on the title of "Professor of American History and Literature" when he was hired away from Michigan in 1881 by Cornell University.[22] Tyler's blurring of history and literature had antecedents as far back as Samuel Knapp's *Lectures on American Literature: With Remarks on Some Passages of American History* (1829). By the early twentieth century, when complaints about insufficient attention to American literature reached a fever pitch, courses with titles like "Democracy in American Literature" and "American Ideals in American Literature" were being offered at Oregon (1917), USC (1918), Wesleyan (1918), Princeton (1918), West Virginia (1920), Pennsylvania (1920), Bucknell (1921), South Dakota (1921), and Colorado (1924).[23] From an institutional perspective, at least, it appears that complaints about the supposedly missing American literary curriculum were not grounded in reality.

The more potent line of attack on literature departments was methodological, and this is where American Studies made its most significant contributions. As we have seen, scholars like Vernon Parrington felt that turn-of-the-century literature departments were ensnared in esoteric methods such as "philology" (i.e., tracing words and texts back to classical sources) at the cost of the very things that made literature relevant to everyday life. These concerns were not limited to Americanists. In 1906, Harvard University established an interdisciplinary program in "History and Literature" that came to be seen as an important forerunner of American Studies, even though it did not include American content until the 1930s.[24] Likewise Yale University's "History, Arts and Letters" program, which laid the groundwork for its American Studies major, was originally dominated by medievalists who "broke down disciplinary barriers in the interests of depicting a medieval culture as a whole."[25] These "straddle programs," as Willard Thorp called them, were founded on the premise that literature was about more than words and sentences.[26] Some of the deeper truths of literature required tools that could be found in other departments such as history and economics.

Far from embracing cultural nationalism, the purpose of this more expansive view of methods was quite often to expose flaws and find solutions, and it drew on the sensibilities of the Progressive Era, pragmatist educational philosophy, and, later, the New Deal. In this respect, literature was only one piece of a much larger movement to make academic life relevant to American democracy. Recall the 1930 launch of the interdisciplinary major in "American Problems" at Sweet Briar College in Virginia, which sought to address "problems facing America today" (figure 10). In this same period, the University of Wisconsin tested an American Studies curriculum as part of its experimental college, and shortly thereafter launched a formal degree program in "American Institutions" that included a cluster of courses on "American and world problems."[27] Likewise the University of Michigan's Program in American Culture, founded in 1935, was inspired by a sense that,

INTERDEPARTMENTAL MAJORS

Two major courses are offered which give the students who elect them the opportunity to study certain topics in the correlated courses of several departments.

THE MAJOR IN AMERICAN PROBLEMS

Supervising Committee: ASSOCIATE PROFESSOR FRASER, Chairman; PROFESSOR SPARROW, PROFESSOR RAYMOND, ASSOCIATE PROFESSOR BEARD, ASSOCIATE PROFESSOR HUDSON, ASSISTANT PROFESSOR BOONE, MRS. WAILES, MR. LAUKHUFF.

Many problems facing America today result from the reciprocal play of forces which can be understood only by the study of their interrelations. The departments of History and Government, and Economics and Sociology cooperate to offer a course of study with major interest centered in American Problems. This covers the work of the junior and senior years and is open to candidates for the A.B. and B.S. degrees. The requirements for this major subject follow:

A. Courses required	Hours
1. History 111-112	6
2. History 211-212	4
3. Economics 101-102	6
4. Economics 203 or 206 or 212	3
5 Government 101-102	6
6. Government 203 or 207	2 or 3
7. Sociology 101-102	6
Total	33 or 34

FIGURE 10. *Bulletin of Sweet Briar College,* 1932–33. Image courtesy of Sweet Briar College Archives.

as Howard Mumford Jones put it, the university had "too little connection with the problems of a state as complex as Michigan."[28]

The practical orientation of these programs was epitomized by Amherst College's major in American Studies, established in 1938 as a collaboration between the departments of history, political science, economics, philosophy, and English. Its founding director, economist George Rogers Taylor, viewed American Studies as "the discipline of conscious choice" and built this idea into the curriculum.[29] All students in Amherst's major were required to take a team-taught course called "Problems in American Civilization" that cast American Studies as practice for democratic participation. Each year, the course's faculty collectively selected a number of "problems" that would reflect their political and methodological differences, and students were asked to make reasoned decisions about which tools would best help them arrive at answers. Like riding roller coasters, Taylor argued that students should "actually practice the difficult art of analyzing problems, considering alternatives, and choosing a course of action." This approach, he believed, would "more deeply and realistically" involve them "in the process of democratic education."[30] According to another Amherst faculty member, Allen Guttmann, intellectual disagreement was the "driving force of the entire program," and dissent was baked into the cake of the curriculum. Often this meant finding guest speakers for the explicit purpose of contradicting an earlier lesson. Guttmann once invited "three different people who had quarreled with me in the past, but all three declined."[31] Rather than seeing political consensus as a virtue, the course asked students to practice democratic decision-making through critical reasoning, even if they disagreed with their instructors.

The Amherst model offered a useful curricular blueprint, one that continues to resonate today. Other programs took different, equally challenging approaches. In the 1940s, for example, Barnard College's American Studies major recommended courses in "economics, English, geology, government, history, philosophy, and sociology."[32] The inclusion of geology in Barnard's curriculum was no fluke. American Studies in its early iterations was not only interdepartmental but inter*divisional*—bringing together the humanities, social sciences, and natural sciences. Wittenberg College's American Studies program offered a class on "Nature Study," and Florida State's included "not only humanists and social scientists, but also a botanist, a geographer, and educator, and the University Chaplain."[33] This explains why Carl Bode, the first president of the American Studies Association, reached out to editors of the journal *Land Economics* to try to plan a joint meeting, citing "the relation of Connecticut's town planning to the economics of the land" as a sample American Studies topic, bringing together very different tools to solve a real-world issue.[34]

In short, the boundaries of early American Studies were by no means dominated by the humanities, and one finds significant emphasis placed on finding ways of "teaching by means other than the larynx and the printed word."[35] Even after the ACLS granted recognition to the ASA in 1958, it was still unclear how, exactly, the nascent field would harness this challenging breadth. Would it become "the discipline of conscious choice," as was happening at Amherst? Or would its rebellious sensibility keep it largely "freewheeling and eclectic," as *Mademoiselle* put it in 1954? The answer, at least for a time, was that it depended on where you lived and worked.

THE LOCAL AND THE GLOBAL

Today, the annual conference of the American Studies Association attracts hundreds of papers and plays a critical role in setting the intellectual agenda of the field. Its power is such that it is easy to see the ASA as the driving force in the institutionalization of American Studies. This, too, has been a familiar narrative in American Studies. But in fact, such was not the case until quite recently. In its early years, the ASA was largely supported by regional chapters rather than vice versa—a dynamic that set it apart from many other disciplines. Among the most active in the 1950s were the American Studies Group of Minnesota and the Dakotas ("Tremaine McDowell's empire," according to ASA records), the Ohio-Indiana American Studies Association ("needs suggestions and help but not in the form of commands"), and the New England American Studies Association (the chapter "least wedded to the national organization").[36] The result of this decentralization was that American Studies, as a discipline, looked different depending on where you were studying it. As Louis Rubin, Jr., wrote to Charles Hirschfeld, president of the American Studies Association of Michigan, in 1954, "The regional chapters *are* the ASA."[37]

This decentralized model was the brainchild of McDowell, who proposed "a national society made up of informal and loosely linked regional groups" in a letter to Carl Bode on April 10, 1950.[38] As the founding editor of *American Quarterly,* McDowell was concerned that the University of Minnesota (which provided its funding) would shut down the journal unless he could prove that some sort of national professional society was in the works.[39] Bode, meanwhile, was already on the lookout for a periodical that could help him consolidate power away from the Society for American Studies (SAS), a competing group founded in 1946 by Robert Spiller of the University of Pennsylvania. Spiller strictly limited membership to fifty members, a practice that rankled people like McDowell who were left out.

One classic narrative of the development of American Studies takes Spiller—elitist, organizational, Hamiltonian—and Bode—democratic, free-wheeling, and Jeffersonian—as metonyms for two competing currents in the field. A focus on McDowell suggests a more complicated story. The establishment of the ASA can be understood as an effort by both Bode and McDowell to move the discipline in a more democratic direction, each for very different reasons. McDowell's gambit worked, with Spiller joining the ASA and agreeing to turn the older SAS into a Middle Atlantic regional chapter. In exchange *American Quarterly* was moved to Philadelphia—a move that McDowell quickly regretted. In 1951, McDowell complained "that the show is dominated by Easterners."[40] His concern was only partly a matter of geography; the real problem was that the move seemed to be turning the ASA into "an organization dominated by American literature people."[41] He believed that, in order to remain viable, American Studies had to aggressively recruit scholars from across the disciplinary spectrum as well as librarians, journalists, artists, and, as *American Quarterly* put it, "the serious-minded man on the street."[42]

McDowell's concerns proved unfounded. Not only did the University of Minnesota's broadly interdisciplinary American Studies program remain a leader in the field, but the various regional chapters continued to grow in strength relative to the national ASA throughout the 1950s and 1960s. In that sense, Spiller's gambit—to abandon national aspirations and focus on a regional organization—also proved successful. As late as 1965, the Kentucky-Tennessee chapter's newsletter scoffed at the nationalizing ambitions of the ASA, noting that: "The operant fiction that ASA possesses a national structure is at odds with observed fact, but the national secretary has hopes of coordinating the regional organizations with the mythic superstructure of the national body."[43]

If the ASA's ability to coordinate was indeed a "fiction," what was happening at the regional level to give these chapters so much power? Some activities were driven by place, such as an international exchange program in 1956 called "A Visit to the Factories and Forests for the Teachers of France." This program brought teachers from France to the Pacific Northwest to visit logging camps, tour manufacturing plants, and attend seminars held at the University of Washington to reflect on the experience. A pamphlet on the program in the ASA's records even included a glossary of "Logger Language" to help the visiting teachers interact with the lumberjacks.[44]

But most of the activities of the regional chapters did not focus on local culture; rather, they hosted meetings with themes that reflected the discipline as a whole, attracting participants from other chapters and working on an ad hoc basis with whatever resources were close at hand. In other words, regional chapters hosted national meetings in local settings. Many of these meetings revolved around archival collections of Americana (from bric-a-brac to wartime letters) that had been acquired by western and southern libraries during the nineteenth century while the wealthier universities of New England "gobbled up" manuscripts from Europe.[45] The Wisconsin–Northern Illinois chapter, for example, sponsored a conference in 1957 on "Three Chicago Institutions: Their Setting and Influence" that partnered with representatives from the Newberry Library, Chicago Historical Society, and the Art Institute of Chicago. According to the University of Minnesota's Mary Turpie, such partnerships could help realize the field's capacious approach to the archives. As she noted in 1952:

> Study of Puritan gravestones and New Mexican *santos* [religious folk art], for example, serves to sharpen and vivify understanding of the contrasting religious climates in New England and the Southwest in the seventeenth century. Similarly, the entire gamut of modern artistic expression, from calendar art to abstractions, from juke-box tunes to twelve-tone symphonies, is the legitimate and rewarding concern of students of the American present. Teachers of American civilization who venture into this field must be prepared for criticism as esthetic levelers who crassly disregard all values save that of illustration.[46]

What looked to cultural elites like "aesthetic leveling" was, from the perspective of American Studies scholars, an embrace of values like inclusion, capaciousness, and the intersection of the academic and the public. The involvement of artists and collectors in regional activities was reflected, for example, in a 1953 conference that included presentations by "a French-Canadian folk-singer, a Virginian folk-singer, a folk song collector, a blues singer, a ragtime piano player, a Dixieland band, a Trinidadian group, [and] an Afro-Cuban drummer."[47] Two years later, the ASA of Michigan organized a conference on Walt Whitman together with Charles Feinberg, a private Whitman collector in Detroit.[48] Such activities were accompanied by bibliographical projects such as a partnership with the National Society of Autograph Collectors "to take a census of the holdings of the libraries of several hundred American private collectors."[49] The Northern California chapter's activities, meanwhile, were shaped by the leadership of Alfred Frankenstein, a *San Francisco Chronicle* editor who organized several sessions on American Studies beyond the academy. The Midcontinent chapter similarly invited a technician from Anheuser-Busch to speak at one of its annual meetings.[50]

At best, the national ASA served as a clearinghouse for sharing news about these activities; it was not the driving force in organizing them. What the ASA did do was win grants, often from large philanthropic organizations. The ASA proudly announced such grants in its newsletter, most notably a major three-year award from the Carnegie Corporation in 1954 intended to strengthen the national office. With money came power—or so it seemed. This foundation funding has emerged as a key piece of evidence used to indict American Studies as a cultural arm of Cold War statecraft.[51] Robyn Wiegman, for example, positions the original project of American Studies as "a protonationalist one, beholden to the ideologies emanating from the security state, and dedicated to forging an entire symbolic vocabulary to accompany the worldwide defense of capitalism that the Cold War spawned."[52] Eva Cherniavsky likewise explains that during the Cold War, American Studies was "adopted as a state-sponsored academic export to a range of actual and potential U.S. client states."[53]

The reality was much more muddled. One might take the grants—for there was a range of them—as evidence of the ideological orientation of an emergent academic discipline. It is perhaps more accurate, however, to see them as evidence of the ASA's malleability and lack of a clear intellectual agenda. Unlike the regional chapters, the ASA found itself constantly struggling to placate the changing whims of these foundations, thereby undercutting its responsiveness to individual members at the grassroots level. As Bode complained in a 1951 letter to a colleague regarding a meeting with the Rockefeller Foundation:

> In sum, the Foundation officials felt that a society like ours should have an extensive, detailed, and realistic intellectual program to present to its membership from the very beginning. My own feeling is—and I wonder if you agree?—that our program should evolve out of the needs and desires of the membership and that it would be premature to begin with a series of theses and formulations.[54]

Three years later, even as the ASA publicly celebrated the Carnegie grant, several of its leaders met with the ACLS to discuss what they perceived as an intellectual trap created by the ad hoc funding structure of American philanthropy. The foundations, argued Daniel Boorstin, were causing "pervasive and deplorable" damage to the nascent field with the "pressure to think something up." This dynamic created incentives to ignore the slow work of institution-building in favor of short-term projects that would serve the foundations' "own vested interests."[55]

In effect, this meant that the ASA found itself in a devil's bargain, tangled up in a series of political agendas that were often explicitly contradictory—when all it really wanted was to fund travel for the executive secretary, who sought to unify the independent regional chapters. Two of the most lucrative avenues of funding were also the most contentious: first, projects to support American Studies abroad, and second, projects to spread appreciation for American "heritage" in the United States. The latter was widely lampooned by scholars in the field, even as they turned around and accepted the funding. As Arthur Bestor, Jr., put it in 1952, "If programs of American studies are to retain their good repute, their sponsors must be on guard against jingoistic allies who offer support in return for a betrayal of liberal education itself."[56] The same year, Tony Garvan attacked the "pitfall of jingoism" even though his position at the University of Pennsylvania was funded by the Rockefeller Foundation.[57]

The more nationalistic programs announced by *American Quarterly* included a $105,000 grant ($898,000 in 2016 dollars) from the Ford Foundation to fund the Center for Information on America, which offered brochures to "business and industrial organizations for distribution through racks to their employees" in order to "help build up among the mass of Americans a greater awareness of America's heritage and its importance to our present day democracy."[58] Its programming included "a pilot summer session for teenagers in American studies."[59] Individual institutions received their own grants, with the same kinds of strings attached. In 1955, an even larger $250,000 grant ($2,241,000 in 2016 dollars) from the Fund for the Republic was secured by individual ASA members Daniel Aaron and Donald Egbert to study "the influence of Communism, past and present, on all aspects of American life."[60]

By comparison, the ASA's own $39,000 grant from the Carnegie Corporation was paltry, yet it still resulted in pressure from the foundation to create an ASA ad hoc committee "to discuss ways and means of furthering the knowledge and appreciation of American art among the general public and among scholars."[61] With a lightly staffed national office consumed with such demands, it is no surprise that the practical work of program development was mostly left to the regional chapters. Willard Thorp, president of the ASA in 1958, went so far as to declare that the organization was "living on borrowed time because of the impending loss of Carnegie support."[62] The national organization was barely national, it turns out, and barely an organization.

The most notorious philanthropic organization involved with American Studies in the 1950s was the William Robertson Coe Foundation. Coe built his fortune in New York through the insurance industry around the turn of the twentieth century. In 1910, he purchased William "Buffalo Bill" Cody's ranch in Wyoming and spent the next several decades collecting western ephemera, which became the nucleus for the Yale Collection of Western Americana when he donated it to the Beinecke Library in 1948. In addition to endowing a professorship at Yale University, Coe donated $750,000 ($6,800,000 in 2016 dollars) to establish the University of Wyoming's American Studies program. In a personal letter to a colleague in 1956, Carl Bode referred to Coe as "a neolithic millionaire" who had given a "nationalistic flavor" to Wyoming's new program. He cautioned: "Yale too has taken Coe money, and gladly, I gather. Nevertheless, my own feeling is that any money we take ought not have even the most silken of strings tied to it. I don't know what idea of American civilization Mr. Coe has, but I'd be surprised if it's yours or mine."[63]

Bode was right to worry, as indicated by a number of donations aimed at turning the field into a vehicle for Cold War nationalism. The ASA itself received funding from a nonprofit, the Asia Foundation, that claimed "communist literature is given away or sold at extremely low prices" in Asian countries. In addition to sponsoring travel, members of the ASA were urged to donate books that could supposedly give "Asian peoples a fairer presentation of Western thought and life than they have hitherto received."[64] At the local level, at the University of Wyoming, red-white-and-blue promotional materials focused on appreciation for "the American way" and its roots in a "Judeo-Greco-Christian past." In a reflection of the anticommunist politics that inspired Coe's philanthropy, one pamphlet warned of "massive threats" to democracy emanating from "ideologies of a different sort" that supposedly thrived when youth were ignorant about "their great heritage."[65] Coe also sponsored a summer "Conference on American Studies" that was intended for high school teachers to learn how to defend against communism in the classroom.

And yet, Wyoming was as much local exception as it was national rule. Bode's contempt for the nationalistic approach was shared by many of his colleagues around the country. According to Mary Turpie, some students "accused the Minnesota faculty of being not merely critics of American values and American behavior past and present but utterly vicious and destructive debunkers of everything American."[66] Such critiques—familiar to some contemporary American Studies faculty—began in classrooms that challenged nationalistic ideologies.

Conventional narratives of American Studies treat Coe's politics as a metonym for the field as a whole during the Cold War. One major reason for this was the widespread involvement of American Studies scholars in the postwar rebuilding process in Europe. The Austria-based Salzburg Seminar in American Studies—which included instructors such as Margaret Mead and F. O. Matthiessen in 1947 and Henry Nash Smith in 1948—was touted in the first issue of *American Quarterly* as a model of cultural diplomacy. In 1952, John Hope Franklin, director of American Studies at Brooklyn College and author of *From Slavery to Freedom* (1947), served, along with Bode and McDowell, on the first ASA Committee on International Exchange of Persons and Ideas.[67] Bode also took a leave of absence from his faculty position to serve as cultural attaché to Britain, and Spiller spent time as a visiting professor in Norway.

It would be a mistake to dismiss these activities as simple propaganda. For one thing, American Studies teaching abroad was under way well before the war, and not simply at the behest of the United States. In 1931, the student newspaper of Sarah Lawrence College announced that "the first courses in American Civilization and Literature to be given in a European university" had been inaugurated at the Université de Rennes in France.[68] In fact, the Norwegian scholar Sigmund Skard found much earlier examples in his archival study, *American Studies in Europe* (1958), including a French graduate subject offered in 1912 addressing the "Economic and Social Life of the U. S. A."[69] The study of American society and culture emerged in the 1910s in Japan as well.[70] In German universities, Skard found classes dating back to the American Revolution. He noted that "three German scholarly journals were exclusively devoted to American Studies" between 1777 and 1797, including one devoted to the "literary and intellectual life of the United States."[71]

In the Netherlands, the linguist R. W. Zandvoort of the University of Groningen pushed for attention to American culture throughout the 1930s, ultimately founding an American Institute in 1937.[72] Another Dutch scholar, Arie den Hollander, grew interested in what he called *het onofficiële Amerika,* or "the unofficial America," writing "not about politics at large and the most obvious socio-economic movements, but about the far corners of the country, about the losers and the forgotten: Indians and blacks."[73] Imprisoned by Nazi occupiers in 1942, Hollander went on to become a leader in American Studies in the Netherlands after the war. In short, philanthropists like Coe could not monopolize the study of American culture, even if they wanted to. Within the United States, most American Studies scholars looked critically at Cold War nationalism (even as some of them garnered the grants); outside the United States, one found individuals and programs that brought their own transnational agendas to American Studies.

Of particular importance were the political activities of scholars involved in postcolonial liberation movements, including José Martí in Cuba and, later, the Trinidadian socialist C. L. R. James, author of *Black Jacobins* (1938), which cast the Haitian Revolution as the true heir to the ideals of the French Revolution. In 1948, James started drafting the manuscript for *Notes on American Civilization* but—as we have seen—could not secure a publisher. Likewise W. E. B. Du Bois pushed for a broadly transnational understanding of American culture (studying, for example, the experiences of black American soldiers in World War I) and became deeply involved in the intellectual and political circuits of black internationalism. Although these scholars were not credited as leaders of the American Studies movement in universities in the 1940s, their work eventually transformed the field.

Other unexpected sites of transnational, hemispheric teaching and learning before the war included the Leavenworth Federal Penitentiary in Kansas, which Christina Heatherton has dubbed "the University of Radicalism" due to the exchange of ideas that took place among its "motley crew of war dissenters, radical labor organizers, foreign-born radicals, and Black militants" between 1917 and 1922.[74] Prisons would continue to play an important role in the historiography of American Studies, from Antonio Gramsci's *Prison Notebooks* (1926–35) to Eldridge Cleaver's *Soul on Ice* (1968). Again, such work underscores the marginal impact of Coe's funding for the "American way" on the discipline as a whole. His chauvinism was rejected by everyone from Bode to Skard to Du Bois.

And we can go further in understanding the geopolitics of American Studies postwar cultural diplomacy by remembering the ways that the war transformed the usual calculus of national self-interest. Far from offering a cultural blueprint for Americanization or a picture of "the American mind," the Salzburg Seminar, in Smith's view, sought to "dispel any idea of the

FIGURE 11. F. O. Matthiessen and a Fellow at the Salzburg Seminar in American Studies, 1947.

uniformity of our national personality" and avoid "a mere exchange of dogmas and prejudices."[75] The seminar operated, to a significant degree, on the belief that national chauvinism posed a clear and present danger to the international order (figure 11).

One of the most transformative legacies of the postwar period was the demographic homogenization of Europe along ethnic lines. The assault on Europe's Jewish population did not stop with the liberation of concentration camps, as pogroms continued and 332,000 European Jews sought refuge in Israel between 1947 and 1949. In addition, Allied forces were confronted with millions of displaced persons, including virtually the entire German diaspora of Eastern Europe, which had fled along with the retreating Wehrmacht. Population transfers numbering in the hundreds of thousands further homogenized much of the subcontinent. As Tony Judt put it, "At the conclusion of the First World War it was borders that were invented and adjusted, while people were on the whole left in place. After 1945 what happened was rather the opposite: with [the exception of Poland] boundaries stayed broadly intact and people were moved instead."[76] In short, the Salzburg Seminar was held not just in the aftermath of war, but also amidst the ongoing collapse of European cosmopolitanism. For liberal scholars, a critical understanding of democratic pluralism seemed urgently needed to stop this crisis and create norms of transnational cooperation. In some respects, the Salzburg Seminar was more about the process of conversation than the content of the material being discussed. As Smith put it: "The same people who would almost certainly fall into mutually repellent factions if they were invited to discuss abstractions like international good will or to debate the current problems of Europe could work harmoniously together on such a definite body of scientific and scholarly materials as the facts of American history and the texts of American literature."[77]

Such conversations were baby steps, to be sure. But in a moment when Europe had indeed sorted into ethnonational enclaves on a scale not seen before or since, such bridging mechanisms were necessary for imagining a future of open borders. They paralleled postwar efforts in the social and natural sciences to develop global structures of knowledge through UNESCO and other United Nations organizations. And if, as a number of scholars have argued, the United States offered "American culture" to the world as part of its Cold War strategy, these contexts suggest that there might have been more to the story as well.

"THIS CRAZY DREAM TURNED NIGHTMARE"

Over the past two decades, the "post-nationalist American Studies" movement—which generated numerous anthologies and an annual summer institute at Dartmouth College on "The Futures of American Studies"—has pushed to decenter the United States as an object of study in favor of transnational approaches. At the same time, the very name of this movement has helped entrench the notion that past iterations of the field were nationalist in orientation and chauvinist in affect. But in truth, there was *never* a moment when the most visible institutional manifestations of American Studies—*American Quarterly*, ASA, regional chapters, leading degree programs—were free of at least a strong undercurrent of antinationalist sentiment. This fact has not stopped each generation of scholars from characterizing earlier disciplinary norms as repressive, only to themselves come under critique later in their careers. At its best, this impulse keeps American Studies constantly on the move, changing with the times in the spirit of its earliest practitioners. At its worst, it can become a cycle of rote critique that purges historiographical and institutional memory and forces young scholars to reinvent the wheel when usable pasts—complicated ones, to be sure—sit somewhere close at hand.

Among the most significant examples of generational revolt was a group that called itself the Radical Caucus. Organized at the 1969 ASA annual meeting in Toledo, Ohio, the group received a condescending response from some senior leaders, most notably Robert Walker (who had launched the Coe-sponsored American Studies program at Wyoming), but succeeded in securing, among other demands, ASA subsidies for publication of a caucus newsletter. The central mission of the Radical Caucus was to make American Studies relevant to contemporary social movements, including opposition to the Vietnam War (see "Mixtape, American Problems"). For some members, this meant pushing the ASA to take official stances on issues of the day. As Robert Merideth, one of the group's founding members, wrote: "We urge the executive committee of ASA (if necessary by air-mail vote or phone call) to endorse publicly the march on Washington on November 15 in favor of immediate, unilateral U.S. withdrawal from Vietnam and to urge ASA members to support the monthly moratoriums (note plural) on business as usual until all American forces are out of Vietnam."[78]

Merideth's proposal was resisted by those who wanted to keep the ASA from being politicized, but this position, he argued, was "itself a kind of political decision, a decision in favor of policy-as-it-is by default." Among the main accomplishments of the Radical Caucus was the creation of the ASA Commission on the Status of Women, led by Betty Chmaj, which found systematic discrimination in all aspects of American Studies professional life. To the credit of Chmaj, Doris Freidensohn, Alice Kessler-Harris, Linda Kerber, and others, the organization proved relatively responsive to the critique, with inclusion initiatives increasingly emphasized in newsletters and organizational programming.

Also among the group's initiatives was a push to merge American Civilization with Afro-American Studies at the University of Iowa under the direction of Robert Corrigan. The link was a recognition that African American Studies could be "a potent change agent by forcing re-examination of the structure, courses, attitudes, disciplines, educational goals and processes of U. S. higher education."[79] Of course, that call, in 1971, came shortly on the heels of another series of calls—often based in and supported by Black Studies scholars—demanding the creation of full and autonomous ethnic studies programs. In March 1969, following student strikes at Berkeley and San Francisco State, both universities created institutional structures—a department and a college, respectively—for ethnic studies programs that included Black Studies, Asian American Studies, Raza Studies, and Native American Studies. Each had distinct origins and unique imperatives toward interdisciplinarity; these have often sat uneasily with the forms of interdisciplinarity found in American Studies. Likewise, the institutional linkages of such programs with American Studies can be seen as a productive partnership, a humiliating administrative cost-savings measure, or an act of American Studies institutional imperialism. In many cases, all three are true.

In the long term, the Radical Caucus hoped to create structural change within American Studies that could make it a vehicle for activism for years to come. The ASA's conferences, in particular, needed "to break out of the boring pattern of papers read out loud into something more in line with the tone and spirit of American Studies itself."[80] Chmaj, for example, worked to develop new modes of adult education, including hosting a "lecture-seminar radio series in American studies, in which radio listeners could enroll and thus participate."[81] This program, which was picked up by stations around the country, included interviews with John Dos Passos, Ihab Hassan, Irving Howe, and R. W. B. Lewis.[82]

Other Radical Caucus members had decidedly different ideas. In the group's ASA-sponsored newsletter, Robert Scarola proposed "having 'happenings' instead of conventions. For instance we might meet somewhere in the country. There could be music, films, camping, love-making, etc."[83] Later iterations of the proposal dropped the "love-making" references (calling simply for a "convention—no, HAPPENING!—to be held somewhere in the country"), but the group did host a series of summer retreats that were recorded and transcribed. At the 1973 Kirkland College meeting, Merideth described breaking down in tears as he took his children on the Disneyland ride, "It's a Small World." As he explained:

You get in this boat and you float through and the music plays and the puppets are all dancing and all the nationalities are together. The craftsmanship is just unbelievably great and it lasts a long time. There I was with my kids and I cried as I went through it. My kids were digging it and I was crying.[84]

Today, "It's a Small World" is widely regarded as obnoxious, saccharine kitsch. The director David Lynch has joked that having the song stuck in your head is "like having a disease."[85] By contrast, Merideth earnestly absorbed its message of international harmony, and claimed that his tears were a response to the inevitability of conflict. Doris Friedensohn, who also attended the retreat, framed Merideth's reaction as symptomatic of the fragmentation of radical hope, or what she called "this crazy dream turned nightmare." In Merideth's view, sharing such emotions allowed the Radical Caucus to serve as both "self-help group" and "cultural revolution," which in turn could help articulate "a new, radically humanistic American Studies."[86] Merideth was in the American Studies groove in more ways than one: he sought out new and challenging possibilities; *and* he rejected the past of the field as insufficiently radical and inadequately humanistic.

The visual rhetoric of the Radical Caucus's newsletter was similarly dramatic. One cover depicted a student cowering before an "Old Wave Professor," who is holding a cat o' nine tails marked with the words "authority," "grades," "sarcasm," and "tests" (figure 12). This conflation of teaching with violence was made explicit in an essay by Peter Hartley published by the Radical Caucus. Hartley advocated for what he called "non-method" in order to "discredit the notion of method" and thereby reconcile the politics of American Studies with its practice. As he put it: "Professors think they are called radical because they publish intellectual attacks on the status quo, and exhort students to oppose the policies of Washington, while every day the same professors reinforce student acquiescence to the social forms of authoritarian fiat and rigid bureaucratic impersonality."[87]

Hartley did not use the term "authoritarian fiat" as hyperbole; methodological training was tantamount, in his view, to psychological warfare. Regardless of whether students wanted to spend their energy "kicking around ideas instead of people," professors robbed them of this freedom by trying to teach methodology instead. Above all, Hartley wrote, American Studies had undermined his confidence. Failure had become a catastrophe to be avoided at all costs. In short, the vision of American Studies as "the discipline of conscious choice" was impossible, since too much was riding on getting the right

FIGURE 12. Cover illustration from *Radical American Studies,* the short-lived journal of the ASA's Radical Caucus. Box 42, Folder 1, ASA Records, Library of Congress.

answer. The fundamental problem with Hartley's reasoning was that few of the consequences he imagined had actually come to fruition; instead, the bulk of the essay consisted of conjecture about what supposedly *would* have happened if he had taken more intellectual risks instead of playing it safe. Any affirmative vision of method as an avenue for creativity was left unexplored, overshadowed by an internalized suspicion of being told what to do with his life and the challenges of robust debate and disagreement.[88]

Unfortunately for the ASA, the antagonistic stance toward rules articulated by Hartley did not simply manifest in scholarship. It also shaped the day-to-day operations of the national office. Since 1952, one of the key roles of the executive secretary had been to edit the ASA's newsletter, *American Calendar,* with news about regional chapters, fellowships, publications, and special projects.[89] In the early 1970s, under executive secretary Allen Davis, *American Calendar* greatly reduced its coverage of the regional chapters. One might see the move as part of a consolidation of the national organization, but it actually represented the beginning of what Gene Wise would call the "coming apart" moment in American Studies. Wise's influential essay frames "coming apart" in intellectual terms—the end of the possibility of paradigms and syntheses in the field. But an equally apt description is of the decline of the already-tenuous national organization. *American Calendar* ceased publication altogether in 1974. Two years later, when Davis was replaced by Roberta Gladowski, the ASA stopped filing tax returns or paying its $1.00 annual registration fees with the District of Columbia Recorder of Deeds, which eventually led to the loss of its charter as a nonprofit organization.

As a result, when John Stephens assumed control of the national office in 1983, he was alarmed to discover that his new employer did not exist under the law, which meant any contracts signed in its name were fraudulent. "Since the Association had no legal existence between 1979 and 1982," Stephens explained in a memorandum, "the officers and administrators of the Association are personally liable for debts, obligation, and court appearances."[90] The issue came to a head when the National Endowment for the Humanities demanded a formal audit. It turned out that the ASA had ignored financial and performance requirements for eighteen different grants between 1975 and 1980. This situation severely strained the relationship between the ASA and its institutional home, the University of Pennsylvania. The ASA's budgets, Stephens found, were "unrealistic and continually broken, especially items carried on the Penn ledgers, e.g. telephone, publications, postage, and office supplies."[91] In 1993, the University of Pennsylvania decided to close its American Civilization program altogether, even though it had been headquarters for Robert Spiller and a central force in American Studies for over three decades.

Such administrative neglect left the ASA in shambles. The regional chapters were largely abandoned in terms of both financial support and publicity, with correspondence from chapter officers routinely left unanswered. The collapse of the regional chapter model was perhaps the most significant consequence of the turmoil. The national ASA survived largely through the administrative efforts of John Stephens, who cleaned up its finances, strengthened ties to other disciplinary organizations, and implemented aggressive new strategies to boost membership.

While presidential addresses had been part of the ASA since the first meeting planned by the national organization in 1971 (meetings in 1967 and 1969 had been organized by regional chapters), Linda Kerber's 1988 address inaugurated a new tradition: the publication of the address in *American Quarterly*. As Kerber noted, the speech was to address the conference theme. "Our presidents," she observed, "are not free to be self-indulgent."[92] Indeed, the first several addresses did some heavy lifting for the ASA, explicitly trying to consolidate a sense of unity for the reconstituted field in relation to the challenges of intellectual and institutional diversity. Kerber, Allen Davis (1989), Martha Banta (1990), and Alice Kessler-Harris (1991) all recounted personal narratives of the field that sought *not* to discipline American Studies, but to offer coherence nonetheless. They recounted the meetings of the Radical Caucus, the 1972 retreat to Kirkland, the achievements of feminist scholars, and the ambiguities of the field's new engagements with ethnic studies. Each traced their own history as an example of the various ways one might fit into the field. Davis observed that the quest for a single method had failed in the 1950s through 1970s, and that the turn to theory would likewise fail in the 1980s and 1990s. Banta assumed the position of insider / outsider, diagnosing a series of sometime bitter exclusions and offering twelve ways in which American Studies scholars could, quite literally, *be good to one another.* These included making a renewed effort to engage regional chapter activities, embrace cross-generational collaboration, and resist an attitude of "indifference toward one another's material, methods, and points of reference."[93] Her advice remains relevant today.

From a historiographical perspective, such addresses both recognized and anticipated power shifting dramatically in the direction of programs built around partnerships with adjacent fields such as critical race studies, borderlands studies, queer theory, gender studies, disability studies, and emergent "interdisciplines" such as food studies, animal studies (the focus of an *American Quarterly* special issue), and fat studies. Indeed, it became unclear whether American Studies had any independent purpose apart from connecting *other* interdisciplinary movements in a single national meeting.

This risk of obsolescence would preoccupy the ASA well into the twenty-first century. On the one hand, scholars recognized that the mainline disciplines had themselves borrowed from, and been transformed by, American Studies' willingness to explore and expand disciplinary edges. One could sit in a history or literature department and ask, "Do we even need American Studies anymore?" On the other hand, ethnic studies and other adjacent fields proved vital in their own right, and often resistant to American Studies' expansive interests. In 1997, Mary Helen Washington built a landmark presidential address around the question, "What Happens to American Studies If You Put African American Studies at the Center?"[94] Washington framed the issue in larger terms: what would it take to make the ASA an intellectual home for ethnic studies scholars of all sorts? The following year's address by Janice Radway was also built around a question, "What's in a Name?"[95] By this Radway sought to rethink the term "American" in "American Studies" in light of the field's shift toward transnational and hemispheric studies.

These shifts were echoed in changing institutional landscapes. Older programs, such as American Culture at the University of Michigan, refocused themselves even more explicitly around ethnic studies through a series of faculty hires in the 1990s and early 2000s. At Michigan, this investment supported units in Latino / a Studies, Asian American and Pacific Islander Studies, Native American Studies, and Arab American Studies, and complemented a diasporic African and African American Studies program. Relatively new programs such as the University of Southern California's Department of American Studies and Ethnicity quickly became leaders in the field. In 2012, *American Quarterly* published a special issue, *Las Américas Quarterly,* and the ASA held its conference in San Juan, Puerto Rico. The journal and the annual meeting had become productive—if sometimes contentious—points of intersection and connection among a host of emergent fields.

In light of these later developments, the disarray of the national office in the 1970s has been largely forgotten, partly because Stephens (who remains executive secretary to this day) was able to pull it from the brink of disaster. But in fact, this brush with legal sanctions helps explain the vexed relationship between the national ASA as an *institution* and the discipline of American Studies as a *practice.* In 2013, for example, the ASA voted to endorse an academic boycott of Israeli academic institutions, in protest over the violations of Palestinian human rights. It was exactly the sort of public stance that the Radical Caucus had urged the ASA to take against the

Vietnam War. But apart from the merits of the cause, it quickly became apparent that the national office had not developed a coherent communications policy. In an interview with Richard Pérez-Peña (a *New York Times* reporter), Curtis Marez, president of the ASA, "did not dispute that many nations, including many of Israel's neighbors, are generally judged to have human rights records that are worse than Israel's, or comparable," but stated, "one has to start somewhere."[96] This makeshift approach gave the impression of an organization flying by the seat of its pants.

By looking to its near-collapse in the 1970s, however, it also becomes apparent that the ASA never achieved anything approximating the power of other academic professional organizations. It basically began again from scratch in the 1980s. And it immediately dove into complicated waters in the 1990s and 2000s, as each new president offered different initiatives and directions. Some pursued various forms of ethnic studies; others, transnational partnerships; others, public scholarship; still others, various thematic or topical interests. The Call for Papers for the 2014 Annual Meeting of the American Studies Association went so far as to suggest that participants consider delivering "a presentation in a ball gown with piano accompaniment, commenters arrayed like backup singers, interacting during the course of the lecture"—an idea that wasn't taken up by any individual members. Moreover, this lack of top-down control was not a bug, but a feature. In other words, the discipline of American Studies is—and has always been—an ad hoc movement that draws on the methods and resources at hand.

This did not stop many newcomers to the field from seeking a standard answer to the old and familiar question, "What is American Studies?" In 1970, *American Quarterly* published a special issue edited by ASA executive secretary Robert Lucid, who reported that numerous people had written to inquire about whether the national office had any "blueprints" for starting American Studies programs. When he checked with the regional chapters, he found surprising consensus—about the folly of consensus! Well, not quite, but close. As Lucid explained: "Consultation revealed a consensus that there was no chance of compiling a single blueprint—no more than there was a chance of devising a single method for American Studies scholarship. But it seemed possible to sketch out a range of kinds of programs, aiming at maximum variety, and to ask informed individuals around the country to write essays about them."[97]

The resulting issue embraced the inevitability of "holes in the collection" and chose to limit its coverage to eleven case studies. It was, in essence, a mixtape. Lucid felt that an intentionally small number of case studies, each explained in depth, could prove more useful than a list of hundreds of programs. Look backward in time from 1970: a similar approach—perhaps best described as "descriptive with a hint of advice"—inspired the 1962 publication of the ASA's Occasional Paper No. 1, "Recipe for an American Civilization Week," which offered "step-by-step details on how one week-long institute was organized and carried out at an institution having no American Studies program in its curriculum."[98] Now look forward: in 2015, the ASA published a series of online "white papers" that sought to provide summaries of the field, its research, and several programmatic goals relative to university administrations. The definitional essay by George Lipsitz, "What Is American Studies," ably summarized the keywords we've also suggested in these chapters: interdisciplinary, open, eclectic, democratic, nexus, capacious, sometimes ungainly, socially relevant, politically engaged, and a "never completed work of living sculpture, a place where strangers can meet, where ideas are aired, where problems are diagnosed and where solutions are imagined, envisioned and enacted."[99]

The metaphors of the "recipe" or the "living sculpture" describe well this user's guide. American Studies enjoys an embarrassment of riches—both archival and methodological—which is why its "blueprints" often take the shape of curated collections (or mixtapes). This includes Lucy Maddox's popular anthology, *Locating American Studies: The Evolution of a Discipline* (1998), which selected seventeen essays previously published in *American Quarterly* and invited scholars to write introductory remarks for each one. Or Janice Radway, Penny Von Eschen, Kevin Gaines, and Barry Shank's excellent greatest hits collection, *American Studies: An Anthology* (2009). Or John Carlos Rowe's set of commissioned essays, *A Concise Companion to American Studies* (2010). The problem with mixtapes, unlike recipes, is that they are often descriptive *without* that useful hint of advice. They don't always go into detail about *how* to actually use them, as a recipe might.

Before we close, therefore, we want to offer you the opportunity to practice using one of the archival documents that we relied on to cook up this chapter: a portion of a page from a 1956 directory of ASA members.[100] The full document is sixteen pages long, but for the purposes of this exercise we are pulling only about half of a single page, or 1 / 32 of the document as a whole. Although it might appear to be a raw jumble of information, this document is from a larger curated collection: the ASA Records at the Library

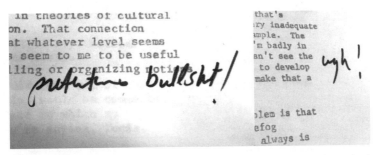

FIGURE 13. Marginalia from an unknown reader on a transcript of a Radical Caucus dialogue. Box 82, Folder 6, ASA Records, Library of Congress.

of Congress. The 351 boxes of files in this collection were organized and preserved over the course of decades, first in the ASA national office in Philadelphia and later by archivists at the Library of Congress. Some of the documents are marked with tantalizing scribbling in the margins from the people who originally saved them. One reader, for example, wrote things like "pretentious bullshit!" and "ugh!" in the margins of a Radical Caucus document (figure 13).

Who wrote these comments? Why did they read this document? Why was it preserved? When it comes to archives, the challenge is piecing together a story out of such traces. American Studies takes this challenge even further by allowing extreme flexibility in terms of constructing your archive; you are not stuck with libraries, but can build archives out of almost anything, from beauty pageants to breakfast menus. For now, though, let's focus on that page from the 1956 directory (figure 14). As you look it over, try coming up with a list of as many questions about this page as possible. Instead of looking up answers online, try to keep generating questions. See if you can fill a full page of your notebook.

The reason for writing down questions is to avoid jumping to conclusions. As the behavioral economist Daniel Kahneman has noted, in his book *Thinking, Fast and Slow* (2011), our brains have a bad habit of replacing difficult questions with easy questions. When faced a difficult question like "Is this person making a valid argument?" we might swap it out for something easy like "How does this person make me feel?" By slowing down to write a bunch of questions, we can move in the opposite direction—toward complexity instead of away from it. Here is the start of our own list, which is by no means exhaustive.

HAUGH, ROBERT F. English. Univ. of Michigan, Ann Arbor. *Relationship of social studies to fiction.*

HAUPTMANN, JERZY. Political Science & American Studies. Park Coll., Parksville, Mo. *Amer. politics.*

HAVIGHURST, WALTER. English. Miami Univ., Oxford, Ohio. *Midwestern social hist., early settlers of Ohio Valley.*

HAWES, RICHARD E. English. Univ. of Pennsylvania, Philadelphia. *Amer. civ., jazz novel & its relation to the real world of jazz.*

HAYES, BARTLETT H., JR. Addison Gallery of American Art, Phillips Academy, Andover, Mass.

HAYFORD, HARRISON. English. Northwestern Univ., Evanston, Ill. *Amer. lit., Melville.*

HAZARD, PATRICK D. *Scholastic Teacher,* 33 W. 42nd St., N. Y. C. 36. *Amer. intell. hist., Amer. popular cult., John Fiske.*

HEATH, HELEN TRUESDELL. English. Los Angeles City Coll., Cal. *17th cent., Samuel Pepys, Son of the Middle Border, the familiar letter.*

HEBERLE, RUDOLF. Sociology. Louisiana State Univ., Baton Rouge. *Changes in class structure in the South.*

HEDGES, WILLIAM L. English. Goucher Coll., Towson, Md. *Amer. fiction, Washington Irving.*

HEFFERNAN, MIRIAM M. English. Brooklyn Coll., N. Y. *20th cent. Amer. lit., Vachel Lindsay, genesis of James' The American.*

HEFLEY, J. THEODORE. History. 670 Ivanhoe St., Ypsilanti, Mich. *20th cent. social hist.*

HEFTEL, VIRGINIA LEE. 1623 Dewey St., Manitowoc, Wis. *Amer. lit., Amer. woman novelist.*

HENDRICKSON, WALTER B. History. MacMurray Coll., Jacksonville, Ill. *Amer.*

HINTZ, HOWARD W. Philosophy & American Studies. Brooklyn Coll., N. Y. *Amer. philosophy, ethics, value theory, ethical concepts of A. N. Whitehead.*

HIRSCHFELD, CHARLES. Humanities. Michigan State Univ., East Lansing. *Amer. social & intell. hist. from 1870, Amer. political thought 1900-20.*

HISLOP, CODMAN. American Civilization. Union Coll., Schenectady, N. Y. *19th cent. Amer. hist., N. Y. hist., Eliphalet Nott.*

HOBBS, RANALD P. Executive Vice President, Rinehart & Co., Inc., 232 Madison Ave., N. Y. C.

HOBEN, JOHN B. English. Colgate Univ., Hamilton, N. Y. *Amer. lit., Mark Twain.*

HOCHSCHILD, HAROLD K. President, Adirondack Historical Assn., 28th Floor, 61 Broadway, N. Y. C. 6. *Adirondack museum.*

HODGMAN, DONNA H. Remedial Reading. Grosse Pointe Univ. High School, Mich.

HOELTJE, HUBERT H. English. Univ. of Oregon, Eugene. *19th cent. Amer. lit., Hawthorne.*

HOFFMAN, FREDERICK J. English. Univ. of Wisconsin, Madison. *Changes in 20th cent. lit. views of mortality.*

HOFFMAN, LEONARD R. English. Oberlin Coll., Ohio. *Amer. lit.*

HOFSTADTER, RICHARD. History. Columbia Univ., N. Y. C. *Amer. hist.*

HOGAN, PATRICK G., JR. English. Mississippi State Coll., State College. *Renaissance, southern Amer. lit., Faulkner & hist. of ideas in South.*

HOGLUND, A. WILLIAM. History. Univ. of Wisconsin, Madison. *Amer. hist., Finnish immigrants & U. S. 1880-1920.*

HOLLAND, ROBERT B. English. Mississippi State Coll., State College. *Amer. lit.*

HOLLIS, C. CARROLL. English. Univ. of Detroit, Mich. *19th cent. Amer. lit., New Eng. circle, Orestes Brownson, Whitman.*

FIGURE 14. Excerpt from a 1956 ASA membership directory. Box 123, Folder 3, ASA Records, Library of Congress.

1. What's the deal with Jerzy Hauptmann?

2. How about Codman Hislop?

3. Or Virginia Lee Heftel?

4. Did any of them receive degrees in American Studies? If not, why did they join the ASA?

5. Why did the ASA compile this directory?

6. Why did it include interests instead of contact information?

7. Was this data self-reported? If so, were the questionnaires preserved in the archives?

8. Can we infer from this data what "counted" as American Studies in 1957?

9. Was any of this data fact-checked?

10. Where can we find more information about these members?

11. Were the disciplines on this page representative of the ASA's membership as a whole?

12. How did these members share their work with a wider audience?

13. Were any members listed here people of color?

14. Were any members listed here students?

15. This page seems to be overwhelmingly male—how did this gender balance compare with the ASA as a whole and its regional chapters?

16. Are there commonalities to be found among the women on this list?

17. Did any of these members actively participate in regional chapters?

18. How was this directory used?

19. Looks like some members, like Ranald Hobbs, had jobs outside the university. Was this unusual for academic professional organizations at the time?

20. Why are so many of these members employed by departments such as History, English, or Political Science rather than American Studies programs?

The list could go on and on. A quick google search can generate preliminary answers to a few of these questions, if only to gather more information on individual names. The School of Public Affairs at Park University appears to be named after Jerzy Hauptmann, who, it turns out, was involved with the Polish resistance during World War II and survived imprisonment by the Nazis. Virginia Lee Heftel, on the other hand, only has one hit on a google search—a letter to the editor of the *Chicago Tribune* published in 1954, two years before this membership directory. What would it take to track her down?

With each figure we might take the very slow route of figuring out who published academic (and nonacademic) writings, accessing their books and articles, and then following the trail of their citations in hopes of piecing together a broader intellectual mosaic. Some of the most prominent scholars on this page, including Richard Hofstadter, have been cited so widely that such a task would take months if not years. Things change, though, when we move from the individual entries to the wide-angle questions about the institutional structures that linked this list of names together. We know they were members of the ASA, which in turn saw fit to create a directory. But their reasons for joining, and the weight of their hopes for the future, are more opaque. Some were building careers, changing lives, fixing the country; others just wanted to read *American Quarterly*.

You might locate some of them on a mixtape, an intellectual entry in a long history of American Studies, traced through a past of words and utterances. All of them show up here, however, in a directory that reflects the institutional pasts that underlie, complicate, and sometimes even contradict the intellectual history of the field. Somewhere in the relation between these narratives, in the messiness of overlaps and alignments, in the gap between the social dream and the practical everyday work, lies American Studies. With the same recognition of complex ambiguity that has characterized the field at every step of the way, we turn—somewhat nervously!—to the recipe box and the difficult question of method.

PART TWO

———

Methods

FOUR

Methods and Methodology

IN THE SECOND SHERLOCK HOLMES STORY, *The Sign of Four,* published by Arthur Conan Doyle in 1890, Dr. John Watson continues a game that he and Sherlock Holmes began in the first story, and that they are destined to play throughout the series. The game has been a hallmark of the many versions of Sherlock Holmes that can be found both in the United States and around the world. There are a lot of them, ranging from the Basil Rathbone films of the 1930s to the exhaustive new fiction writing of David Stuart Davies, Marvin Kaye, Laurie King, June Thompson, Graham Moore, and others, to the 2009 and 2012 remakes starring Robert Downey Jr. and Jude Law, the gender inversion and New York location of the CBS series *Elementary* (first aired in 2012), the BBC version, *Sherlock,* with Benedict Cumberbatch as a latter-day Holmes, or the 2015 film *Mr. Holmes,* which rewrites the game for Ian McKellen's aging forgetful Holmes (figures 15 and 16). Perhaps, as you read this, you're multitasking with another version, yet to be conceived. Rewriting Sherlock Holmes, it turns out, is irresistible, which suggests that the detective scratches a kind of cultural itch, that Holmes himself is a cultural form or template. That template is evocative of many things: puzzles, mystery, problems, the skills of devising solutions, arrogance, and eccentric genius, among others. We'll talk more about the idea of the cultural form later. Back to the game!

All versions of Holmes replay, in one form or another, the same game Doyle first created in *The Sign of Four.* It is explicitly a game about method: Holmes will make a seemingly unknowable claim, and Watson will react with disbelief. Then, Holmes will explain his methods, and Watson (and the reader or viewer) will come to understand the way that knowledge, observation, and logic meet in the art of deduction and inference.

FIGURE 15. Classic Holmes and Watson: Basil Rathbone and Nigel Bruce in the film adaptation *The Adventures of Sherlock Holmes* (1939).

In *The Sign of Four,* Watson challenges Holmes, handing him a pocket watch and daring him to work his detective magic. Holmes begins by suggesting (correctly, of course) that the watch had been Watson's father's and that it had been in the possession of his older brother, until coming recently to Watson: "The W. [inscribed on the watch] suggests your own name," Holmes points out. "The date of the watch is nearly fifty years back, and the initials are as old as the watch; so it was made for the last generation. Jewelry usually descends to the eldest son, and he is most likely to have the same name as the father. It has, therefore, been in the hands of your eldest brother."

For Holmes, this is all very basic, and Watson is impressed but not surprised. Watson imagines that Holmes has reached his limit ... but no. Holmes proceeds to outline the embarrassingly low character of Watson's brother: "He was a man of untidy habits very untidy and careless. He was left with good prospects but he threw away his chances, lived for some time in poverty with occasional short intervals of prosperity, and finally, taking to drink, he died. That is all I can gather."

Watson is furious, for he cannot believe that Holmes has deduced these facts: "You have made inquiries into the history of my unhappy brother, and

FIGURE 16. Updated Holmes and Watson: Jonny Lee Miller and Lucy Liu in the television series *Elementary* (2012).

you now pretend to deduce this knowledge in some fanciful way. You cannot expect me to believe that you have read all this from his old watch!" And Holmes, as usual, explains his method:

> What seems strange to you is only because you do not follow my train of thought or observe the small facts upon which large inferences may depend. For example, I began by stating that your brother was careless. When you observe the lower part of that watch-case you notice that it is not only dinted in two places, but it is cut and marked all over from the habit of keeping other hard objects, such as coins or keys, in the same pocket. Surely it is no great feat to assume that a man who treats a fifty-guinea watch so cavalierly must be a careless man. Neither is it a very far-fetched inference that a man who inherits one article of such value is pretty well provided for in other respects. . . .
>
> It is very customary for pawnbrokers in England, when they take a watch, to scratch the number of the ticket with a pin-point upon the inside of the case. It is more handy than a label as there is no risk of the number being lost or transposed. There are no less than four such numbers visible to my lens on the inside of this case. Inference—that your brother was often at low water. Secondary inference—that he had occasional bursts of prosperity, or he could not have redeemed the pledge. Finally, I ask you to look at the inner plate which contains the keyhole. What sober man's key could have scored those grooves? But

you will never see a drunkard's watch without them. He winds it at night, and he leaves these traces of his unsteady hand. Where is the mystery to all this?[1]

One of the key words in the Holmes stories is, not surprisingly, "method." Sherlock Holmes is constantly battered by the good but dull constables of Scotland Yard. "His methods," they say, "are highly irregular, but nonetheless effective." And Holmes himself is both fanatical and protective of "his method." Indeed, Holmes refers to "his method" frequently and with reverence. So what is it that Holmes *does* when he looks at a watch or a murder scene? What, exactly, do we mean by "method"?

A GENERAL SENSE OF METHOD

If you are interested in creating American Studies work, one of the key questions you will confront is that of method. As we've seen, American Studies writers have spent decades worrying about, defining, refusing to define, or rejecting "method" altogether. It is a term that is (not surprisingly) fluid in its definition—and its fluidity is made more acute by the challenges of interdisciplinarity, the difficulties of saying something firm about "culture," and the shifting meanings of this thing called "America." The question of method, it turns out, is challenging to say the least.

- Is method a set of skills that we can all develop—the ability to work in a formal, document-based archive, or to interpret texts, or to read books critically, or to write well?

- Or is method a school of thought? If one claims to be a Marxist or an economic conservative, do these intellectual identities imply a certain method?

- Does method flow from the subject of an inquiry? Does labor history or the study of early American novels demand a particular method?

- Or, is method simply a set of questions—who, what, where, when, how, why—that one asks of a subject and then goes about answering?

- Is method different from methodology?

Method. Approach. Theory. Style. Procedure. All these words describe, in one way or another, just what it is that we do when we set out to interpret the evidence of the past and the present, and to put those interpretations into a meaningful analysis. And yet these words are not exactly the same. It's worth our time to pry them apart, just a little. A "procedure," for example, is a set of steps taken to accomplish something. It's close to what we mean by "method," but it lacks that sense of mystery, that thrill of *investigation* that keeps us stuck on Sherlock Holmes. "Procedure" is something a doctor does to you. American Studies methods are more individual or distinctive, based somewhat on personal style, but "style" seems too superficial a word for what we're after. It has the right spirit of creativity, but without a foundation in research questions or problem solving. A term like "theory" has more gravity, but although an abstract body of understanding is critical to good analysis, theory lacks the step-by-step clarity of what Holmes gives us. And an "approach"... well, that word is pretty vague—more so even than theory, though it is quite common. "Approach" signals a direction—or perhaps a position—*from which* one interprets. It may also signal a kind of uncertainty about just what one's method really is.

Then, there is the question of *methodology*. If "method" has something to do with steps and procedures toward an uncertain answer, "methodology" reflects the bigger questions underlying "method." Methodology, we might say, describes the philosophical and disciplinary underpinnings concerning objects of knowledge, and how these objects might be known. Methodology makes these abstract ideas concrete by studying the various "methods" that have characterized a field of inquiry over the course of its development. How, in other words, have the steps and procedures changed over time? And what do these changes say about the ways *we think about* the act of figuring things out? Let's make these questions the ones that define methodology.

In this sense, methodology sits closely adjacent to two similar concepts that are also worth touching upon: historiography and epistemology. *Historiography*—which you now recognize as the "history of history-writing"—refers to the study of past scholarship. It concerns itself with the development of schools of interpretation, the rise and fall of specific approaches to evidence, the ascent of certain key questions or categories, and the role of particular audiences or writerly conventions in these changes. Not surprisingly, historiography is *also* interested in the question of methods, particularly as these can be seen in light of bodies of exemplary or representative writing that produced a *canon*—that is, a general body of "standard works."

Epistemology approaches similar questions from a philosophical perspective, asking just what we mean by a term such as "knowledge." What is it? How do we acquire it? How do we know what we know? Here too, amidst sometimes abstract discussions of belief and truth, "method" occupies an important place, for method is implied in *any* theory that concerns the acquisition of knowledge. To summarize: one of these adjacent words (epistemology) points us to abstract questions *about* knowledge; the other (historiography) to a concrete accounting of actual practices that have *made* knowledge. Methodology sits astride the two, and the philosophical and historiographical aspects of a methodology might be seen to produce the concrete practices we can call "methods."

So, after qualifying all these other descriptions, we might offer the following tentative definition:

Method is an orderly sequence of observation and analytical thought, supported by preexisting skills, knowledge, and theory, which structures an investigation into something not yet fully understood. While an investigation may begin with a standard procedural template, each individual case will also require flexibility and adaptation, so "method" will always be something more than rote procedure. In that sense, method is fundamentally creative.

Method has order to it, but—in its creative sense—can (and probably should) complicate and transcend that order. As we have done with other keywords, let us look at a couple of previous articulations of "method," as a way of pointing toward a richer understanding of what is involved in identifying a particular method for American Studies.

The seventeenth-century French philosopher Rene Descartes offered one of the first systematic treatments on the subject, *Discourse on the Method* (1637). He identified four key principles necessary to thinking well, which we might paraphrase as follows:

- Carefully use your senses and perceptions; accept only the things you know with absolute certainty. Maintain an attitude of skepticism toward all else.
- Divide problems into the smallest constituent parts.
- Solve simple and small problems first; use these solutions to build more complex understandings that move beyond the evidence of perception. Understand relationship more than sequence; visualize problems and evidence through lists and graphics.
- Omit nothing.

These principles might remind you of that powerful engine for the creation of knowledge, the "scientific method," which took shape over many centuries. Some writers trace the roots of this method to medieval intellectuals such as the physicist Ibn al-Haytham of Cairo; others to Galileo Galilei, who published *Discourses and Mathematical Demonstrations Relating to Two New Sciences* in 1638, only one year after Descartes's treatise. As it stands today, the scientific method is generally understood to rest on four sequential steps:

- Observation: the evidence of one's perception, formalized in measurements and definitions.

- Hypothesis: A possible (or "hypothetical") explanation of the things observed. This explanation must be "falsifiable," which means there has to be a way to disprove it.

- Prediction: A process of logic that asks: "If the hypothesis is true, then what are the consequences? And how can those consequences be observed?"

- Experiment: A test case that establishes the conditions under which consequences can be observed. If the consequences are observed as predicted, then the hypothesis might be true; if they are not, then either the hypothesis is wrong or the experiment is faulty. Importantly, experiments are not designed to prove, but rather to *disprove,* a given hypothesis. Scientists who are scrupulously following the scientific method try to defeat their own hypotheses in every way possible, so as to avoid false positives based on coincidence, correlation, or confirmation bias.

In the scientific method, experiments build on one another. A "no" answer, or "null result," is still a valid outcome. It simply tells the scientist to consider the problem again, develop alternative hypotheses, and keep trying. Scientists are careful to avoid "confirmation bias," or the temptation to rig an experiment to produce the desired outcome while ignoring contradictory evidence or explanations. Over time, and if carried out correctly, a series of hypotheses and experiments will produce enough pieces of knowledge that they can be woven together into a "theory," which seeks to explain the various outcomes by jumping up to a higher level of abstraction. In the world of science, a "theory" has a fairly high degree of confidence since it has been confirmed from many different angles. With even more certainty, a theory can become a "law."

In American Studies, we live in a very different world, one of *interpretation and argument,* which has far less certainty about it. Our questions are not like those of scientists who seek clear, simple explanations as part of a long sequence of investigations. This is not to imply that American Studies is somehow more sophisticated than the sciences (or vice versa); explanatory simplicity, or "parsimony," is a hard-fought virtue. Some scientists spend decades filtering through alternatives in order to find the simplest and most direct explanations for a given phenomenon. By contrast, scholars in American Studies (and other interpretive fields) actively seek out open-ended questions. In our line of work, a question that does *not* have multiple possible answers is, quite simply, a bad question. This is partly because human action is difficult to explain. Where some natural sciences are able to postulate laws and theories, fields that place human experience at the center—the humanities—generally despair of such clean explanatory devices. And academic disciplines only scratch the surface of the many different ways of making sense of the world. Some emphasize "factual" aspects of the world that, if hard won, are nevertheless knowable. Others emphasize that life is messy, that any human action has multiple causes, and that consequences reverberate in multiple directions, almost none of which can be anticipated.

In American Studies, we have to support our conclusions as best we are able, and to accept that at least some of what we do has the creative quality of art, deeply influenced by our own subjective selves. On the other hand, it would be a mistake to write off Descartes or the scientific method as irrelevant to American Studies. Indeed, consider a method that comes from the field of material culture studies. This particular method was developed by Jules David Prown and advanced by his students.[2] As summarized by Kenneth Haltman (and further paraphrased by us), it has five basic steps, all of which should sound familiar:

- Description: close observation and statement of basic characteristics of an object, artifact, or text (broadly speaking).
- Deduction: Logical analysis, applying general understandings and premises to the specific object of analysis.
- Speculation: Creative speculation, based upon one's own reaction to the object, though remaining within the bounds established by the original description. Speculation generates questions that can be answered through further research.
- Research: Using primary and secondary sources to confirm speculations, to raise additional questions, and to place the object in historical, social, and cultural context.
- Analysis: Using the data now assembled to put forth an argument or claim about the object of analysis, its meanings, and its importance to our understanding of the world.

In these three disparate examples—Descartes, Prown, and the scientific method—we can see enough commonality and overlap to advance a set of basic principles on which to build a *general sense of method.* The first step might revolve around observation:

Pay attention, use your senses, make detailed observations, omit nothing, and never be satisfied with superficiality.

A second step turns on the linked processes of deduction, inference, and creative thought:

Divide into manageable problems, apply general rules and knowledges, deduce, infer, speculate, hypothesize, and predict.

A third step involves the question of evidence:

Conduct experiments, undertake research, return to your initial observations, and gather data.

A fourth step points to the larger questions:

Chart relationships, pull experiments together into theories, and move from the interpretation of evidence to the analysis of connections, which will take the form of an argument.

It turns out that these steps characterize—almost exactly—Sherlock Holmes, who constantly sang the praises of perception, deduction, evidence, and analysis. Of course, anything that encompasses laboratory sciences, humanities work, and turn-of-the-twentieth-century English detectives can offer little in the way of practical, concrete guidance. But now that we have these general principles knocking around in our heads, we can turn to the question of how we might arrive at a specifically *American Studies* practice.

AMERICAN STUDIES: SHIFTING DISCIPLINARY GEARS

One way to think of our enterprise is something like the shifting of gears on a car. In this metaphor, each gear is a set of disciplinary tools for a specific kind of task. In American Studies, *we begin as literary critics* (depress clutch and shift . . .), *morph into curators* (shift again . . .), *turn into historians and contextualizers* (twice more . . .), *and finish as social theorists* (cruising in fifth gear). Much of this book will be devoted to exploring this idea in greater detail, and complicating this sequence with other ideas and other disciplines, all of which will come more clearly into focus as we depress the clutch and shift our gears. What we've sketched out is not a hierarchy. Note that the engine works just as hard in each of these gears—usually around 2500 rpm—and a major reason for the transmission or gearbox is to make this possible. Situationally, first gear gives your car the torque to get up a steep hill, whereas the fourth or fifth gear is optimal for highway speeds. Let us chart out what we mean, and then explain further.

Method	Object	Action
Interpretation	Text	Perceive
Curation	Archive	Collect
Analysis	Genre	Categorize
Contextualization	Formation	Expand
Generalization	Power	Connect

There is an implied sequence here of analytical moves, which is why the metaphor of a gearshift works better than, say, a menu. A skilled driver can jump a gear—moving directly from second to fourth, for example—but this also risks stalling the engine. We'll complicate that later. For the moment, though, let us walk through each "gear" briefly.

- Texts. As literary critics, we will first concern ourselves with the act of *interpretation*. By that we mean a detailed reading of *individual texts,* which will become evidence. To make our interpretations, we will mobilize all the tools of literary and textual analysis available to us. Indeed, our analysis will expand beyond the literary to encompass art history, material culture studies, and performance studies, among other strategies for looking up close and personal at texts. We will apply those tools to many different kinds of sources.

- Archives. Any time we move beyond the individual text, we are in the business of *curation*. But instead of simply collecting texts at random, we need to develop the logics that allow us to bundle those texts together purposefully. We might juxtapose films, reviews, fan fiction, internet commentary, and congressional actions. Or material objects, newspaper reporting, judicial decisions, and public demonstrations. Or any number of possibilities. In this process—an important pivot point in American Studies—we will, in effect, create our own *project archive,* an assemblage that will help situate our interpretations in relation to a range of other texts.

- Genres. We'll read the texts in our project archive for their commonalities and their differences, for what we can usefully call generic evidence.

We will move from the one-text-at-a-time focus of interpretation into a mode of *analysis*; that is, the discovery and articulation of *connections among multiple texts*. This new kind of genre evidence will be more amenable than individual texts to historical readings—or at least to the kinds of analytical tools commonly wielded by historians, anthropologists, and sociologists. The key question, then, is how we find insights in our archives, and how we put archives in relation to one another in order to make visible hidden possibilities.

· Formations. Having discovered generic commonalities through the interpretation of multiple sources, the American Studies writer will then move to yet another methodological register in order to *contextualize* those commonalities in light of different kinds of social, political, and economic *formations*. These range from the traditional institutions of government or business; to the circuits and networks that characterize the global world; to the various forms of community that make up public life. When possible, we want to "follow the money" through the structures of cultural production, distribution, and consumption. Who made the texts and the archives? How, why, and with what consequence? When possible, we also want to track the formation of new kinds of structures, connective networks of mobility and meaning built and used by people.

· Power. Because our interest will be in people, human social relations, domination, and uneven power, we will move to the broadest methodological register, that of *social theory*, where we will develop *generalizable arguments* that explain the significance of our study to other examples. Theory, in this case, simply means an ability to take an analysis and suggest the ways that it might apply, in a general sense, to other times and places. That makes theory an important goal, since it tells our readers why they should care about our analysis. The ability to theorize is the ability to make connections with others at the broadest and most general level. In particular, we'll trace American Studies theoretical interests that have focused on four interconnected areas: theories of *subjectivity* that seek to understand the constitutive relationship between human subjects and social institutions; theories of *identity* that examine the public faces of ascription, performance, and resistance on the part of individuals; theories of the *state,* which try to explain the ways that political institutions—nations, states, and empires—organize the lives of their members, and influence people across the globe; and theories of the *market,* grounded in the economic structures that shape societies, but equally interested in the complicated place of culture in relation to those structures.

The strategies that we've charted above reflect very different kinds of methods, each requiring different skills and knowledges. This sequence may seem to translate into a kind of hierarchy, with interpretive grunt work at the bottom and lofty theorizing at the top. But no! One is not superior to another. Each of the methodological strategies we've charted and described influences and changes the analyses going on "above" and "below," so we should imagine a relentless interpretive dialogue *among* these distinct analytical registers.

As important—and this is where our gearshift metaphor is less useful— you can enter a project at *any* of these registers. Some American Studies writers enter at the level of theory, and they look for discrete texts, multiple examples, and contextual evidence to support a theoretical argument about, say, the discourse of a "state of emergency," the shifting expressions and demands of "neoliberalism," or the changing nature of "empire." Other writers will enter through institutional formations and context. If you are interested in the underground newspaper circuit of 1960s queer San Francisco, you might be starting with institutions, asking questions about production, consumption, distribution, location, and network. Some writers will have in their minds an archive of texts. If you are mostly interested in a particular film, or novel, or television show, you are entering at the level of the text and the interpretation. In all cases, your mind will almost immediately start to play with insights from across these different registers. The best American Studies work imagines and communicates that dialogue in creative ways.

Though it may be tempting to think that a writer with a political commitment will be more likely to enter through *social theory* and *generalization,* in fact any one of these registers offers a chance to live within the American Studies tradition and say something important about social relations and power. And indeed, it is our sense that the strongest arguments come from the richest engagements across *all* these registers. Politics wants to give the writer an answer based on moral and ethical principles that are already held. That's fine. There's no need to abandon principles and commitments. But the art of political communication is the art of *compelling simplification,* of moving quickly—perhaps too quickly?—to core convictions that are hard to shake, even for the most fair-minded and open person. If you care deeply, for example, about contesting U.S. imperialism, heteronormativity, or patriarchy (as many American Studies scholars do), then these things may quickly become not the *questions* that animate your project, but your *answers.* They may be perfectly correct conclusions, but there's a good chance you'll be telling, not showing, offering answers that are ready-made and obvious. Our goal is to show complexity within structures of power and domination—and thus to build a more convincing argument.

The gears on this chart, these methodological registers, are a template, nothing more. It's flexible, not rigid, and indeed it requires you to be adventuresome and creative. But it also offers a guide. And since a book does, in fact, need a logical, orderly sequence, we've adopted this one. Our hope is that you'll be better positioned to think about American Studies as a field after you've absorbed a sequence of *possibilities* that can be configured in any number of ways. We've tried to represent both *methodology* (this book offers a philosophical strategy for producing knowledge, one that crosses disciplinary lines and thus produces a different way of seeing) and *method* (it also offers the possibility of a procedure for moving through an analysis, while leaving room for a creative engagement with complex pieces of knowledge that may never be fully understood).

With that thought in mind, let's turn to our first toolkit, beginning as literary critics of the wide world of culture, looking first at just what that might mean—and then working our way through a set of different strategies for paying close attention to individual texts.

FIVE

Texts

AN INTERPRETIVE TOOLKIT

WE BEGIN AS LITERARY CRITICS

What do we mean when we say that you might begin as a literary critic? Really, "literary critic" is just our shorthand for a person who reads and interprets texts. A text might be a novel, poem, or play—but it also could be a film, photograph, song, or even a place. Even though we'll branch out into the worlds of art history, material culture studies, and anthropology, starting with literary criticism offers a revealing window into the ways we define "texts" and think about how we "read" them.

This focus on the text is a surprisingly recent development. Before the 1930s, as we have seen, many critics devoted their careers to philology and biographical criticism. Others, like Vernon Parrington, studied not only texts, but authors, their histories, and their social milieu. This changed with the arrival of a rigid new school of thought called "The New Criticism," driven largely by conservatives (including several around Vanderbilt University in Nashville) who were skeptical of the progressive political orientation of writers like Parrington. Its hallmark was methodological dogmatism, explicitly rejecting everything outside of "the text" itself. That is to say: no discussions of the biographies of authors, their psychological issues, the amount of time books did (or did not) spend on the bestseller lists, the circles of writerly friends who inspired one another, or the generational tensions between mentors and disciples. Farewell to all that! The thing that mattered most to the New Critics was "the text"—that is, the words themselves. The method they applied was called "close reading," and it offers a useful starting point.

Close reading is, in one sense, simply another way of talking about some of the general methodological principles we discussed in the previous chapter. A close reading begins with deep attention to detail. The close reader often focuses on a small (that is to say, manageable) portion of text, noting repetitions of phrases and forms, unusual grammatical choices, and, for the New Critics in particular, devices such as ambiguity, paradox, tension, tone, and irony. Rather than moving lightly, in concert with the text (as one might do when reading for pleasure), one moves slowly and, in the process, makes the text *strange and unfamiliar.* This, in turn, opens the mind up to seeing new kinds of meanings. Here's an example of the analytical potential that comes with focus, attention to detail, and the resulting state of hyper-aware estrangement. In the passage below, from Robert Pirsig's *Zen and the Art of Motorcycle Maintenance* (1974), a student has proposed to write a "500-word essay on the United States." The instructor suggests that she narrow her topic to Bozeman, Montana, the setting of the novel. She tries, but finds that she has nothing to say. "Write on the main street of Bozeman!" he says. But, again, she returns empty handed:

> She still couldn't think of anything to say, and couldn't understand why, if she couldn't think of anything about *all* of Bozeman, she should be able to think of something about just one street.
>
> He was furious. "You're not *looking!*" he said. A memory came back of his own dismissal from the University for having *too much* to say. For every fact there is an *infinity* of hypotheses. The more you *look* the more you *see.* She really wasn't looking and yet somehow didn't understand this.
>
> He told her angrily, "Narrow it down the *front* of *one* building on the main street of Bozeman. The Opera House. Start with the upper left-hand brick."
>
> Her eyes, behind the thick-lensed glasses, opened wide.
>
> She came in the next class with a puzzled look and handed him a five-thousand-word essay on the front of the Opera House on the main street of Bozeman, Montana. "I sat in the hamburger stand across the street," she said, "and started writing about the first brick, and the second brick, and then by the third brick it all started to come and I couldn't stop."[1]

Narrowing the scope to a single brick forced the student to *see* with unfamiliar—and thus original and perhaps even creative—eyes. In effect, she was dragged into the method of close reading—detailed attention to the particular, and to the ways sentences and paragraphs (and even bricks, buildings, and towns) are arranged and organized.

If New Criticism and close reading demanded tightly focused attention on the text itself, another (sometimes overlapping) group of theorists moved interpretive analysis in a parallel direction by proclaiming "the death of the author." These critics argued that an author's *intent* did not matter nearly so much as a reader's *response* to the text—and we're not talking about just any reader here. Ideally, the reader in question was an abstract reader, a kind of everyperson. For these scholars the creative act that mattered most in an encounter between human being and literary text was *not* the authorial act that produced the novel or poem, but rather that the act of reading, which *created* (indeed, some would say "authored") meaning out of the texts themselves—regardless of whether these meanings corresponded to the intentions of the original writer. If you take this argument seriously, you can see again how, from this slightly different perspective, the *text* itself came to hold primary importance, with the actual author much less important. With the rise of "the text" came two corollary ideas: first, an emphasis on the centrality of reading (rather than writing and authorship); and, second, an increase in the status of interpretation (as opposed to historical concerns such as biography and philology). Our own emphasis on interpretation has a genealogical ancestry in this line of thinking.

There is a certain amount of irony in these developments, since American Studies as it was practiced at the mid-twentieth century was fundamentally *interested* in historical and cultural contexts surrounding the production of "the text." Indeed, as we have seen, scholars in American Studies bridled against the dogmatism of the New Criticism—and saw American Studies as a way to escape it. Anything that sought to blur the lines and put history (that is, context) in conversation with literary form was an affront to New Critical practices. And yet, *close reading* continues to underpin the methodological practices of American Studies to this day. To understand how this seeming contradiction came about, let us make a quick detour into the world of anthropology, which offered to American Studies and other fields new theories of culture. In the early twentieth century, anthropologists rejected social evolution and racial essentialism, arguing instead that cultures were equally valuable relative to one another, and that they served well the people who lived in and by their structures. This line of thought was driven by Franz Boas at Columbia University and his students, including Margaret Mead and Ruth Benedict. Over time, the development of these ideas crossed disciplinary lines into the literary, expanding the very idea of what was, and what was not, a text.

WHAT IS A TEXT?

The concept of culture I espouse is essentially a semiotic one. Believing, with Max Weber, that man is an animal suspended in webs of significance he himself has spun, I take culture to be those webs, and the analysis of it to be therefore not an experimental science in search of law but an interpretive one in search of meaning. It is explication I am after.

CLIFFORD GEERTZ
The Interpretation of Cultures (1973)

Here is a methodological statement if ever there was one—and it points exactly to the intersection of interpretive technique with an expanding notion of "the text." Clifford Geertz's 1973 book *The Interpretation of Cultures* was transformative, precisely along these lines. Geertz does two things in this short passage that are worth our attention:

- He defines culture in a new way: as a practice that rests on signs, meanings, and interpretations, all of which fall under the term "semiotic" (which we will discuss shortly). Culture, in effect, is a *textual* thing.

- He moves the anthropological study of culture away from an experimental model based in natural and social science and toward an interpretive model that emerges from the humanities. It is not laws and general rules that Geertz thinks we should seek, but rather specific interpretations of particular meanings that, taken together, shape that large complex of meaning we call "culture."

Geertz argues that "culture" is, in essence, a web of meaningful "texts." And *anything* that is produced in a creative relation involving human beings becomes such a text. Cultural interpreters are therefore like literary critics, trying to unpack the meanings of texts as they appear in a myriad of interconnected forms—not simply printed texts, but oral communication, individual and social performances, material culture, film, television, tweets, websites, and so on. This is a broad definition of "text," and it has proven incredibly productive. Imagine culture as an infinite silken web, subtle, complex, and connected in multiple ways, with interpreters sitting, like very cool spiders, in the center of everything. As "literary critics" of culture, we are licensed to look at anything as a text and to bring our interpretive skills to bear. Music. Graffiti. Video. Performances. Political violence. Street culture. Blue jeans. Prisons. Crazy made-up teen cultures. Toilet paper dispensers. You name it! *Everything* is up for interpretation. That is what we mean when we say that you'll begin as literary critics.

Though American Studies has always been willing to think about a wide range of texts—including folklore and popular culture—the early years of American Studies scholarship were marked by close attention to writings in American literature. Indeed, as we have seen, American Studies helped canonize the writings of now-familiar authors such as Herman Melville, Mark Twain, Walt Whitman, and Emily Dickinson, among others. During the late 1960s and early 1970s—the same moments that Clifford Geertz was theorizing an interpretive approach to the study of culture—American Studies writers were expanding their own range of possibilities. Popular culture studies became increasingly important, as did film studies, architecture, and the study of vernacular expression. Methodologically, American Studies remade itself around a four-way convergence between:

1) The techniques of attentive close reading of texts.

2) The understanding of culture itself as a linked collection of texts.

3) A newly expansive definition of what kinds of texts might be included.

4) An interdisciplinary interest in connecting textual interpretation and cultural analysis with rich historical and sociological context.

Indeed, we might find this convergence—especially the move to rich context—licensed around yet another methodological premise, also offered by Geertz—what he (after the philosopher Gilbert Ryle) called "thick description." Think of it as an intermediate step, between the close reading of texts and a set of larger contexts.

THICK DESCRIPTION

Cultural texts required the interpretive techniques of close reading. Detailed observation, logical deduction, creative speculation, and internal evidence were critical. But for Geertz (and for American Studies writers), *context*—that is, the world *outside* the text—proved every bit as important, if not more

FIGURE 17. Involuntary muscle contraction, flirtatious wink, conspiratorial wink, and parody of a wink (left to right).

so. "Thick description" offered a way to think about these contexts as cultural. And it involved an explicit treatment not of a single context, but of a *range* of cultural contexts, nested within one another (or perhaps stacked one atop the other). In a famous passage, Geertz riffed on a thought experiment offered by Ryle, involving the act of winking:

> Consider, he says, two boys rapidly contracting the eyelids of their right eyes. In one, this is an involuntary twitch; in the other, a conspiratorial signal to a friend. The two movements are, as movements, identical; ... one could not tell which was twitch and which was wink, or indeed whether both or either was a twitch or wink. Yet the difference, however unphotographable, between a twitch and a wink is vast; as anyone unfortunate enough to have had the first taken for the second knows. The winker is communicating, and indeed communicating in a quite precise and special way: (1) deliberately, (2) to someone in particular, (3) to impart a particular message, (4) according to a socially established code, and (5) without cognizance of the rest of the company.[2]

The twitcher has done only one thing: contracted his eyelid. The winker has done two: contracted his eyelid *and* winked. That wink is, as Geertz phrased it, "a fleck of culture."

But the experiment continues. What if a third boy parodies the wink? He, too, will be contracting his eyelid, but his act will be neither twitch nor wink (figure 17). Parody has its own cultural codes, contexts, and meanings. And what if this third boy wants to ridicule and parody the first, but is not quite sure he is really getting it right? Perhaps he sits in front of a mirror at home, rehearsing. Well, rehearsal too has its own cultural contexts and meanings, which are distinct from parody, winking, and twitching, even though all of these acts may be physically indistinguishable. Ryle and Geertz, then, would make a distinction between thin description ("contracting the right eyelid") and *thick* (in Geertz's words, "practicing a burlesque of a friend faking a wink to deceive an innocent into thinking a conspiracy is in motion"). The analytical goal is clear: revealing as thoroughly as possible the range of *possibilities for meaning* that accompany a cultural act.

Thick description runs smack against the grain of the text-centered formalism proposed by the New Criticism. Within American Studies, however, these two ways of proceeding have found a productive interdisciplinary common ground. In terms of method, American Studies would apply the tools of close reading to a range of texts, seeking out multiple and overlapping contexts in an effort to arrive at a telling thick description. And that thick description—a rich cultural context—opens the door to more familiar acts of contextualization that would draw from disciplines such as history ("what happened before this?"), sociology ("what are the human networks in which the text operates?"), or economics ("how and where does the text function as an object of exchange value?").

Close reading. Thick description. Let's consider these the first two tools in our first toolkit, which focuses on *interpretation*—the way we engage "texts," broadly speaking. These tools ground a number of other practices, to which we'll turn shortly. As we look at these other tools, remember that not all of them will be equally useful in all situations. Sometimes, it is the wrench, not the hammer, that is right for the job. So think, as you adopt these tools, of where and when they will be most useful. Most importantly, we encourage you to go out into the world and practice. Make no mistake, interpretive skill is not a mystical gift. It is, like all skills, the result of *practice*. Next time you visit a new city, try "reading" it like a text instead of simply seeking out the famous landmarks. Is there a logic, a grammar even, in the way the streets are laid out? What are the elements that make a given neighborhood feel different from the rest of the city?

CONTENT ANALYSIS AND DISTANT READING

Content is the basic building block of meaning in any kind of cultural text, whether it be a novel, a poem, a film, or an image. It is simply what a text or image *says*—or seems to say. Accordingly, we'll want to look closely at words, speech, and imagery in order to find the *topics treated* and their *sum and substance*.

Content may be *manifest* or *latent*. Most of what follows in our toolkit will treat *latent* content—meaning that isn't obvious, that might be hidden in some way and needs to be uncovered, or that is not necessarily intended by the author or image-maker. There are lots of ways to figure out all that stuff, as we will see. But before we are able to deal with the latent content, we need to pay attention to messages that are manifest, that is, the ones that carry explicit meaning. And here we might make a further distinction: between *quantitative* interpretation on the one hand, and *qualitative* interpretation on the other. The first requires us to count, measure, and map; the second points us to an examination of the nature of the content itself.

Quantitative content analysis can include what the literary critic Franco Moretti has called *distant reading*. With the aid of digital tools, we might step back from the plot altogether and count up, or quantify, specific words in a text. If you return to our friend Sherlock Holmes, for example, close reading might draw your attention to a particular feature in Arthur Conan Doyle's vocabulary. He seems to use the word "singular" a great deal. "Why is this?" you wonder. Perhaps you might hypothesize that the frequent repetition of "singular" suggests Doyle's insistence upon uniqueness, even as the form was repeating itself—and thus growing less "singular" with every short story he wrote. Such a claim demands a different kind of reading to make sure, among other things, that your intuitive observation about the frequency of the word "singular" in Doyle's writing is accurate. So you might run a keyword search for "singular" in *all* the Sherlock Holmes stories. This sort of counting and quantifying is called "distant reading" because it steps back from small details like the brick on the opera house in Bozeman, and instead finds patterns across vast swaths of textual material. Using a tool like Google's Ngram Viewer, you can expand your search even more broadly to include *all* the historical texts that have been digitized through the Google Books project, not just stories by Doyle (figure 18).

Using a date range of 1700 to 2000, we find a curious and unexpected pattern. In 1800–1830, the word "singular" was roughly twice as common as it was when Doyle published his first Sherlock Holmes story, *A Study in Scarlet*, in 1886. By the time he published the last story, in 1927, the word was even less common—it appears that Doyle did little to popularize it, even though Holmes and Watson became two of the most enduring characters in British and American popular culture. So what does this pattern tell you? One possible explanation could be that Doyle's own education was steeped in books from the early nineteenth century—the heyday of romanticism.

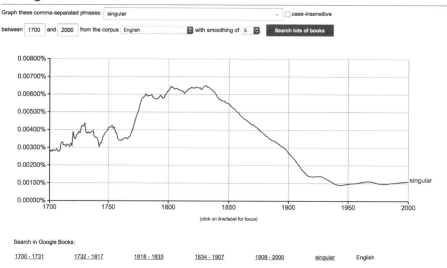

FIGURE 18. Google Books Ngram Viewer: https://books.google.com/ngrams.

This period, in turn, could prove useful as a seedbed for other aspects of the Holmes series beyond simply individual words, or diction. Another explanation might be that Doyle's use of "singular" wasn't actually that, well, singular. Remember, one of the foundational principles of the scientific method is that "null results" are still worth observing.

As it turns out, Franco Moretti—the critic who introduced the term "distant reading"—has written extensively on Sherlock Holmes. In his landmark essay, "The Slaughterhouse of Literature" (2000), Moretti describes bringing twenty detective novels to a graduate seminar and, in a modified version of crowd-sourcing, having his students comb through them for "clues." His goal was to figure out whether something about the use of "clues" in Doyle's work might explain why the Sherlock Holmes series became so popular—and why thousands of other detective stories of the era were forgotten. Distant reading allowed Moretti to apply the insights of evolutionary biology to literary studies. Through the quantitative observations of his students, he was able to build a "tree" of plot devices that appeared in some texts but not others. These functioned much like Darwinian adaptations that allowed Doyle to dominate the nascent literary ecosystem (or market) of detective fiction. Later adaptations would surface in the twentieth century, like the hard-boiled antiheroes of Dashiell Hammett and Raymond Chandler, or Agatha

Christie's "framing" of the least-likely suspect in the final round of manuscript revision.

The possibilities of quantitative content analysis extend well beyond literature. You might examine coverage of a particular event in a particular venue. During the first half of 2008, coverage of the Iraq war in the *New York Times* dropped from an earlier high of 15 percent of available newspaper column inches to approximately 3 percent. Why was this so? Or you might try to quantify positive or negative coverage of individual politicians or issues. How did saturation coverage of Donald Trump affect the 2016 presidential race? How have the media frames around "terrorism" changed over the past decades? Each of these questions requires a bit of distance from the individual text in order to track analytical categories across a fairly substantial data set.

Qualitative content analysis is a little different. Instead of distance, it operates more at the level of the individual text, often in the form of case studies. But unlike close reading, it looks mainly at the manifest content of a given cultural text rather than digging for latent meanings. Advertising, for example, often gives us both manifest (buy this!) and latent (and you'll be thin, virile, rich, etc.) content. The most direct advertisements want simply to "inform," or to provide information. Public Service Announcements—perhaps the most boring kinds of media ever created—often fit into this category. But even here there are exceptions! In 2012, Metro Trains Melbourne in Australia produced a spellbinding PSA about train safety, "Dumb Ways to Die," which as of January 1, 2017, received 143,648,311 views on YouTube. This animated cartoon with vocals from the indie singer Emily Lubitz only briefly mentions train safety, instead cycling through other calamitous deaths such as dressing up like a moose during hunting season or selling both your kidneys on the internet. Of course, advertisers have always sought to quantify circulation through things like Nielson ratings for television. But the granular data about *distribution* and *consumption* made possible by social media—remember, the video had precisely 143,648,311 views!—allows the *producers* of cultural texts to figure out that a hilarious and catchy video that only briefly mentions train safety is likely to generate far more views than a PSA operating strictly on the level of manifest content.

Other examples include the Legal Notices section in a newspaper or television pharmaceutical commercials. In these cases, the content *must* be manifest, in part because it is fulfilling certain legal obligations such as the requirement to disclose side effects. You know these: you're presented a vision of smiling people—sunny, active, and exuding happiness—in an antidepressant commercial, or skiing and swimming in an ad for an arthritis drug. And then you're bombarded by a long, frightening legal disclaimer that lists the potential side effects of the drug, which escalate quickly from nausea and dizziness to death. The images carry the latent meaning; the words carry the manifest content. Most texts contain both types. Before we can proceed to unpack cultural texts, then, it is important to ask what the text itself seems to want (or need) to say. That means *not* killing off the author, but taking him, her, or it (in these contexts, authors are often anonymous and speak for institutions rather than human individuals) seriously.

READING IMAGES

Images—such as those pharmaceutical ads—offer a particularly vivid illustration of how we might go about seeking manifest and latent meaning through both close reading and qualitative content analysis. Indeed, one of the most important analytical tools in our kit is the ability to read images, whether they take the form of photographs, paintings, video, film, or other possibilities. The concept of the "image," though, is a complicated one, and it turns out that before we can explore the interpretive tools for reading images, we need to pause for just a moment to get clear on what exactly we are talking about.

On the one hand, an image is a copy, an imitation, a likeness—a replication of something existing in the physical world. On the other hand, images are mental representations, symbols, pictures in the mind. They convey real information about people and things, but they also carry with them the extra meanings that accompany symbols and representations. In 1894, the philosopher Charles Sanders Peirce sought to make sense of this tension with the terms *index, icon,* and *symbol.* Each of these terms has a long, complicated genealogy, and each is estranged, in some way, from "the real thing" that it seeks to represent. An *index* is the most concrete kind of image. It creates meaning through the physical trace of something, like forensic evidence at a crime scene, or a passerby who points their finger at something. By contrast, *icons* convey meaning through imitation, as with a seated portrait or still-life. The most abstract kind of image is the *symbol,* since it does not necessary bear any mimetic or physical relationship to the people or things it represents. Rather, the meaning of a symbol is acquired socially (or linguistically) through mutual agreement, as in the case of flags that represent a given country.

FIGURE 19. Preparations on the CBS set before the first presidential debate between Richard Nixon and John F. Kennedy, Jr., on September 26, 1960.

Images are powerful precisely because they blur the lines between the "representational" and the "real." The image *shows* us something, but it also *tells* us something. Some images can be so powerful and evocative that they carry not just meanings but also *narratives*. For many readers, an image of the first Nixon-Kennedy presidential debate of 1960 brings to mind (at least) *two* powerful stories: the youthful John F. Kennedy, Jr., laying the foundations for an administration that would be seen as "Camelot," an almost-mythical golden era in U. S. politics; and the new age of televised politics heralded by Richard Nixon's failure to appear telegenic, but instead shifty-eyed, makeup-free, and dogged by five o'clock shadow (figure 19). These stories—each with characters, plot, and a moral—came to define the Nixon-Kennedy debates in such a way that a single clip could do the work of several thousand words of explanation, for several million people. This debate offers a particularly evocative example of the blurriness between the "real" and the "representational"—the capturing of an "authoritative" likeness and the creation of layers of meaning around it. All images demonstrate this dynamic, in one way or another. Intuitively, we recognize that a photographer is making choices, that the photograph is not exactly congruent with the actual world. And yet it is tempting (especially with old untouched photographs, taken before the advent of Photoshop and other digital manipulation techniques) to let our experience of the photograph drift into a complacent sense that, sure, it is a more-or-less straightforward document.

If we slow down to read an image more carefully, dozens of questions might come to mind: Where are you? What time is it? What season? Who or what are you looking at? What are the dominant shapes and forms in the image? Is something centered? Is something noticeably large? Does something have a color that stands out? Are there points of light or darkness that stand out? Are there geometrical patterns formed by the elements of the image? Do these repeat? Are there "visual funnels" that direct your eyes to certain places? Does the image have a foreground, middle ground, and background? Are there particular kinds of "framing" within the image? Does it refer to other, familiar imagery or iconography? Where does the image place you as a viewer? Are you asked to identify with something in the image? Or are you placed at a distance? Does the image use the frame to create emotional character? And we could go on. These kinds of observations create the basic data set with which you will read the image. They require a willingness to describe in detail and refuse to overlook anything—and in that sense they resemble the first steps in all the general methods we described earlier.

But we can also try to set an image in motion, to let it suggest a narrative that unfolds over time, even for images that are not as well known as the Nixon-Kennedy debate. Can you get a sense of what has just happened? Or of what will happen? Are there characters (not simply people) in the image? Can you see, in the image, causes for past or future effects? Does the setting itself imply a storyline? These things are sometimes embedded in manifest ways in the image itself, as in the case of a detour sign (an index) that points toward where a car is likely headed next. On other occasions, however, this kind of image-in-motion work takes you into the realms of deduction and speculation. In the first case—deduction—you might ask what you can logically say, given the information present, about what is likely to happen, or what has just happened. In the second case—speculation—still working within the confines of your observational data, you allow yourself a bit more in the way of creative imagination. You ask: what are some reasonable possibilities?

Nowhere is the possibility for placing images in motion more disorienting than in historical photography, where one is often able to anticipate—in the

FIGURE 20. Streetcar accident, 1929. Photograph by Charles Libby. Courtesy of Joel E. Ferris Research Archives, Spokane.

image—events that have already taken place. Or, conversely, to see in the image the effects of an event already known. Images that involve violence— executions, war photos, accidents, destruction—often demonstrate such a vivid sense of narrative motion that they can confound our sense of past and present tense. The soldiers will charge the beach at Normandy and die. Dzhokhar and Tamerlan Tsarnaev are about to drop backpacks that will later explode at the finish line of the Boston Marathon. Onlookers gather around a fatal accident nearly a century ago (figure 20).

Most historical photographs are not so dramatic, often evincing only the kind of drama one finds proliferating on so many of our smartphones— which is to say, generally uneventful shots of people and places. There are a surprisingly large number of such images, produced in the past, that live on in the present. They present the interpreter of images—and all texts—with a serious problem: how do we understand the content of the utterly unexceptional?

Let's give it a try, with a detailed example (figure 21).

FIGURE 21.

Streetscape

Here is a simple image, of a street in a town. Local libraries and historical societies are full of such photographs. These pictures are almost completely unremarkable, of interest mostly to local history buffs who might care passionately about, say, the architectural history of that big stone building on the left. But really, why should anyone *else* care very much about this street? It's no impassioned diary, no secret spy document, no dramatic hanging. It's an everyday scene from an uneventful past. Indeed, the mundane character of an image like this poses a challenge to the interpreter: What kinds of knowledge of the past can be determined from such a source? Can that knowledge be compelling enough to pursue? And what are the tools one uses to get at that knowledge?

It's time for us to put some of our ideas about method into practice. We will aim for a close reading of the content of the image, looking to use manifest content to open the door to latent content. With that in mind, we'll begin with an attentive *description* of the image. Then we will turn to *deduction,* which allows us to connect our specific description with knowledge internal and external to the photograph. Finally, we will conclude with *speculation,* raising questions and hypotheses and digging, if we can, into things not readily apparent.

Description You will be surprised, perhaps, at how precise we want you to be. But here's the thing: each tiny point in a description may well lead to further insights. If you have failed to truly *see* the image in all its detailed glory, your interpretive work will be flawed from the beginning. You will miss things. So keep this as your mantra: "Until I *say* what I am seeing, I have not yet actually seen it." Do your best to *defamiliarize* yourself from what you think you know; that is, do not simply say that the picture is of a street with some buildings. Rather, imagine that you are seeing the image for the very first time, as a complete stranger, and are trying to make sense of it. What follows are a few examples of the kinds of descriptions you might make.

The photograph is black and white. It measures approximately 6 inches by 9 inches. The camera was positioned in the middle of the street. The image shows perspective and depth, as the two sides of the street draw closer together to form a point in the far distance. The street is not paved. Two shining, parallel lines (notice that we're not quite ready to say that they are "rails") are positioned within the street; they make a sharp curve to the left to pass in front of a large stone building that dominates the image's middle ground. The building has a circular tower structure at its corner, with a turret and window at the very top. Wooden poles hold up wires that are strung above the street. Seven horse-drawn carts or buggies are visible on the street. One bicyclist is visible, as is a dog. People are walking in front of stores on the left side of the street. On the right side of the street, there are trees, which are leafed out. There is an awning visible in the right foreground, but it is very hard to see any buildings on the right side of the street. There may be buildings in the background. The street seems to run for many blocks. In the far background a steep hill rises from right to left. The first two buildings in the left foreground have three stories (or more). A number of buildings have two stories; some have only one.

And you can continue with even more descriptive work. The more detailed you can get (it will, perhaps, be worth getting out a magnifying glass), the more possibilities you will create for yourself. We've only scratched the surface . . . but we've scratched enough of that surface to move to the next step.

Deduction You already know, simply by looking at the train tracks and electrical lines overhead, that this town has a trolley system. But if you described what you were seeing as "a trolley," rather than as a series of what *might* turn out to be its constituent parts (wooden poles, wires, shining parallel tracks, etc.), you would have jumped ahead too quickly, to the next stage in your interpretative work: deduction. Deduction is usefully defined as a kind of analysis that moves from general rules to specific instances. The general rules are premises. If we accept that the premises are true, and that the specific case aligns with the general rule, then we are able to say that the conclusions are true as well. So let us say that the general rule or premise, that thing we (think we) already know, is this: trolley systems run through streets in towns, have two parallel tracks, and require electricity, often carried in wires overhead, and this makes them unique among transportation systems. Seeing these particular details in this image, you might deduce that a trolley was present in this town:

Premise: Trolleys run on tracks through towns, and require electricity.

Observation: In this picture, tracks run through a town, with electrical wires overhead.

Conclusion: A trolley existed in this town when the photo was taken.

But here is where we run into trouble. We take things for granted ("that's a trolley track") when they might turn out otherwise. This town, in fact, also had a railroad line passing through it. Those are two very different things. As interpreters, we should always be on guard against the possibility that our unexamined assumptions might trip us up (this happens *all* the time!). One goal you might have for yourself, then, is to hold off on deduction—on thinking you already know what the evidence says—for as long as possible. That's how Sherlock Holmes did it, always cautioning Watson to take a full inventory of the evidence before making deductions. If your premise or general rule is not absolutely true, then your conclusion will be flawed as well. What we've stated as a general rule ("Trolleys run on tracks through towns, and require electricity") suddenly doesn't look so solid anymore.

Fortunately for us, the practice of interpretation is not confined to the practice of logic alone. We are able to step outside of our deductions and search for concrete corroborating evidence, such as a letter saying "I rode the trolley line today," or a newspaper story reporting on the opening of the trolley line, or a contract between the city and the trolley's operator, or . . . well, the list is long. The larger point is that these interpretive practices usually alternate in a kind of dance with one another. You are always moving between the abstract and the concrete, the logical and the evidentiary, the relation between what you see in a piece of evidence and what you already know (or think you know!).

Let's imagine some general knowledge that you have—some "rules"—that might be applied to this particular image. It turns out that you know a few things about transportation. Trolleys began to be installed in cities and towns in the late nineteenth and early twentieth centuries. Automobiles (which are conspicuously missing from the picture! Did you catch that? A description can also say what is *missing!*) entered common use around the second decade of the twentieth century, at which point trolleys slowly began to disappear from the landscape of many towns. Deductive reasoning—moving from these general pieces of knowledge to the specific case—might tell you that the picture dates from (to be safe) a forty-year period between 1890 and 1930.

Deduction creates out of your observations *facts*—things about which you can be quite sure. These facts are of a different category than the *empirical* facts that you created through your observations. They are new facts have been derived through an exercise in logical thinking. In the case of the trolley, the process may have gone by so quickly you never even noticed it—you simply named the fact of a trolley. But you can apply that same process—slowed down, now—to other elements in the photograph.

Take a moment and practice deduction by asking yourself what you can figure out about these things:

- A large, multistory building occupying a street corner on a trolley line.
- A line of stores along a street, many of them multistory and made of stone.
- A grove of trees alongside an otherwise busy street.
- The length of the street.
- The curious sheen on the surface of the street.
- Anything else that you find compelling in your own description!

We mention this last point because, while we find most interest in the buildings, the street, and the trees, you—being a different person—may find something far more interesting. Perhaps you are a cyclist and you find yourself drawn to the figure of the bike rider. Or you're an animal lover and want to think more about horses and dogs in the town. Each of us brings our own unique personalities to bear on the questions we ask—which is why interpretation is *never* a finished thing, but instead a constantly changing series of stories and readings. Our objective, of course, is to observe and consider as many elements as we can, to offer a thick description.

So, pause for a moment and think about what you think you know. What kind of town is it? How old might it be? Is it prosperous? What year might the photograph have been taken? Who might have taken the picture and why? Where in the town is this street? What season is it? What time of day? Those are just a few of *our* questions about this photograph. You should develop questions of your own. It's no joke: your ability to function as a critical thinker is fundamentally dependent upon your ability to ask interesting and creative questions.

Speculation Most of the questions we asked above have answers that you can arrive at through deduction. You can argue confidently about certain "facts," created out of your deductive reasoning: A medium-long street full of multi-story stone buildings is evidence of the main street in a town—not a city, but a town—at the turn of the twentieth century. The residents drive horse-drawn carriages (not farm carts, but more urbane carriages) even as they enjoy the benefits of an electrical trolley system. No cars are in sight, and the street is unpaved. The existence of the electrical system is itself evidence that the town has a power plant nearby and suggests that some of the stone buildings have electrical lighting. The leaves on the trees are evidence that the picture was taken sometime between May and October. The sheen on the streets suggests that the picture may have been taken after a rainstorm. The grove of trees opposite the buildings might be a park.

Hey, wait! Did you just see the shift in our language? From saying that we are (factually) *confident* that there is a trolley system, we have moved to words like "suggests," "may have been," and "might." These words signal that we have reached a kind of boundary—between those things that we willing to say with a high degree of confidence ... and those things that we are only guessing at. That line is *always* a murky one. We play at its very edges, as the things we can confidently state as premises or general rules start to get a little shaky. The sheen on the streets *might* be from a summer shower—or it might be oil spread on the street to keep the dust down ... or it might be an artifact of the photograph and its printing ... or it might just be a couple of funny patterns of light. The grove of trees *might* be a park—but maybe not. At this point we're offering a reasonably educated guess, but we cannot say the following:

Premise: All groves of trees are parks.

Or

Premise: All shiny dirt streets are the result of recent rainstorms.

Those claims just don't work. We've moved into the realm of *speculation.* Interestingly, what makes Sherlock Holmes seem so superhuman is author Arthur Conan Doyle's way of making the speculative seem like it bears the factual weight of deduction.

In speculation, we can't just make stuff up. We have to try our best to remain within the bounds of our observations and what is logically possible. In that sense, speculation is like a slightly more adventurous form of interpretation. The language we use has to reflect this new status ("might be," "suggests," "perhaps"), which has us playing at the far edge of deduction. We cannot speculate that the picture was taken on market day or that it was taken in Oregon or that it was taken in 1908. There's just not enough information for us to say such things. We can speculate, however, that the large building might be a bank, or that the grove of trees might be a park. Judging from the barren quality of the hill that rises quickly across the background, we can legitimately speculate that the town may be in the arid West rather than the East or Midwest. Considering the time period (turn of the century) and the relatively sharp quality of the photograph, we can speculate that the photographer was a professional rather than an amateur snapping with an early mass-market camera. If we take one more step down this road, we could speculate that he or she was taking the picture to sell. This makes a certain amount of sense. The citizens of this town might be more interested in images of their commercial district and (what seems to be) its largest and most impressive building.

As you can see, deduction and speculation are quite similar in nature, with deductions carrying you up to a certain point ("the large stone building is an important site in this town") and speculations allowing your mind to play a little more freely ("perhaps it is a bank"). The gift that speculation gives us is this: it creates questions ("is that building a bank?"), which we can answer through other sources. Good interpretation relies upon the creation of good questions. Disciplined speculation—from sources that we have thoroughly considered—is a *great* way to develop those questions.

We haven't yet exhausted this source, but at this point, we can take some of our speculations, turn them into questions, and set out again to find answers. Those answers will lead us to other photographs, or perhaps other kinds of sources—maps, city directories, newspapers. If you had found this picture in a photo archive, or in a book, some of the questions will perhaps be answered for you. In fact, this image comes from an archive and was published in a book. Here is the credit and caption that we left out:

> Figure 1. Boulder, 1907. Looking West on Pearl Street after a summer shower. Photo by Ed Tangen. Boulder Historical Society Collections, Carnegie Public Library. From *Ed Tangen, The Pictureman: A Photographic History of the Boulder Region*. Text by Thomas J. Meier (Boulder: Boulder Creek Press, 1994).

So now you know. The town is Boulder, Colorado, which is indeed a western town. We were right about the broad time period, right about the season, and right about the rain and the streets (Boulder's streets were not paved until 1917). The photographer was Ed Tangen, who indeed had commercial interests in taking numerous images of the growing town.

Many of these pieces of knowledge are simple and factual. They emerged from qualitative examination of the content found in the image. This kind of interpretive strategy can be extended, of course, to other kinds of texts, and it can be mixed with quantitative content analysis as well. The manifest meanings of this photograph—and of texts in general—provide the building blocks necessary for a deeper examination of the many other meanings that are latent, buried beneath the surface, or expressed in other ways. It is to some of these other ways of reading that we now turn.

SEMIOTICS

Semiotic interpretation comes out of a complex intellectual history dating back to the late nineteenth century. There are a couple of useful key ideas to understand before we can figure out what is meant by "sign" and how we can use it. The first idea is that words in a language are *arbitrary* and *relative*. What do we mean by this? Simply put, there is no innate connection between a word and the thing to which it refers. The spoken sound "cat" is simply a sound. We've assigned it to a furry, four-legged creature, but we could just as easily have called it something else—"*popoki*" for instance ("cat" in Hawaiian). That's the arbitrary part of it. The *relative* part is a little harder, but not much. The word "cat" gets its meaning *relative* to the other words in the closed system that is a language. That is, we assign meaning to "cat" by understanding that it is not "bat" or "rat" or "mat." Nor is it "car" or "cab" or "cap." Nor is it "cut" or "cot." "Cat" takes on meaning only in a closed system, in this case, the English language, which (like all languages) is full of little segments of sound, able to be combined in a nearly infinite variety of patterns.

A second key idea. Words like "cat" can be split into two functioning parts: a *signifier* and a *signified*. The spoken or written word "cat" is the *signifier*. The idea that comes into your mind (furry, four-legged, not dog) when you hear the word is the thing that is *signified*. When you put them together— a representation and a mental image—you have the communicative act we call a *sign*. Semiotics, then, deals with the meanings that come together in the form of signifiers and signifieds to form signs. Think of a sign as a process or practice rather than a thing.

And a third key idea. Signifiers (that is, the word or image) can mean different things at the same time. This is one of the preconditions for artistic literature and popular culture alike. A sign is something like the ability of the muscle contraction of an eyelid to take on multiple meanings understandable to members of a particular culture. So when you articulate the *signifier* "red," it can be attached not simply to one *signified,* but to several. In other words, the sign built on "red" can refer to American Indians, to communists, a color, love, danger, blood, or the command "stop" (among other meanings). Cultural analysis that is centered on signs, then, has to consider the ways that signs can *overload* us with meaning.

When we use semiotic interpretation in dealing with cultural texts, we need to strive for the multiple meanings created by signs. And we need to expand our definition of signifiers and signs to include not only words (in fact, often not words at all), but also images, gestures, clothing, and the whole broad world of things represented in cultural texts, be they popular, mass, or self-consciously "high art." Semiotic interpretation may be thought of as a particularly useful tool for single images or other kinds of texts that aim to "sign" messages quickly and efficiently. The meanings that signs create do not come from the signifying practices of the words alone; rather, they are the products of shared cultural meanings and thus they convey *both* word-level meanings (color, for example) *and* cultural meanings (love). Indeed, the keywords that we saw earlier from Charles Sanders Peirce—icon, index, and symbol—are really best understood as a semiotic taxonomy. A splatter of red on a T-shirt might be an *index* of a terrible injury (if it's blood) or a wild party (if it's wine), but it can also be closely mimicked through paint splattered on a shirt—and hence become an *icon*. Either of these, in turn, might be worn to a political protest, in which case the shirt would bear socially constructed meanings as a *symbol* (of, say, opposition to police violence).

An Example: Montana Highway Map

Consider the image from 1942, when the United States was in the thick of World War II (figure 22). This is the cover, folded open, of a highway map printed by the Montana State Highway Commission. It's also a collection of signs, some in the form of words, some in the form of pictures. The manifest meaning of the words at the bottom—"Travel Strengthens America"—seems to imply that tourism is a patriotic duty, much like how President George W. Bush encouraged Americans to "go shopping" in the wake of the 9 / 11 terrorist attacks to help prevent a recession. The key difference is this: on December 1, 1942, mandatory gasoline rationing went into effect for the entire country after a year of piecemeal action by states. The purpose of this measure was to conserve fuel for the jeeps, tanks, and planes being used to fight the war, and it was part of a larger effort that included taxes and mass military conscription. In this context, why would Montana *encourage* automobile tourism? Wouldn't this message fly in the face of the sacrificial logic behind rationing? With this historical context as our starting point, let's carry out a semiotic reading of the image itself and see what we can find.

First, we should avoid getting ahead of ourselves with the term "advertisement." Despite the slogan at the bottom, there are actually several elements of this "sign" that raise doubts about whether the Montana State Highway Commission was actually trying to promote tourism. On the surface this is simply an elaborate illustration for a functional tool—a highway map—used by people who are presumably already in the process of finding their way around the state.

To locate the latent meanings of this sign, recall Peirce's taxonomy of *index, icon,* and *symbol.* Let's break down examples of each.

- Index: As a physical trace of this image's function, the vertical crease running down the middle might be considered an index. This is not a piece of art hanging on a wall, but a folded-up map that would usually get torn and crumpled.
- Icon: We can catalog numerous icons, or mimetic likenesses, in this image: the cars, the road, the mountains, the trees, the cloud, the sword, the horse, the rider. Each of these is drawn to try to approximate as closely as possible the actual physical thing or being in the world that it seeks to represent.
- Symbol: The words, of course, are all symbols, since as we noted there is no necessary relationship between a word like "highway" and an actual

FIGURE 22. Montana Highway Map, 1942. Courtesy of Joel E. Ferris Research Archives, Spokane.

street. But there are other symbols as well, most notably the American flag being worn as a cape (representing the nation) and the lightning bolt coming down from the cloud (representing the strategy of *blitzkrieg,* or "lightning war," used by Nazi Germany).

Several of these elements fall into the hazy space between icon and symbol. The woman who towers above the right side of the image wears a distinctive Trojan helmet—its iconicity is what makes it recognizable as such—which in turn functions as a *symbol* of the fact that the United States was in the midst of fighting a war. The woman herself is *Libertas,* the Roman goddess of freedom who had long been a staple of transatlantic republican iconography, from the 1830 painting by Eugene Delacroix, *Liberty Leading the People,* to the Statue of Liberty dedicated in New York harbor in 1886.

So how do these elements come together to produce meaning? For that, we might look to the way they are arranged on the page. In examining the different elements of this image, you might have missed the triangle of empty sky in the middle of the page, punctured only by the lightning bolt. This triangle divides the image into three distinct zones, or frames, almost like a cartoon. The menacing cloud at top left carries with it the war machine of the Axis powers, including artillery, a bomber, tanks, and a battleship. On the right side stands *Libertas,* or America, with her sword ready to defend the country. While we might expect her to be surrounded by soldiers, however, the figures at her feet depict some of the industries that dominated the Montana economy in the 1940s, including a cattle rancher, a land surveyor, a miner, a construction foreman, an oil well, and two industrial smokestacks from what is presumably a factory. The positioning of the sword suggests—by *proximity* and *pointing* (two common forms of indexical representation)— that these trades *are* the tools with which the United States will fight the war. This sector of the document includes the words, "Travel Strengthens America," which are bracketed by quotation marks, as if it is a truism rather than a marketing message. The third and final sector of the image, at bottom left, includes no emblems of war. Instead, we see the beautiful Montana landscape—evergreen trees and the Rocky Mountains—with a highway running through it.

Put these three sectors together, and the image becomes a complicated semiotic argument for why traveling to Montana is still justified, even in a context of rationing and war. The vehicles crossing the Montana landscape on the bottom left directly strengthen the "America" on the right side of the image, which turns out to be a cross-section of the Montana economy. Indeed, the presence of an oil well reminded viewers that the state was not simply a consumer of energy, but a producer as well. At the level of latent meaning, this document implied that spending money on leisure in Montana was like investing in war bonds. In other words, despite the climate of collective sacrifice reflected in rationing measures, the State Highway Commission was finding a roundabout strategy for casting tourism as a way to support, rather than hinder, the war effort. Incidentally, the only dissenting vote against declaring war on Japan in 1941 was cast by Montana's at-large representative, Jeannette Rankin—a move that ended her career but suggests that the state harbored an undercurrent of antiwar sentiment (Rankin was already a well-known pacifist when elected to office in 1940). Regardless, the political climate of the time meant that advertising for tourism was taboo. If this was indeed a promotional document, the State Highway Commission had to maintain plausible deniability, and it did so through clever semiotic strategies for generating latent meaning. In 2001, by contrast, when tax cuts and an all-volunteer military meant that the costs of war were largely hidden from voters, President Bush could explicitly connect shopping and nationalism without fear of a significant political backlash.

STYLE

A quick summary: close reading asks us to defamiliarize ourselves with a text in order to see both manifest and latent meanings. Semiotic analysis asks the same thing, but it also relies upon our ability to mobilize *thick descriptions*— our knowledge of cultural codes that are evoked by individual signs. The metaphor that has emerged—visible surface, hidden depth—is not without problems. It points us to the psychoanalytic framework espoused by Sigmund Freud. It stands in for other metaphors—center and margin, for example— that would take us into the realm of social relations and power. For the moment, though, its virtues—the puzzling out of obscured meanings—make it a reasonable way to begin.

Another interpretive strategy for seeking out such cultural meanings in individual texts centers around the question of *style*. The critic Jules David Prown has offered a useful summary of what we mean by this word:

> In any age there are certain widely shared beliefs—assumptions, attitudes, values—that are so obvious that they remain largely unstated. As such, they are most clearly perceivable, not in what a society says it is doing in its histories, literature, or public and private documents, but rather in the way in which it does things. The way in which something is done, produced, or expressed is its style.[3]

Style permeates everything, from writing to music, visual culture to games. It is often useful in interpreting the texts authored by a specific individual, or produced by many different people in a particular historical moment or location, or in a particular industry. Stylistic differences can be read out of *national* or *regional identities* (K-pop or West Coast hip hop), *corporate structures* (Apple as opposed to Samsung), *social groups* (gospel), *circuits* (Northern Plains powwows or networks of biker clubs), or any number of other circumstances. In these cases, style is something that has been named and identified.

More interesting are the cases in which style lies waiting to be surfaced. And particularly interesting is the tension between the named and the not-yet-named. Sometimes, the style displayed by an individual or a group is both visible, as a quality of the making or doing, and less visible, as a "naturalized" expression of cultural values. Stylistic analysis is often useful with objects, machines, buildings, landscapes, and other material artifacts. However, it is important to resist confusing style with function. Let's think first, as an example, of shoes, and let's think of them functionally—that is, in terms of their purpose or role. Here's a short list: dress shoes, hiking boots, running shoes, military boots, ice skates, curling shoes, track spikes, soccer shoes, sandals, and flip-flops. One is good for hiking; another will stay on your feet in a raft. One will let you slide down the ice to release a curling stone; another will keep you from slipping on the soccer field or a running track. One is great for a shower; another offers your feet stability and support. Each shoe has a specific *function*.

Now picture the following objects: a carved eighteenth-century wooden chair; an early-twentieth-century art deco chair of steel; a vintage 1960s fiberglass "shell chair"; the "pillow chair" of the 1970s (a giant blob of plastic filled with millions of tiny pellets); a naugahyde-covered brown and copper kitchen chair; and a hipster-office retro chair. Can we make the same functional distinctions among these chairs as we did with the shoes? Maybe not so much. Sure, there are functional definitions that we can apply to chairs in general (an ergonomic office chair, a portable folding chair, a utilitarian classroom chair, a technologically complex dentist's chair), but the chairs in the list above don't have strong *functional* differences. We simply sit in them. What really seems to differentiate them is *style*—the distinctive way in which they are made. And given that chairs, in general, have four legs, a seat, and a back, and are meant for one person only, *stylistic* innovation is both constricted by form (if you stray too far from the form, your creation stops being a chair and turns into a stool or maybe a couch!) and is infinite (each of the "chair elements" can be expressed in limitless ways). Style often expresses interests so characteristic of a culture that they begin to seem "natural" in that moment—which is why style is a useful tool for surfacing latent cultural

FIGURE 23. Eames Chair.

meaning. In the 1950s and 1960s, so many people put their bottoms in those hard fiberglass shell chairs that no one ever questioned whether those chairs were in fact the way chairs ought to be. They seemed omnipresent in public and institutional settings, and many people made them the everyday chairs in their homes (figure 23).

If you pursued the stylistic elements of those chairs, you would discover interesting complications. Their style marked them as the work of the design pioneers, Ray and Charles Eames, who innovated with form, material, and manufacture in order to achieve specific goals. They wanted to offer usable designs that helped move consumers to lower levels of energy and material consumption. Charles Eames famously sought to design "the best for the most for the least." The style of the chair itself marked a philosophical position based on making excellent design available to the masses at affordable cost. In this sense, the chair expressed both a personal position and a particular cultural logic about scarcity, technology, class position, and democratic access to high-end style.

The chairs became pieces of an everyday common sense. They had a streamlined space-age look to them—a look that proved evocative to Americans in the era of Sputnik and the space race. Sit in one of those chairs in *that* moment, and you would have experienced—not dramatically, but in a "normal" sense—a feeling about a particular cultural complex of science, technology, and the possibilities of the future. Sit in one of those chairs today and you can almost *feel* the people of the 1950s and 1960s thinking optimistically ahead. As Thomas Hine has described it, this postwar "populuxe" style permeated all aspects of American design, from appliances and automobiles to countertops and, yes, chairs.[4]

Contemporary style markers add additional layers of meaning. On the one hand, original Eames chairs have become collector's items, drenched with new cultural meanings about rarity and the positive judgments we've made over time about the Eames design. On the other hand, it also means there's a booming business based on continuing and replicating the Eames style, which is now distributed by high-end furniture maker Herman Miller. In the Herman Miller chairs one finds old style conveying new meanings about nostalgia, design excellence, and the circularity of design cycles among producers and consumers. If we had a third hand, we could also identify the culture of the "knock-off" Eames chair, replicas sold at low cost by producers other than the Eames-licensed Herman Miller, sometimes blurring the lines into parody. One style: three meanings emerging out of three particular moments.

A FINAL NOTE

In this first toolkit, we have offered overlapping ways of engaging closely with a text. We've pushed the very definition of "text" from pictures and words into the terrain of structures and narratives, and caught a glimpse of how complex texts require the use of multiple tools. At the same time, we have started the task of putting an individual text in relation to other texts and into richer and more complex systems of meaning.

There are other strategies for reading texts, to be sure, but what we hope you will take from this chapter are the common methodological practices that those other strategies will include as well. Other angles, other complex texts, will still require similar work. Close reading, distant reading, thick description, painstaking focus on detail, deduction, creative speculation, comparison, and extraction of narrative: these things can all be put to the task of interpreting individual texts, sorting out the many ways they make meaning, and then connecting them to larger cultural forms and formations.

We began our exploration of American Studies methods by charting out five different domains of analysis.

Method	Object	Action
Interpretation	Text	Perceive
Curation	Archive	Collect
Analysis	Genre	Categorize
Contextualization	Formation	Expand
Generalization	Power	Connect

This first toolkit has emphasized the kind of knowledge that begins with perception, and the interpretive opportunities that come with thoughtful attention to a text. In the next chapter, we'll consider the ways that texts sit in relation to one another, and can be bundled together in a project archive in which individual texts can speak to one another. We began as literary critics; now, we become *curators*.

SIX

Archives

A CURATORIAL TOOLKIT

SO FAR, WE'VE BEEN IN AN (inter)disciplinary first gear, thinking something like literary critics. We've been doing the work of reading, challenging our senses and minds to perceive and interpret the meanings found in texts. We've thought about these texts in terms of *content* (what a text says it is doing), *speculation* (what we suspect it might be doing), *semiotics* (the sign systems that articulate how texts work in the world), and *style* (the distinctive ways we do things). To put it simply, we've been looking for meaning through individual texts, images, and stories.

But despite the alluring ability of Sherlock Holmes to discern a life story from the scratches on a pocket watch, one clue is rarely, if ever, enough to solve a mystery in the real world of research. Instead, scholars need to assemble multiple sources together and understand the *relationships* between them. We saw a glimpse of this with the method of "distant reading," where the Google Ngram Viewer allowed us to speculate on Doyle's use of the word "singular" in relation to the frequency of its use by other writers over a long period of time. But much of the analytical work of American Studies happens in the middle ground between individual texts and data mining. In the next chapter, we will discuss some of the analytical relationships—trope, genre, and formation, among others—that can be found when you put texts in dialogue. First, though, we will spend some time thinking about the challenges of assembling texts, or *curation.*

This step might seem straightforward, but it is actually one of the most difficult and important elements of research. In the criminal justice system, a significant portion of wrongful convictions stem from flawed archives of evidence. This includes the failure to investigate alternative suspects (an inadequate archive), interrogation techniques that increase the risk of false confessions (a contaminated archive), and tainting the process of witness identification (a deceptive archive). These errors are not failures of interpretation and analysis so much as curatorial hubris, or unjustified confidence in the validity of a given archive. As Dean Strang—an attorney featured in the Netflix documentary *Making a Murderer* (2015)—put it in an interview:

> Most of what ails our criminal justice system lie[s] in unwarranted certitude on the part of police officers and prosecutors and defense lawyers and judges and jurors that they are getting it right. That they are simply right. Just a tragic lack of humility in everyone who participates in our criminal justice system.[1]

Strang's point is, at its core, methodological. Each of the many archives produced for a given investigation offers the tempting shortcut of *confirmation bias.* In other words, it is easy to only look for sources that support what you already believe is right. This does not only apply to criminal investigations but to any context—including American Studies—in which the functions of curation and analysis are carried out by the same entity.

In many humanities disciplines, curation is handled largely by institutions such as libraries, special collections, and historical societies, which serve as an important check on the dangers of confirmation bias. These collections are presumed to be assembled without regard for the expected conclusions of a given research project. Nevertheless, institutional collections are still a product of creative labor. Curators must make difficult choices about how to assemble and organize materials based on assessments of intellectual significance. In this sense, we are *all* curators. Both librarians and researchers are in the business of making decisions about how to assemble texts and other data in order to draw meaningful conclusions. Even a decision to focus exclusively on an individual text has a hidden curatorial dimension, insofar as it involves the purposeful exclusion of other texts.

One of the long-standing attractions of American Studies has been the ability to build one's own archive. Earlier generations of scholars in the field took great joy in assembling diverse source collections that included literary texts, historical primary sources, technical work from both the social and natural sciences, journalism, art, and more. Archivists from institutions such as the Library of Congress played an active role in the development of the ASA, and one of the field's early leaders, Henry Nash Smith, went on to become the editor of the Mark Twain Papers at the Bancroft Library in Berkeley, California. The field's flagship journal, *American Quarterly,* has a long tradition of announcing and reviewing archives, from microfilm collections in the 1960s to innovative digital archives today.

Though you may not have realized it at the time, we have already given you an extended example of an archive. We're talking about the *mixtapes* that we used to frame the historiography of American Studies. You'll recall that we focused on four of these mixtapes, each one an *archive* arranged around an important writer:

The Vernacular mixtape (F. O. Matthiessen)

The American Problems mixtape (Vernon Parrington)

The Anthropological mixtape (Margaret Mead)

The American Spaces mixtape (Henry Nash Smith)

These archives were circumscribed by our self-imposed limitation of ten books per mixtape, but we considered a much wider range of materials. In essence, we created and labeled a set of "buckets" (vernacular, anthropological, etc.) and dumped a bunch of stuff into each. In so doing, we hoped to reveal four distinct strands in the intellectual history of American Studies. We then complicated those archives further, suggesting the ways that those four buckets actually splashed into one another.

We do this kind of thing all the time. We make sense of a proliferation of possible meanings by gathering texts together in meaningful *categories*. We set them up in order to create clarity and shape arguments. This is what categories do so well. But then, if we're being honest with ourselves, we allow that our categories are also, to an extent, artificial. The minute you place something into a category? It starts yelling at you that it doesn't really belong there. This process—bundling texts into meaningful categories, working within the categories, and placing different categories in critical relation to one another—is the essence of the *archive*. It's one of the main ingredients in the secret sauce of American Studies.

OFFICIAL AND UNOFFICIAL ARCHIVES

It is easy—and appropriate—to think of archives in a technical sense, as repositories for historical information. This information is often (but not wholly or necessarily) in the form of paper documents. Let's start there. You might, for example, imagine the National Archives, or a local historical soci-

Main purpose is to preserve.

ety, or a collection of papers generated by a famous person, or a film or music archive, or an archive of oral history interviews, or . . . the list of stuff that can be categorized and collected is nearly endless. An archive is something like a museum (an "archive of objects") or a library (an "archive of books"), but it's not exactly either of these. At the same time, the digital world of Pinterest and Instagram has transformed older meanings of "the archive" from something almost inevitably *historical* into something rooted in the present. The problem of preserving the internet for future historians has become a very real and pressing issue for professional archivists, who see not only the latest memes but also a digital wasteland of broken links, dead websites, and disappearing content.

An archive is, first and foremost, a *collection*. Library archives have a family relationship to other collections like a yearbook, or a blog, or the valuables in a safety deposit box. You might think of an archive as "a collection plus a purpose." The human intent behind an archive could be *individual:* some archives are the products of people with sufficient interest and resources to collect things from a range of locations. Or the intent could be *institutional:* many archives result from the record-keeping practices of companies, state bureaucracies, churches, organizations, publications, and other institutions. In both cases, the act of curation consists of bundling together objects with some sense that they are, or will be, significant to future readers.

Bundling not the

Perhaps the most common form of institutional archive is the manuscript collection. Let's take as an example the American Studies Association Records at the Library of Congress. What is the advantage of consulting a source like this instead of browsing the ASA website or reading our own humble user's guide? For one, the ASA Records include materials from as far back as 1946, whereas the ASA website is more focused on announcements and activities. In addition, manuscripts can offer an inside glimpse into the daily activities and correspondence of a person or institution, including records of conflict. Although record-keeping practices do reflect institutional priorities, they are not usually as sanitized as websites, which are edited for a wider public. The ASA Records collection is also huge: it includes 123,000 items contained in 351 boxes. That's a lot of stuff! And it is chronically underutilized in histories of American Studies, which tend to rely heavily on secondary sources such as *American Quarterly.* Part of the reason for this comes down to time and money: the ASA Records collection is not digitized, so the only way that you can access it is to travel to Washington, DC, and view it in the Library of Congress manuscript reading room.

why is info not public?

Even when dealing with a collection as big as the ASA Records, you should be on the lookout for gaps. For example, the transition to email has put a major dent in the range of ephemera saved by the ASA, since correspondence is saved on servers instead of filing cabinets. It is critical to avoid the trap of treating an archive as a *totality,* or an all-encompassing repository of information about a topic. But neither is it an *aggregate,* or a random collection of parts. We prefer to think of archives as *assemblages.* An assemblage is a whole composed of heterogeneous parts that, when subjected to analysis, becomes more than the sum of its parts. Assemblage theory is rooted in the work of philosophers Gilles Deleuze and Félix Guattari, who emphasized that assemblages can be disassembled or changed, since their meanings are generated by the exterior, contingent relations of their parts. In other words, an assemblage does not draw its essential character from a single necessary part, or from some essential quality thought to exist in the collection, but rather from the way its parts work in concert, as that working is revealed through our own analytical insight.

The concept has been further elucidated by Jane Bennett, Manuel DeLanda, Mel Chen, and others. Bennett uses the provocative example of a trash heap as a potential archive—something alive with analytical potential. We might imagine, according to Bennett, that there is an "ontological divide between life and matter," with historical agency firmly on the side of life. But this is a mistake, she argues. Not only do objects have a sort of "vital force," but organic bodies themselves are simply "temporary congealments of materiality," much like a bird landing on a floating pile of trash (figure 24).[2] At the other end of the spectrum, DeLanda argues that social movements might be productively understood as assemblages with moving parts. Indeed, projects within the anthropological current of American Studies have long grappled with the inherent flux resulting from treating large-scale categories like the "community" as an archive.

To put it another way, archival curation is always a partial and incomplete endeavor. Some items are saved; others are discarded. Some people have the power to select and collect; others do not. So while "official" archives—by that we mean formal collections like the Library of Congress—often appear to be neutral sources of data, writers in American Studies widely acknowledge that all archives have *interests.* They are, in and of themselves, collections that function as *representations* of someone's picture or vision of reality. Due to the costs of collecting and saving and storing, those pictures have often reflected the interests of those with relatively more social, political, and economic power. But this is not to say that archives are only—or simply—an

FIGURE 24. Heron standing on a pile of trash on the Anacostia River. Photograph by Emilie Gill.

expression of power. Hundreds of archives are explicitly devoted to records of the everyday, the marginal, and the oppressed. Consider the crowdsourced archive generated by sex advice columnist Dan Savage's It Gets Better Project, in which users uploaded videos about their lives to give hope to LGBTQ youth facing bullying.[3]

There are many, many such archives. Indeed, the dynamic through which "unofficial" archives are assembled may hold lessons for us. An archive begins with the assembly of a collection, a group of individual objects that bear enough similarity that they can be usefully seen as a connected category, a bucket worth filling up. Whether the objects are baseball cards or finger puppets, the act of collecting and the passage of time creates a sense of value that is not economic so much as cultural: these are possibilities for reflecting upon the past, and they produce a curious and dynamic relation between collecting (an active process) and the archive (an assemblage that can become a locus of meaning-making).

As practitioners of American Studies, we have three primary forms of engagement with archives:

- We *look skeptically* and critically upon existing archives, especially those that claim to speak for, to, and through powerful institutions. We interrogate every archive, asking: Who collected it, who cataloged it, who made it available, and why? What was included and what was left out? What was deemed important and what unimportant? Who can see it and who cannot?

- We *create our own archives,* bundles of texts that we assemble for the purposes of a specific project. Like all archives, ours are also self-interested; they point in some directions and not others. We have an obligation to be honest with ourselves and our readers by interrogating our own archive. Are we leaving out texts that are inconvenient? What are the "rules" through which we select some texts into our archive and exclude others? How do we balance the need for efficiency and clean argument with the reality of inconvenient complexity? How do we avoid *confirmation bias,* a particular danger when curation and analysis are inextricably tied together? These are methodological questions.

- We test and deepen our archives by placing them in *critical dialogue with other archives.* Pursuing cultural meanings, for example, we may select primarily cultural texts: images, art, music, performances. We would do well, in that instance, to link our analytical conclusions to archives focused on legal, political, social, or economic analyses. Such linkages represent important tools and techniques that American Studies scholars have used with great success.

We'll say a word about each.

LOOKING SKEPTICALLY

In American Studies, we commonly claim to read archives "against the grain." What exactly does that mean, and how do you do it? First, if you assume that the archive was collected with *interests,* you should try to identify those interests. During the Great Depression, for instance, the WPA Federal Writers' Project Slave Narratives collection had two primary objectives: employing writers and preserving the testimony of former slaves. But it also involved secondary interests like romanticizing the Old South. These interests structured the questions, the recording, the editing, and the cataloging of the narratives, producing an archive that many have considered to be highly compromised. As we have seen, some scholars have refused to use it. Others have argued that a critical focus on the archive's interests can allow one to peer beneath those interests to discover information that goes beyond the restrictions of the archive.

Second, since archives are the result of processes of collection, you should try to understand how those processes shaped the texts within the archive. WPA interviewers were given a standard set of questions, which put boundaries on what was and was not recorded. They were instructed to capture "dialects," which meant that the slave narratives would immediately and forever reproduce a kind of white fantasy of black speech. The very structure of the project—white interviewer / black subject—established power relations and limited what might and might not be said. The raw texts were then processed through a collection, transcription, and editorial pipeline that introduced opportunities for alteration. And they have subsequently been subjected to further organizational logics: by state, by gender, by experience.

Can you learn anything from such an archive, and if so, what? It's a fair question. Understanding the archive's limitations has allowed scholars to critically engage both the folkloric intent and the collection practices of the WPA archive—and to argue that its best information is experiential and impressionistic, offering the feel and texture, if not the economic structures or historical specifics, of slavery. In this sense, we engage any archive by looking not only for its obvious limitations and interests, but also for what James Scott once called its "hidden transcripts"—critiques of domination by the dominated that take place "offstage," out of sight and illegible to those controlling the "public transcripts" that seem to structure the creation of so many archives. The texts that reside in many "official" archives demand that the conscientious reader search for such hidden transcripts.

Third, you need to take the archive itself as a text, an object requiring interpretation. What does the WPA archive suggest about the rising interest in the study of folklore and slavery in the 1930s? Or about a shared sense of the impending and irretrievable loss of a collection of testimonies? Or about the cultural power of the New Deal government? Or perhaps about the linguistic and social dynamics of race in the so-called New South? The answers to such questions are not always straightforward.

Fourth, any archive has complications that blur the lines between "official" and "unofficial," and we need to look for these. The WPA project had at least seven black interviewers and took its inspiration from a project in Florida that featured the folklorist Zora Neale Hurston. If we look carefully, can we find counter-archives hidden in plain sight that don't even require reading against the grain? How do individual positions and personalities complicate the overall shape of an archive? Should the National Museum of

African American History and Culture collection be seen as an explicit counter-archive to the WPA project, a parallel archive, or a tangential archive?

Finally, your own subjective experience with the archive is distinct. Your handling of sources carries a kind of "you-ness" that can be critically embraced rather than repressed. But please be careful. Your "you-ness" is a tool for reading, not a special claim to authority. It's a useful tool—but everyone reading an archive should be aiming for the same kinds of critical engagement. Your strongest arguments are the ones legible to all, not the ones that are idiosyncratic to yourself. Subjective archival experience is successful when it generates insights that are persuasive to others.

ASSEMBLING YOUR OWN ARCHIVES

Your "you-ness" comes directly into play as you create your own archive. Your archive—let's call it a *project archive*—is the sum total of sources that you locate, interpret, and assemble into analytical categories. This archive is distinct from (but certainly might include) the institutional archives that you might visit in search of evidence. In other words, a project archive is something that you personally put together on an ad hoc basis for the purposes of a given project. The freedom to build such archives is a key ingredient in American Studies. But this does not mean that scholars in American Studies simply throw texts together at random and call it an archive. Rather, a project archive demands the purposeful extraction of *analytical* elements from a collection of texts, such that these elements become objects of analysis. The archive is the tool that lets us move beyond the individual text to this register of analysis.

Given the seemingly endless range of potential archival sources, as well as the demand for analytical rigor, how do you go about assembling *your archive* without ending up with a random aggregation of texts? One of the most common approaches is a back-and-forth cycle of inclusion and exclusion, with an increasingly strict criteria for entry as you move further along in a project. In other words, in the early stages of a project, you should try to cast as wide a net as possible, inevitably losing a degree of depth in exchange for glimpsing the array of possibilities. Think of it like brainstorming. Do not simply focus on institutional archives, but look for other places where you might find texts and objects. This initial stage might result in multiple possible topics, and your goal is to find unusual, interesting, or anomalous texts or patterns. In the next chapter, we will discuss some of the common analytical patterns—tropes, genres, and formations—that you might sense emerging through the process of curation, even at an early stage. As you begin to narrow down a topic and develop preliminary research questions and hypotheses, these analytical patterns will move to the forefront.

Again, the range of possible sources is endless, so it is critical that you find ways of excluding items without prematurely cutting short the possibilities of your archive. However, you should avoid the temptation to exclude texts that seem to contradict your preliminary hypotheses; these are the most important sources of all. You should also feel free to wander off the beaten path in search of original sources. Even within the category of "institutional archives," the possibilities are more expansive than you might realize at first glance. A great example is Katherine Lennard's work on the history of Ku Klux Klan robes. Drawing on her background in theatrical costume design, Lennard went on a cross-country road trip to dozens of museums and archives that held Klan robes in their collections, examining the fabric and stitching to determine how and where the robes were made. Were they factory produced? Homemade? Only by physically examining an extremely wide range of robes was Lennard able to identify and analyze the garment manufacturing industry that sustained the reemergence of the KKK in the 1910s and 1920s. The clues in these garments led her to more traditional documentary sources such as advertisements, business records, and correspondence, all of which constituted the *project archive* for Lennard's research.[4]

We encourage you to scour the footnotes of American Studies books and articles for other ways of assembling sources. There are many—but you'll find one point of commonality. The curation of a project archive will always face chicken-and-egg problems around where to start, what to include, and what to exclude. Chicken: an archive becomes more than a random collection of texts when it is capable of being subjected to analysis. But (egg): the work of analysis cannot take place without the raw material of the archive. In practice, therefore, American Studies scholars often find themselves employing various heuristics, or shortcuts, for inspiration. This might involve browsing existing institutional archives (often through networks of libraries such as OCLC WorldCat or the Online Archive of California) for manuscript collections that seem particularly rich with possibilities. But be careful: some heuristics can be hazardous to the validity of your research. As we noted, it is tempting to engage in confirmation bias by building an archive consisting of evidence that supports your predetermined argument. This is a serious problem since one of the core responsibilities of academic freedom is the accurate handling of evidence. Filtering out sources that might disconfirm your argument is a violation of trust between the scholar and reader.

The risk of confirmation bias is particularly acute in the case of ethnography, which involves gathering data through interviews and observation. It is easy to seek out people who will say what you want to hear, and it is just as easy to ignore people who might muddy your findings or cast doubt on your hypotheses. This is why anthropologists have developed a battery of ethical safeguards such as the expectation of detailed field notes. If you are affiliated with a university and seeking to carry out ethnographic research, you likely will have to obtain approval from your university's Institutional Review Board, or IRB, before embarking on your project. This is to protect people from being harmed as a result of your work. But assuming it is carried out with integrity, ethnography can open whole new vistas of possibility. Any conversation—any experience, even—can become part of your archive. Anthropologists are among the staunchest defenders of the notion that experience is epistemologically significant, which is another way of saying that books aren't the only way of generating knowledge. Good ethnographic research can draw on both book smarts and street smarts.

Regardless of the particular methods you choose to employ, you will need to compile a *project archive* that can provide valid data for analysis. We will illustrate this process by walking through a couple of examples. First, we will put together a project archive around Lin-Manuel Miranda's musical, *Hamilton,* which opened on Broadway in 2015 and went on to win eleven Tony Awards and a Grammy. The musical is itself based on an assembled archive, self-consciously drawing on a wide range of references, from historiography to hip hop. Our challenge will be to distinguish Miranda's archive (created for the musical) from our own project archive (created in order to write *about* the musical), and to place the two in critical relation to each other. Next, we will carry out a structural interpretation of James Fenimore Cooper's novel *The Last of the Mohicans* (1826) to examine how individual texts can be situated within broader webs of meaning.

SAMPLE PROJECT ARCHIVE: *HAMILTON*

> What does it mean to be examining, absorbing, feeling, reflecting on, and writing about the archive as it is being produced, rushing at us—literally, to entertain an unfolding archive?
>
> JASBIR PUAR, *Terrorist Assemblages: Homonationalism in Queer Times* (2010)

The news that Lin-Manuel Miranda was working on a "concept album" about Alexander Hamilton, the first Treasury Secretary of the United States, began to spread in earnest on May 12, 2009, when the writer and composer was invited to perform at the White House.[5] With Barack and Michelle Obama in the audience, Miranda described Hamilton as somebody who "embodies hip hop" and "caught beef with every other founding father." Miranda then performed a draft of what would become the opening number of *Hamilton* six years later. Today, it is difficult to watch this performance without thinking ahead to the musical. But imagine that you decided to write an essay on this performance sometime between 2009 and 2015. Could you have predicted that the musical would become such a smashing success? Maybe. Would you have guessed that one of Donald Trump's first tweets after getting elected president in 2016 was to criticize the cast of *Hamilton*? Of course not. You would have had no way of knowing that Trump would become the next president, let alone that Twitter would be his medium of choice. This problem underscores Jasbir Puar's quotation at the start of this section. When writing about very recent events, you might discover that your archive is changing faster than the academic publishing cycle will allow. This doesn't mean you need to abandon topics like *Hamilton,* but rather that you need to be careful to account for the possibility of change when constructing your archive (as you might imagine, the onrushing archive of new history and materials poses a challenge central to the book you hold in your hands!).

Anything in the musical is, of course, grist for the mill of scholarly analysis, but your decisions about what to include would hinge on the demands of your project, including research questions and expectations for presentation. Are you writing an essay on musical theater audiences? Your project archive might be shaped by the observation that *Hamilton*'s early years were marked by paradox; it was a highly influential musical that hardly anyone had actually seen, since it was so hard to score tickets. But this is just a guess. Was it actually hard to score tickets? You could test this question by tracking ticket prices on resale vendors like StubHub. You could also build an archive of popular musicals such as *Oklahoma!, Jesus Christ Superstar,* and *Rent* in order to think analytically about the discursive spaces (including film, soundtracks, and social media) in which theater publics are constituted.

The core imaginative leap made by Miranda is that he points to the revolutionary spirit of hip hop youth culture as an explanation for how Hamilton was able to "rise above his station." At first glance, this doesn't seem to make sense. How can a cultural style rooted in the late twentieth century explain a story from two hundred years earlier? Piece by piece, however, the connections in the musical become clear, particularly its decision to emphasize Hamilton's birth on the island of Nevis and impoverished childhood in St. Croix, a detail rarely remembered in conventional narratives of the history of the early republic (unlike Jefferson's roots in Virginia, Adams's roots in Boston, or even Lafayette's roots in France). Many of hip hop's early pioneers were also immigrants to New York from the Caribbean. The key to Miranda's innovation—which relies on a leap across historical chronology—relies on his archive, which included *both* Hamilton's biography *and* a reading of hip hop culture.

Our own project archive can help us step back, analytically, to explain and elaborate on this move in relation to hip hop historiography. In *Can't Stop, Won't Stop: A History of the Hip Hop Generation* (2005), Jeff Chang argues that socioeconomic and racial marginalization served as a source of stylistic inspiration for the black and Latinx youth who pioneered hip hop in the Bronx in the 1970s. Chang explains this feeling of "invisibility" as follows:

> It put you on a relentless quest to prove to them that you were bigger, wilder, and bolder than circumstances dictated you should ever be, to try to generate something from nothing, something no one else had, until everyone around you had to admit that you had something they might never have, something that might even make other people—big, important people—stand up and take notice themselves, offer you money, give you power, or try to crush your very soul.[6]

This spirit is at the center of songs like "My Shot," where Hamilton describes both himself and his country as "young, scrappy, and hungry." Rooted in the undercommons, hip hop was a brash, unapologetic vehicle for making the invisible visible—and Miranda reads this spirit back into the past. In the song "The Room Where It Happens," Hamilton is referred to as "the immigrant" (as Jefferson and Madison are called "the Virginians"), and one of the musical's biggest applause lines comes at the Battle of Yorktown, when Hamilton and Lafayette exclaim, "Immigrants: we get the job done!" At the Grammys, the cast unfurled a large Puerto Rican flag when accepting their award—underscoring for millions of viewers who hadn't seen the musical that it was celebrating the Caribbean roots of both hip hop and the American republic. That flag, in the context of the Grammys, occupies an important spot in our project archive. It's a text that helps us understand—and prove— the connection.

The links between past and present, structure and free verse, tradition and revolution—all draw on *music history* as a sort of archival "bucket" that allows *Hamilton* to paint historical connections impressionistically, through latent meanings, and that you, in turn, can repurpose for your own project. An example is the song "The Farmer Refuted," in which Hamilton debates Samuel Seabury, who had criticized the American independence movement in *Letters of a Westchester Farmer* (1774). The ideological division is echoed in music, with Hamilton rapping while Seabury delivers his points to the sound of a harpsichord. In the second act, *Hamilton* turns to the familiar structure of a rap battle (a form we might add to our archive), with Jefferson and Hamilton each taking turns making policy recommendations by hurling insults at one another.

The tension between manifest and latent content is a hallmark of the style or aesthetic known as *camp*, which has its roots in gay male culture. Camp revolves around performances of cultural clichés—from love stories to the violence of horror films—that are so exaggerated or in such bad taste that they generate opposite latent meanings. Camp is closely related to *satire* and can have a strong political edge. Concepts like camp and satire are useful tools for understanding many other Broadway musicals, which can be woven into your archive by way of contrast. You might reveal something about *Hamilton* by including in your archive the movie musicals of Vincent Minelli like *Meet Me in St. Louis* (1944), starring Judy Garland, which was influential in introducing the camp aesthetic to mass audience. Camp hinges on the ability to move among worlds and undermine normative cultural scripts through a humorous, over-the-top embrace of those scripts. A more expansive project archive can therefore help explain anomalies in the text of *Hamilton,* including the decidedly campy aesthetic of the songs featuring King George III.

George's role invites a range of possible meanings, depending on how you choose to build your archive. Miranda wrote the song while on his

Lin-Manuel Miranda ✔
@Lin_Manuel

 Follow

Dick Cheney attended the show tonight.
He's the OTHER vice-president who shot a
friend while in office.

RETWEETS   LIKES
430   1,064

8:30 PM - 20 Mar 2015

FIGURE 25.

Overumal-sis
or
well-detailed

honeymoon in the South Pacific, a part of the world where the impact of
climate change is most visible.[7] Adding this context to our project archive
gives a new depth of meaning to George's admonition that "oceans rise,
empires fall." What did President Obama think of this line when he attended
the musical in 2015 within a month of the United Nations Climate Change
Conference in Paris? Can we understand George's line as an unexpected
inversion of a king speaking truth to power? The same might be said for Vice
President Dick Cheney's attendance at the musical, which Miranda himself
tweeted (figure 25). The tweet jokingly compared Vice President Aaron Burr's
murder of Hamilton to an embarrassing (but nonfatal) episode in 2006 in
which Cheney accidentally shot a friend while hunting. But the deeper context includes the ill-fated American invasion of Iraq, which Cheney spear-
headed with promises that U. S. soldiers would be greeted as liberators, and
which bears an unmistakable echo of King George's own overseas ambitions.
George's first number, "You'll Be Back," is a threat disguised as a love song,
promising the colonists that he will "send a fully armed battalion to remind
you of my love."

The scope
of
our
Contemp.
History is
always
being
Reevaluated

Still, as we noted, the challenge of working with a recent text like
Hamilton is that its archive is, as Puar puts it, "rushing at us" as we write. Its
archive is neither in the past nor even really the present, since the contours of
its cultural impact are continually changing. Even during the publication
process of our book, new additions to the *Hamilton* archive kept emerging.
Shortly after the 2016 presidential election, Vice President Elect Mike Pence
attended a performance of *Hamilton* and was met with pointed remarks
from the cast afterwards. As we noted, Donald Trump responded by criticiz-
ing the musical on Twitter (figure 26). The fact that Trump took time away
from the presidential transition to lambast a musical generated considerable

Our wonderful future V.P. Mike Pence was harassed last night at the theater by the cast of Hamilton, cameras blazing. This should not happen!

The cast and producers of Hamilton, which I hear is highly overrated, should immediately apologize to Mike Pence for their terrible behavior

FIGURE 26.

controversy. As we write, it is not yet clear exactly how Trump's immigration policies will take shape, but there is no doubt it will change the political context in which the musical is encountered, and in which you'll read these words. Like the very title of "President Elect," the *Hamilton* archive is rushing at us—something materializing in the future that will become the present, and then the past, even as still more possible futures take shape on the horizon.

As you can see, *Hamilton* requires multiple forms of *archival* skill. We find ourselves mapping the archive out of which Lin-Manuel Miranda constructed *Hamilton:* scholarly books, musical styles, immigrant texts, sexualities, racial formations, and uncertain futures. At the same time—indeed, in an interwoven process—we create our own project archive that includes everything from presidential politics to the New York hip hop canon. In both cases, we find ourselves placing archives in relation to one another and using the juxtaposition to produce new ideas and new analytical insights. But as we situate texts within larger webs of meaning, we sometimes find that certain specific patterns appear again and again. In these instances, interpretation (chapter 5), curation (chapter 6), and analysis (chapter 7) start to flow together in a sensation of *déjà vu*. When you find yourself feeling this way (asking "haven't I seen this before?"), there's a good chance you might be onto something. It is a signal that your collection of texts is pulling you in the direction of *structures*.

STRUCTURAL INTERPRETATION
(IN A POST-STRUCTURAL WORLD)

The intellectual movement called "structuralism," which flourished in the mid-twentieth century, grew out of language theory, and in particular, the idea that the meaning of words in a language is arbitrary—a product of social convention rather than necessary correspondence. That is to say, you'll recall, there is no reason why we call a white fluffy thing in the sky a "cloud" rather than a "gliblinkf." Words get their meaning relative to other words in a finite language system. This insight—that *meaning is relative to that which surrounds it in a closed system*—powered the semiotic analyses of the linguist Ferdinand De Saussure, the ideological analyses of the literary theorist Roland Barthes, and the narrative and social analyses of the anthropologist Claude Levi-Strauss, among others. Though the heyday of structuralism has passed (for a surprisingly cogent summary of this shift, check out the two-part illustrated *BuzzFeed* article by Chris Rodley, "Post-Structuralism Explained with Hipster Beards," published in 2014), its insights continue to provide useful tools for American Studies.

In structural interpretation, we are chasing the meanings that are communicated through the *interrelation of the parts that come together to make a whole*. Structural interpretation works well when one is looking at a richly conceived story, complete with plot, character, setting, and developing relationships. Anthropologists have always been fascinated with "kinship" relations—which are, in effect, a closed system of human relationships within a society—and so it is perhaps not surprising that kinship offered Claude Levi-Strauss a particularly powerful way to think structurally about social relations and their role in narrative. One of Levi-Strauss's most famous analyses,

FIGURE 27. Scene from Season 20 of ABC's *The Bachelor* (2016).

for example, was of structural relations in the Oedipus myth, so rich with killings and couplings. Films and novels are often ripe for similar kinds of interpretation. The parents, children, spouses, relatives, in-laws, friends, enemies, and competitors featured in such narratives take us directly to a kinship system of finite possibilities, and a way to chart structural relationships.

Among the best examples are ensemble reality shows—*Survivor, The Biggest Loser, Tool Academy*, and others that trade on "teams," "tribes," "families," or other closed social units—which pull viewers in through "plot" shifts that are little more than realignments of interpersonal relations (figure 27). In ABC's *The Bachelor*, which featured twenty-four women competing to marry a single man in its first season in 2002, these structural expectations have proven durable enough to sustain at least three spin-off series (*The Bachelorette, Bachelor Pad*, and *Bachelor in Paradise*) and countless satires (including the online-only *Burning Love* and the dark Lifetime drama *UnREAL*). Television producers are not necessarily interested in the reasons *why* these structures are so durable, as long as they continue to attract viewers. But we scholars of American Studies are in the business of interpretation and analysis. Structural interpretation allows us to find the latent meanings in relationship narratives—and, in so doing, to make sense of a particular kind of archive.

[handwritten marginalia: structure closely relates to hype previously established conventions]

We want to begin by taking you back to a much older American text, James Fenimore Cooper's *The Last of the Mohicans,* published in 1826. The setting is the French and Indian War, in which the British and French fought one another for control over colonial North America, each utilizing Indian allies. The French and Indian War was the North American theater of a global conflict known as the Seven Years War. In the novel, the year is 1757. Professional British troops, aligned with colonial settlers and a few Indian allies, have squared off against the French, who have built much of their North American empire on an extensive Indian alliance system. Our first step will be to identify the key characters, their relationships to one another, and perhaps a little bit about the nature of the characters. Here's the cast:

- Colonel Munro: British commander of Fort William Henry, which is surrounded by the French and their Indian allies; father to Cora and Alice, and both commanding officer and avuncular figure to Duncan Heyward.
- Cora Munro: Older daughter of Colonel Munro, she is the daughter of his first marriage. Spunky and tough, she is half-sister to Alice Munro.
- Alice Munro: Younger daughter of Colonel Munro, and the child of his second marriage. Alice is blond, fragile, and genteel; half-sister to Cora.
- Duncan Heyward: A dashing and capable British Army officer who is in love with Alice Munro.
- Chingachgook: The noble, wise, and good last chief of the Mohicans, and father to Uncas.
- Uncas: The only remaining Mohican of his generation, and a noble, wise, and good son to Chingachgook.
- Nathaniel (Natty) Bumppo (aka "Hawkeye" or "the scout"): American frontiersman and companion of Chingachgook and Uncas. He is tough, smart, honest, and a skilled master of the woods.
- Magua: The novel's resident bad guy, Magua is an Indian outcast who blames his misfortunes on Colonel Munro. He is tough, vicious, and vengeful, and desires Cora.

Whew! That's a lot of names. This is sort of like the whirlwind introduction to characters that tends to bog down the opening episodes of ensemble reality shows. But there's a reason these shows take the time to do so: their viability depends on the availability of lots of moving parts and potential relationships.

Claude Levi-Strauss focused his analyses on a search for opposed pairs: night / day, raw / cooked, young / old, live / dead, hot / cold, and so on. As we interpret the relationship structure found in a text, we might follow his lead in modified form, pairing up characters in order to start forming webs of relations. With eight main characters in *Last of the Mohicans,* there are twenty-eight possible pairings. Some potential pairs cross social boundaries; others reinforce them. There are pairs that satisfy one's expectations—about race, about class, about sexuality—and pairs that do not. So take a moment and think about the pairings that seem most interesting to you. There are a lot from which to choose.

Let's imagine some strategies for picking evocative pairings. What if you considered the nature of the characters? Magua is evil; Uncas is good. Their essential nature defines a relationship, and we can explore it further by focusing our interpretive attention—description, deduction, speculation—on the two. Both are young men, both Indians, both seek women to marry, and the closed pool of the structure suggests that a rivalry will play out over one or both of the Munro women. Ding ding ding! This is exactly what happens in the novel, and it illustrates the critical role of plot (as opposed to, say, style) in the structural interpretation of narratives.

Plot—the sequence of actions that shape the story around a beginning, a middle, and an end—allows us to see not just fixed images or diagrams, but relationships in motion. Cooper's *Last of the Mohicans* is a complicated novel, but here are a few of the key plot developments:

1) Colonel Munro wants to get his daughters to safety. Hawkeye, Chingachgook, and Uncas take up the task.

2) As they flee, they are dogged by Magua, who is able to capture the Munro sisters.

3) Colonel Munro and Duncan Heyward unsuccessfully defend Fort William Henry against a French siege. Numerous English captives are killed.

4) Uncas and Chingachgook confront a separate set of problems, as they are the last of their tribe, caught between the imperial geopolitics of France and Britain and the tribal politics of Indian people under colonial pressure.

5) In the end, Uncas, Magua, Colonel Munro, and Cora all die, and Duncan and Alice get married.

This plot places strain on several of the novel's most important pairings. These include actual kin relations (Chingachgook / Uncas, or Munro / Cora / Alice) as well as "fictive kinship"—nonbiological ties that bind characters together (the marriage of Duncan and Alice, or the partnership of Hawkeye and Chingachgook). Alice and Cora, for example, constitute a partial biological relation. Cora, it turns out, is the daughter of a marriage Munro made while serving in the Caribbean. Her mother was mixed race and Cora is considered a "quadroon"—a woman with a single African grandparent. The sisters, then, represent a particularly evocative pairing of whiteness and color. Alice's blonde frailty is about her white womanhood; Cora's dark resilience signals that she is a possible partner for Uncas or Magua. Not unlike *The Bachelor,* the movement toward marriage (or away from it) is the driving force of the novel's plot. Marriage defines the creation of new families—new social structures—and the possibility of children and futures. It also highlights the failure of other potential pairings (most notably Uncas and Cora) that might have produced a different kind of future. What should we make of that failure? Why are some characters driven together and others apart?

A structural interpretation would have us ask how such pairings reflect the people who produce and consume the text, and particularly the narratives they construct about American pasts and futures. Are there *patterns* visible in the text that can be read in light of their correspondence to, or alignment with, patterns that exist in a given social and cultural world? Since the maker of the text is a member of that world, those patterns are also assumed to exist in his or her mind, often (but not always) in latent or unconscious form. This assumption thus explains how such patterns come to be embedded in the text, and why all texts carry, in some form, *structural imprints* of the social world, unspoken but evocative gestures toward the proper forms of social relations, the constrictions of history, and the possibilities for futures. You've perhaps located other, equally evocative pairings that might (or might not) be reflected in the novel's plot. Let's summarize a few of the other possibilities, and then consider the patterns they might suggest.

- Cora and Uncas: A possible romantic pairing, since neither Cora nor Uncas is truly "white." In fact, Cooper raises the possibility of this union.

- Cora and Magua: Another possible pairing, but this one is explicitly about "savage" Indian desire for white women. In articulating these relationships, we are almost immediately led to see that Cora's racial identity can oscillate between white (in relation to evil Magua) and black (in relation to good Uncas), thus creating dramatic possibilities for social meaning.
- Alice and Duncan: The most likely marriage partnership, between two members of the white, British, military upper class.
- Chingachgook and Hawkeye: Two longtime male partners, nurturing the next generation's future in the form of Uncas, Cora, Alice, and Duncan. One nurtures an Indian future with almost no possibility, the other nurtures—sometimes unwittingly—a white future that is seemingly inevitable. Since neither man has a female partner—and thus will not reproduce—both are forced to see the future in terms of their own lonely limits.
- Duncan and Hawkeye: Two powerful, confident white men, who live out radically different experiences of the new world of North America, the first tied back across the Atlantic to the British empire, the second all about freedom and self-sufficiency in the American woods.

Already, we can see that certain pairings are so rigid, they cannot be transformed in the novel. The Magua / Munro pair, which speaks to the racial distinction "Indian / White," and is framed around mutual hatred, is one such opposition. The white, upper-class reproductive marriage of Duncan and Alice may be another. Other structural pairings, however, will be reshuffled over the course of the narrative, evoking possibilities, driving the story, and playing on deep cultural anxieties and questions surrounding race, class, the frontier, and the nature of the American future.

The manifest content of the book—signaled by its title, *The Last of the Mohicans*—suggests that what matters most is *not* the pairing of Alice and Duncan. Our interpretive work has led us to see that relationship as both obvious and easy. Rather, it is the struggle to find Uncas a marriage partner and thus rescue the Mohicans from oblivion that seems to matter. As we move through the story and see Alice and Cora in constant peril, these various structural possibilities give readers a sense of urgency and a reason to care. More than that, however, the possibilities give us patterns that we might use to look for correspondences in the social world. Our next step, then is to *convert relationships into patterns:*

- There is a *race pattern* in which white-on-white social relation charts the future, while color-on-color (even for good and highly regarded people) does not.
- There is a *gender pattern* in which genteel white womanhood charts a future, while bold, forthright, and sturdy mixed "frontier" womanhood does not.
- There is a *class pattern* in which civilized upper-class elites (Alice and Duncan will return to the mother country for a refresher before they come back to rule the colonies) will define the future, while lower-class backwoods people will not.
- There is a *national pattern* in which Britishness, not Indianness—or even hardy "frontier" Americanness—will shape the future.

These are only a few, but they provide us enough material to think about. Let's pause and summarize what we think we know. The structure of relationships in the novel reflected corresponding patterns of ideas about race, gender, and class in the nineteenth-century United States, ideas that were firmly embedded in the mind of James Fenimore Cooper. America, in Cooper's vision, relied upon white English metropolitan elites who (like Alice and Duncan) had become Americanized through their adventures but who maintained a conservative social hierarchy. In this America, there was no place for race crossing (indeed, we could find literally thousands of cultural texts in which authors play with the possibility of racial romance, before killing off the characters who dared to consider it).

Likewise, Cooper and much of his audience shared a cultural common sense about the roles and place of women, one that emphasized domesticity and male patriarchy over the relative liberty embodied by Cora. And of course, all of these things work in concert: Cora's portrayal as an independent woman was made possible, in large part, through the black racial history Cooper assigned to her. Her touch of blackness, in other words, precluded an elite white marriage and thus allowed her to be presented as one kind of a woman and not another. Uncas is presented as a possible partner for Cora only because he is basically an exceptional, elite Indian, blending a claim to Indian "royalty" and status together with the manly hyper-competence of someone like Hawkeye. Even that competence cannot save Hawkeye, who is too wild to contribute to Cooper's America and who will trek West, with Chingachgook, along the advancing American frontier.

Make sense? Let's turn, very briefly, to a variation on this theme. Claude Levi-Strauss emphasized dualisms—pairs of two. He argued that the human brain built meaning—even complex meaning—around such binaries. Other structuralists asked, "Well, why not structures that build meaning around three?" So we might revisit our characters in terms of triads, not pairs. Doing so reveals new and different structures, and thus different patterns corresponding to other kinds of cultural formations and familiar narratives. This triangulation also reveals other aspects of the characters, which might also be mapped onto social correspondences. Consider how one might complicate the pairing of Cora and Alice with a third character.

Place their father as the third side of a triangle, and you have a *familial drama* of race, multiple mothers, and uncertain affections. That's enough to power a novel of its own! Replace him with Duncan Heyward and you have a *love triangle* in which Cora functions as a third wheel, destined only to bring together the racially pure lovers Duncan and Alice. Place Uncas as the third side of a triangle involving the two sisters, and you have a different sort of love triangle, one well suited for Cora. With such a nicely varied cast of characters, there are a number of these triangles that one might pursue. Perhaps the three characters of the backwoods (Chingachgook, Uncas, and Hawkeye), or the three white men who claim different forms of authority (Munro, Duncan, and Hawkeye), or the three main Indian characters (Uncas, Chingachgook, and Magua). In each case, detailed interpretive work yields insights into cultural patterns and structural meanings.

A COMPARATIVE EXAMPLE

Cooper wrote a number of other books featuring the character of Hawkeye. Other writers produced similar texts. We will talk more about the possibilities of linking such texts together in the next chapter. Here, we would like to close our example by asking you to put another version of the same text in your project archive: Michael Mann's 1992 film, *The Last of the Mohicans,* starring Daniel Day-Lewis and Madeleine Stowe, along with Indian actors Wes Studi and Russell Means (this film is one of at least five film versions of the story, which suggests the importance of this text in American cultural history). Comparison is an excellent strategy for your toolbox, as it allows you to extract even more meaning from the two parallel texts. Establish points of similarity (the characters and the basic plot, in this case) and then look for points of difference (here, the relationships among the characters). Since you're now practiced, we'll move quickly, though we do advise you to watch the film . . . it's pretty good!

Consider the very different structural pairings and actions that appear in the Mann film:

- Duncan and Cora: Duncan, an incompetent English fop, far prefers the spunky dark-haired Cora over the pretty but frail Alice. Though independent-minded Cora rejects him, Duncan sacrifices himself for her, thus proving his worth, even as he is eliminated from the remainder of the plot.

- Uncas and Alice: These two are paired as romantic partners; both end up dead. Alice kills herself when she sees Uncas killed and is herself being carried away by Magua. The film ends with a shared funeral, as they get to spend eternity together, since there is no place for them in the British colonies or future United States.

- Hawkeye and Cora: Far from being the asexual character of the novel, the film's Hawkeye is an explicit rival for Cora's hand. As the film ends, they are together, presiding over the funeral of Uncas and Alice.

Whoa! It's like a whole different version! Mann kills off Duncan and Alice, both of whom survived in Cooper's novel. What should we make of that? The change in the structural relationships forces us to ask why Hollywood screenwriters wanted to tell a different story in 1992. Some of these alterations were undoubtedly manifest and intentional; others were likely latent, unconscious, and *structural,* the products of human beings living in—and creating in—a particular cultural moment.

Recall Cooper's vision: no race-crossing allowed. His implicit message was: "Thanks to all of you pioneers out on the frontier, but please keep moving. Patrician elites ought to, and will, rule." In the film version, that's completely gone. In its place is an America dominated by hardy white frontier folk. Weak Englishmen die out in this version. So do equally weak, pale, scrawny blondes. Where Cooper found no use for the frontier scout, other than to clear the way for white elites, Michael Mann makes the scout the center of everything: Hawkeye and Cora will marry and produce a new American race. Their hybrid histories and their matching long dark hair, streaming out in the wind, correspond—and not by accident—with both the

FIGURE 28. Scene from 1936 film adaptation of *The Last of the Mohicans.*

emphasis on American pioneering that characterized Ronald Reagan's regenerative political rhetoric of the 1980s *and* the multicultural turn of the late 1980s and 1990s. She—though white—has been touched by blackness; he—though white—has been touched by Indianness. In 1992, they were quintessentially American.

Working comparatively, we've mapped similarities and differences. We might also ask, "What remains absolutely constant in both texts?" If you think about it, you'll realize that it is the dying Indians. We should not ignore this consistency. Why didn't the endgame for these characters change? To engage the question, we might imagine a final set of *structural* triangles. In both narratives, Indians are a third party in relation to the imperial struggles of European powers. The war between the British and the French hinges on the Indians allied with both sides. At the same time, Indians are also the mediating force that differentiates American colonists like Hawkeye from British overlords like Duncan. It is Hawkeye's supposed Indianness—his skill in the woods, his affinity with Uncas and Chingachgook—that makes him American. Finally, Indians complicate the dynamics of black and white. The racial codes that would have made Cora "black" are made more complicated by the possibilities of an interracial romance with an Indian (figure 28).

In the end, all these complications are resolved into a final opposition that returns us to the title, *The Last of the Mohicans*—white future and Indian disappearance. In neither text do Indians manage to survive into the future. In both cases, the prime agent of Indian death is other Indians, not white people (thus absolving white audiences of historical responsibility). James Fenimore Cooper will send Chingachgook and Hawkeye off together into the West, where they will vanish in the face of an encroaching civilization. Filmmaker Michael Mann does not even give poor Chingachgook company on his final journey into oblivion. The final shot in Mann's film shows the three—Chingachgook, Hawkeye, and Cora—standing next to one another, conducting a funeral for Uncas and Alice. The camera pulls away and makes the bitter end clear: Hawkeye and Cora, it turns out, have been standing close. Chingachgook has been physically removed from them. He ends the film alone, an Indian with no future.

Our structural interpretation has suggested that the two texts reflect the two distinct historical moments in which they were created. These differences are visible in the *patterns* of relationships that structure the film and the novel. These patterns speak to larger issues—racial crossing, national identity, gender, class status—in ways that correspond to the social and cultural issues at play in the moments the two texts were produced. At the same time, on at least one issue—the place of Indians in the United States—the two texts suggest a similar message that encompasses *both* historical moments. One might use the continuity between these two pieces of textual evidence to argue (as many others have) for the ongoing centrality of the myth of the vanishing Indian in American cultural history.

ONE MORE THING

In the language we've used to analyze *Last of the Mohicans,* we have suggested that the texts represent, through their structures and relationships, the social worlds of the 1820s and 1990s. But both Levi-Strauss and Saussure go much farther, arguing that language (in the case of Saussure) and narrative (in the case of Levi-Strauss) do not *represent* meaning so much as *create* it. That is, as humans, we *only* see the world through the structures we create, namely language, social behaviors, institutions, and stories. The philosopher Ludwig

Wittgenstein called these structures *language games,* and he argued that we could easily get trapped in them. As he put it, "A picture held us captive. And we could not get outside it, for it lay in our language and language seemed to repeat it to us inexorably."[8] This is pretty complicated stuff, and we don't need to belabor it. But it is worth remembering the bottom line: systems that classify (race, gender, class, civilization, marriage, and more) also operate as systems that create meaning. Simple dualisms—good / bad, old / new, ours / theirs—function as categories that structure the ways we perceive and understand. Indeed, the simplest categories are often the most powerful. Category-building is one of the prime functions of language and storytelling. In the process of parsing and naming differences and similarities, we create the world—not as a physical thing, but as a thing capable of being known in certain ways and not in others. Our goal in interpretation, curation, and analysis is to uncover and unpack those meanings as they are represented and created through texts.

It is worth noting just how complex our interpretations became—and how quickly—as we moved from one text to a comparison between two. What holds these interpretations together—ideas such as Indian disappearance, cross-racial romance, and backwoods hybridity—are *tropes,* or ideas that recur across time and between texts. But tropes would not be visible without the curatorial step of bundling texts together into a project archive. That act of bundling will take us into the territory of analysis, which is the subject of the next chapter.

Method	Object	Action
Interpretation	Text	Perceive
Curation	Archive	Collect
Analysis	Genre	Categorize
Contextualization	Formation	Expand
Generalization	Power	Connect

You might recall the chart of methodological functions that we included in the previous chapter. The interpretation of texts posed an interesting series of challenges; no less important are those presented by curation, which requires a wide vision, a discerning eye, an enthusiasm for collection, a creative use of juxtaposition, and an honesty about the criteria for inclusion and exclusion. It is these very challenges, though, that make American Studies such an exhilarating field of study. It offers an unusual degree of freedom to curate your own archives. However, that same freedom is also what makes it vulnerable to shortcuts, especially the temptation of curating an archive that simply reinforces what you already believe. By delaying the process of jumping to conclusions—by taking the time to collect and categorize your sources—you might start to see connections that you never expected to find when you first embarked on your project.

SEVEN

Genres and Formations

AN ANALYTICAL TOOLKIT

HUMAN BEINGS LIKE TO THINK by pairing objects together. As we've seen, we can figure out a lot of stuff by *comparing* ("How are these things similar or different?") and by *connecting* ("What is the relationship between these things?"). In the last chapter, when we considered two versions of *The Last of the Mohicans,* we noted the strong similarities—same characters, setting, title, and basic plot—but then observed shifts in meaning made visible by some significant *differences,* figured around deaths and marriages. In the midst of those shifts, we identified a single idea that remained consistent—the refusal to concede to American Indians a future. These are only a few examples of another methodological register, one we're going to call *analytical.* It's a new gear, and to engage it, we'll need to push in the clutch and shift.

It may be useful to begin with a simple but important distinction between interpretation and analysis, since the two words are often interchangeable. For the moment, let's say that *interpretation* focuses attention on our understanding of single texts, while *analysis* calls us to put multiple texts into relation to one another within a project *archive.* You can see how, in the example above (with an archive of only two texts!), we found ourselves moving easily from interpretation to analysis. Analysis produces larger claims than interpretation, and, in doing so, it creates the building blocks for the generalizations we call *theory.* Analysis works by making comparisons and building categories, creating analogical relations, looking for causes and effects, tracing beginnings, transitions, and endings, and situating bundles of texts in *context.* Those *contexts* prove critically important, for they reveal networks of money, social relations, institutional authority, distribution, consumption, and globally connected (or disconnected) circuits of readership and practice. We call these contexts *formations.* They help reveal the deployments and contests surrounding *power,* which we will be turning to in the next chapter.

Analysis and contextualization might seem at first glance to be dry and familiar things. You've likely been asked "compare-and-contrast" questions for a very long time. But stick with us, please, and we'll try to demonstrate how they actually underscore the *creative* possibilities of an interdisciplinary approach to methods. In methodological terms, we'll try to figure out ways that the curated texts of the archive can be arranged and rearranged into categories that allow us to make broader claims. In interdisciplinary terms, we'll begin shifting gears toward disciplines that offer tools for context: history, anthropology, sociology, and economics, among others.

We are going to make a few stops along the way, each offering distinct opportunities for connecting texts and enabling analysis. We'll begin with a quick look back to our reading of *Last of the Mohicans,* which introduced the idea of the *trope,* a shorthand figure of speech that generates literary and cultural associations. Then we'll look at other ways that texts can be placed into meaningful categories like *form* and *genre.* As with the mixtapes in chapter 2, the focus is not on the specific texts that live within the categories—that's *interpretation*—but rather on the category itself and the ways that it generates meaning—that's *analysis.*

TROPE

When we say that a trope is a kind of figurative language, we simply mean that there's a *substitution* going on: the literal details that seem unique to a text (like the marriage of Duncan and Alice) can fall into familiar patterns, or tropes, that evoke well-worn *figurative* meanings. These meanings often reinforce cultural expectations that are totally false—like the inevitability of Indian disappearance, or the idea that same-race marriage reflects the natural order of things. Tropes are frequently structured around figures of speech— metaphor, metonym, synecdoche, and others—that are useful for swapping meanings, often in ways that move from specific case to general claim. Importantly, tropological analysis is not limited to fictional texts; it can help you understand everything from historical writing to journalism. In history books, the "facts" chosen by a given historian might be true, but they *also* might be organized into tropes that are anything but innocent. To treat a specific detail (such as the marriage of characters in a film, or the election of a president in real life) as representative of a larger meaning of "America" is an example of figurative language in action.

Tropes are created when many different texts offer up the same plot twist or motif, to the point where its larger cultural meanings become second nature. What happens, for example, when Chingachgook—and other Indians—in book after book, game after game, film after film, political utterance after political utterance, *always* seem to die without leaving a next generation behind? This kind of patterning is what distinguishes a *trope* from figures of speech in general. A metaphor, for example, can be found in a private poem with an audience of one, but a trope needs to be recognized by lots and lots of readers or viewers. A metaphor can *become* a trope, but only after it morphs into a convention, pattern, or template that serves as an efficient conceptual shorthand. A cultural producer—a novelist, film director, game creator, or politician, for instance—can expect an audience to quickly glean the cultural meaning of a trope because the audience is already intimately familiar with it, whether consciously or unconsciously, from the wider cultural atmosphere.

A trope is like a stereotype that functions at the level of both plot *and* cultural meaning, and in that sense *trope* reflects something with richness and complexity. For example, the two-note sound used by the TV franchise *Law and Order* to transition between scenes has become such a staple of comedy sketches that it now functions largely as a critique of the lazy conventionality of American crime drama. At first these references were simply *allusions* to a specific series. But as the references piled up, this sound took on *tropic* (pronounce that with a long "o," not a short one!) qualities, thus reinforcing the meanings and creating a durable category. Today, those two quick musical notes can indict an entire genre.

Tropes thus provide the American Studies scholar with a coherent, ready-made object of analysis. It's pretty straightforward: place your individual text in dialogue with other texts that *mobilize the same pattern,* and that are (or would have been) *visible to a wide audience.* In our example of *Last of the Mohicans,* we used two texts to establish the trope of the vanishing Indian. We did so through comparison, noting the texts' similarities (characters, setting, and title), then differences (radical structural rewriting), then finally identifying an important shared structural element: Chingachgook's childless future. We asked you to take our word on the existence of other texts, but in fact you could easily find many other pieces of literature, film, music, popular writing, and bureaucratic writing that utilize the trope of the vanishing Indian. You would be overwhelmed with examples.

As you located these examples, the object of your inquiry would shift. Each individual text would become evidence of a trope. Having demonstrated that trope's existence, you would focus your analytical energy on *it,* in effect *curating* connections across texts in an effort to reveal something about the dynamics of cultural production, transmission, and meaning. This kind of tropic analysis is a powerful tool—but it's not the only way to think about how we work with texts. There are equally interesting possibilities to be found, for example, in looking at bundles of texts united by *form.*

FORM

Let's begin to think about form by defining it against what it is not. It is quite easy—and very tempting—to get "form" mixed up with "structure." Both form and structure give shape to things, and they are indeed similar and related in that respect. But the metaphoric associations we have with each word give us clues to their differences. Consider the idea of buckets, templates, and molds (form) in relation to foundations, scaffoldings, and frames (structure). Form feels more like a pattern; structure more like a supporting skeleton.

We based our understanding of structural interpretation on the proposition that the properties found in a text (relationships between characters, for example) had a certain correspondence to cultural patterns. Structure, as we used it, was primarily about the relationship between parts that make up a whole. Dualistic oppositions and triangular relations among characters proved central to our structural interpretation. Structure was about the hidden girders and beams that hold up the building. Form, on the other hand, is about the visible and shared "rules" that make a cultural text recognizable to both its audience and its creators as one thing and not another. A form can be thought of as a well-established set of conventions within which one can pursue an infinite number of variations.

Take, for example, the literary form of the sonnet, which has a particularly rigid set of conventions or rules. The sonnet makes the notion of form painfully clear. Sonnets have fourteen lines—not thirteen and not fifteen. Each line contains ten syllables—not nine and not eleven. The lines are written in iambic pentameter, which requires an unemphasized syllable followed by an emphasized one. A sonnet has a rhyme scheme, defined by the sound of the final word in each line: A-B, A-B, C-D, C-D, E-F, E-F, G-G. To take an example:

My mistress' eyes are nothing like the sun;
Coral is far more red than her lips' red;
If snow be white, why then her breasts are dun;
If hairs be wires, black wires grow on her head.
I have seen roses damask'd, red and white,
But no such roses see I in her cheeks;
And in some perfumes is there more delight
Than in the breath that from my mistress reeks.
I love to hear her speak, yet well I know
That music hath a far more pleasing sound;
I grant I never saw a goddess go;
My mistress, when she walks, treads on the ground:
And yet, by heaven, I think my love as rare
As any she belied with false compare.

William Shakespeare, Sonnet 130

If you deviate from this form, you will no longer have a sonnet. Within the "rules" of the form, however, you are free to create anything you want. Writers stay within the form; audiences measure the writer's skill by what is said in relation to the form itself. In this case, Shakespeare is parodying more conventional love sonnets, which described the women who were the objects of the writers' love through over-the-top comparisons with admired, sometimes worshipped, natural beauties (the sun, coral, snow, roses). Not only does he overcome the challenges presented by the form of the sonnet, he is able to use the form itself to mock what had developed as a penchant for hyperbole among his peers. For certain cultural texts—such as this one—the form matters a lot.

We thought, at this point, that we should write a sonnet about American Studies, just to remind you of how complex a container this form can be. And we tried. But, precisely because the form is so challenging, writing a good sonnet is really hard. Conversely, writing an embarrassingly bad sonnet is really easy. The good news (for us, and maybe for you) is that there's another form, equally classic, equally structured, and far friendlier and more familiar. It allows, and perhaps even encourages, less-than-perfect writing. We've decided to subject ourselves to its rules:

There's a field of American study
Whose method can seem a bit nutty
But just shift your gears
As an idea coheres
And all will be clear that was muddy

This is a limerick, as you may know. Limericks offer exactly the kind of formal container we've been talking about (five lines, AABBA rhyme pattern, etc.). And some of the content that sits inside that container even verges on becoming part of the form ("There once was a girl from Nantucket"; "There once was a man from Poughkeepsie"). The form of the sonnet is so rigorous and restrictive, we easily (and rightly) associate it with the high-culture world of literary poetry. The form of the limerick, in contrast, is restrictive but easy, and it occupies a very different social world—the folkloric world of bars and bathroom stalls and festive social occasions. It's a poetic form that would fit right in with the Vernacular mixtape. Limericks are often obscene (and indeed, many would say that true limericks *must* be ribald and bawdy); sonnets, not so much. It is worth noting that Shakespeare himself—master of the sonnet—included early forms of limericks in some of his plays.

An Example: The Blues

Let us take, as another example, one of the great *forms* in American cultural history—the blues. Its form is defined by its length (twelve measures) and the formal pattern of its lyrics (AAB). It has a regular, familiar, and conventional harmonic progression, usefully broken into three sections of four measures each. Lyrically, the first and second sections both repeat the A line; the third section offers the punchline (B). When you hear the first line of the lyrics ("I've had the blues so long it's hard for me to smile") repeated a second time over the new chord (A7) that begins the second section, you *know,* without being told, that you're listening to the blues. Likewise, when you hear the punchline (B: "Seems like every day I live . . .") over the distinctive V–IV (B7–A7) chord change that begins the third section, it's a moment when the form, the performer, and the listener all join together in a shared moment of culture. You *know* this sound! You can hear, in your mind, exactly what we're talking about. But if not, it's time to go and listen to the blues. Check out some standards: "Cross Road Blues," "Sweet Home Chicago," "The St. Louis Blues," "Texas Flood"—there are thousands out there. You could play a classic twelve-bar blues tune forever, holding the form constant, while subjecting everything else to infinite variation. This is a perfect meeting point between rules and creative exploration!

So how might you use *form* as an analytical tool? Remember, form is a category, and categories cry out for comparison. Consider the sonnet and limerick. How are they similar? How are they different? Those comparisons

EXAMPLE I.

A: I've had the blues so long, it's hard for me to smile

A: Yes I've had the blues so long, it's hard for me to smile

B: Seems like every day I live, is just one more lonely mile.

logically lead us to a second set of questions concerning *connection.* Is the sonnet an outgrowth of the limerick, or vice versa? How (and when) did the limerick become associated with vernacular culture? These questions ask you to consider other analytical frames: *change over time,* for example, or the possibilities of *cause and effect.* They may lead you to think of an *analogical relationship:* sonnet is to *x* as limerick is to *y.* Or you might situate each form in a rich cultural *context.*

If, for example, you were to compare two formal categories—major and minor key blues—you would find that the difference between major and minor matters a lot. Blues melodies in a major key get much of their power by borrowing notes—so-called "blues notes"—from a parallel minor key scale. A shift in the underlying harmonies from major to minor changes the very nature of a blues melody. It's a shift that is often associated with jazz—a musical form with strong interests in exploring harmonic tone and color. Having established the differences between the two forms, you might then trace the connections. Who has used the minor form? Did it evolve somehow out of major key blues? When and where? How and why? With what consequence?

If you browse YouTube, you'll find lots of blues that take all kinds of liberties with the form. At a certain point, you might find yourself asking just how far one can drift away from the form itself before you are no longer playing the blues, before a singer or a song is just *bluesy*. Consider two of the most familiar kinds of blues: "city blues" and "country blues." The acoustic guitar sound that characterizes the "country blues" of the 1920, 1930s, and 1940s (go listen to Robert Johnson) helps form a set of conventions quite distinct from those found in the piano-based "city blues" (go listen to Ma Rainey or Bessie Smith). You might observe that more women seem to sing "city blues" and more men "country blues," that the women were often backed up by bands, and that their sound drifted well into the range of jazz. Indeed, you might wonder about the number of jazz tunes that are blues-based, and about the men and women who created those songs. Or you might notice the ways that country blues elements drifted into early forms of country music through singers like Jimmie Rodgers, the "Singing Brakeman" of the late 1920s and early 1930s. Are these distinct *forms* of the blues, or are they distinct performance styles?

And it gets more complicated still. You might observe that there's a whole bunch of blues played on electric guitars, and that there is a recognizable cohort of "Chicago Blues" musicians (Howling Wolf, Muddy Waters, and Buddy Guy, for example). You might also wonder about the connections between blues artists and the blues-based guitar wizards of the British invasions of the 1960s and 1970s (such as Eric Clapton, Jimmy Page, and Jeff Beck). In each of these cases (and there are many more) musicians continued to return to the well—the classic *formal* blues—even as they took the blues sound and spirit in new directions. The term itself was used in albums outside the form, such as Miles Davis's *Kind of Blue* (1959) and Joni Mitchell's *Blue* (1971), suggesting that the blues could morph into a sort of trope.

Such transformations of form also present us with evocative objects of analysis. How did specific alterations of form—the agreed-upon containers into which we place content—reflect and create shared cultural meaning at specific moments? Let's go back to our list of blues: city blues, country blues, Chicago blues, British blues. In each case, alterations of the blues form tell us something about the contexts of particular cultural moments and about the ways those contexts have changed. We could explore how these variations in the form might help us think about social categories such as race or gender. We could use them to track historical changes such as migration ("What are the formal connections between Chicago blues and the Great Migration?"), access to technology ("Does the electric guitar change the form?"), or the globalization of distribution networks ("How do we make sense of the back and forth of blues forms across the Atlantic—and elsewhere?").

When we move from individual texts to categories such as tropes and forms, we open ourselves up to new and productive forms of complication and opportunity. In part, that is because the moment you place an individual text in a categorical bucket, it invariably decides that it would prefer to be elsewhere. Chicago blues calls out to us, for example, saying "Hey, I'm not really a form; I'm really a *style*!" Or, "You might think I'm from Chicago, but it's more complicated than that!"

Even as an analysis of form tells us a lot, then, it also has the potential to limit us by tying us tightly to a particular container, even as its contents—the blues, for example—want to slop all over the place. The overspill territory is huge—so huge that we might want also to think of blues music in ways that are not quite so restricted by the rule-based category of the form. Fortunately, we've got a word for that.

GENRE

The tool that allows us to account for fluidity in relation to form is *genre*. Like form, genre is a categorization—applied to art, literature, music, and film—based on the world of form, plot, style, structure, signs, and audience, among other things. When certain familiar elements are commonly repeated, we can begin to see them as *generic conventions*—the agreed-upon elements that let us understand a text as part of a genre. Music that is not, *formally* speaking, the blues, but which is nonetheless "bluesy," might usefully be described as part of a genre. Such music might use classic blues notes—those minor key notes inserted into major key melodies—as generic markers of the blues in a song that does not have the *form* of the blues at all. It might adopt the turnaround harmonic structure of the classic blues form, or perhaps the repetitive A-A-B form of blues lyrics—but still not engage enough of the form to be blues. Yet these things are not exactly *style* either. Rather than merely reflecting "the way things are done," they are sortable into distinct elements or conventions. This is the raw material of genre.

Let's illustrate this concept with an example from film. The "western" has been dying a slow death for several decades. Sure, there are the occasional westerns here and there. But the experience you may have had with westerns is unlikely to match that of earlier generations, who were besieged by them. Nonetheless, you probably know many of the genre's conventions. Take a moment and make up a list.

We're betting it looks something like this: Good guys wear white hats and bad guys wear black ones. Indians lurk up in the hills and there is always ominous music when the camera cuts to them, because they're usually preparing to massacre the wagon train. There's a bold fearless heroine and a rugged handsome man. They don't seem to get along at first, but are destined to fall in love. The stage and the mail have to get through and the black hats are planning to stop it. There's a herd of cattle in there somewhere, and a lawman who stands up against the corrupt railroad baron, or who steps outside the law in order to ensure justice is done. The hero has a sidekick, who is either an Indian or a crusty old geezer. Lots of things seem to be happening in Monument Valley in Utah, or in desolate little towns in Wyoming; no one knows quite why these forsaken little places seem to matter so much. Of course, there's a gunslinger, who heartlessly kills innocent men and pays close attention to his guns, holsters, and surprisingly delicate hands. He probably wears a duster. People fight in bars and destroy pretty much all the furniture. Saloon girls watch from the stairs. And so on.

These gestures have seeped, like so much culture, into our collective unconscious, and this is exactly how genre creates meaning. Their meanings come not (only) from the existence of individual texts to be read, but from the way those texts function as representative examples of *generic* meanings, drummed into viewers through repetition. The generic elements of the western film bear all kinds of cultural meanings, obvious (and therefore often invisible) to us because it has been such a long-running genre. There are lessons about American history as a struggle to civilize the West, lessons about the virtues of farm and ranch economies and individual independence, lessons about the power of technologies, and lessons about doomed Indians, of course. Some of these take shape as tropes. But many of these meanings don't require figurative language, since they are right at the surface. The western itself, as a genre, carries the meanings.

Perhaps the most important message to come out of the western—one that has passed seamlessly into the conventions of countless other genres—is this: if you're one of the "good guys" and have been wronged or threatened, it's okay to use violence. You're not a violent person, of course, but hey, you were forced to do it, right? We could make up a lengthy list of classic films that advance this argument—*Shane* (1953), *The Man Who Shot Liberty Valence* (1962), *The Virginian* (1962), and so on. It would be like a mixtape of films, full of "good" men who have been wronged and threatened, and who are forced to wield violence to save their family or their town or civilization itself, or to somehow rebalance the scales of justice through a justified revenge. We can call this what it is—one of the cultural seedbeds of toxic masculinity—but it's no accident that so many observers around the world choose to view the United States through the lens of the western film genre, a popular American cultural export and a *tropic* form of American self-presentation.

As we saw with the blues, one can create powerful analytical possibilities by placing forms in relation to other forms, looking for comparisons and connections. The same holds true here. Think about the western, and the ways it sits in relation to other genres: sci-fi, romantic comedy, police procedural, and more. Because *genre* is a more expansive category than *form,* texts and conventions can easily fit into multiple genres, generating a kind of traffic in cultural meaning. Consider, for example, the musical *Oklahoma!* (1943), performed on Broadway, in community theaters, and in high schools across the country. *Oklahoma!* helped to create the genre category *musical,* which integrated songs directly into the plot and allowed actors to move seamlessly from speaking parts to singing parts. But it is also part of the genre of the *romance,* with all the appropriate conventions: lovers pretending not to like one another, rivals who come between them, circles of sympathetic friends and confidantes, parental figures who either aid or prevent the romance, eventual happy-ever-afters. And you might argue that it also fits within the genre of the *western.* In *Oklahoma!,* you'll find cowboys and farmers in conflict, good and bad guys in the appropriate hats, a brawl, a murderous bad guy, and aspirations to "grow up with the country" and evolve from territory to state.

We can take the argument one step further: individual texts are not the only things that operate across multiple genres. Critical elements from one genre can cross into the boundaries of another, offering us an opportunity to compare genres as objects of analysis and trace the connected webs of meaning. An excellent example of this kind of crossing is the original cowboy western. In their earliest incarnations, cowboy westerns took shape as nineteenth-century "dime novels." They drew on centuries of familiar narratives of conflict and resolution, but also upon frontier folktales, the urban detective story, and the tales of soldiers and scouts being surrounded by Indians.

These dime novels set the stage for live Wild West shows, which in turn shaped expectations for the western film genre. There's a complex traffic in meaning here, flowing across both time and space. And it will likely come as little surprise to discover that, as western movies faded in popularity in the 1960s, many of their generic conventions moved straight into other kinds of genres.

Consider the actor Clint Eastwood, who had established himself as the archetypal "man with no name"—an amoral gunslinger character who epitomized the so-called "spaghetti westerns" of the 1960s, including *A Fistful of Dollars* (1964), *For a Few Dollars More* (1965), and *The Good, the Bad, and the Ugly* (1966). In 1971, Eastwood took genre conventions that had been developed in the western and moved them straight into the character of Dirty Harry Callahan, a contemporary San Francisco street detective. The original *Dirty Harry* (1971)—a good lawman who stepped violently outside the law in the name of justice—spawned four sequels and carried Eastwood's career throughout the 1970s. Two decades later, an aging Eastwood returned to the western with *Unforgiven* (1992), a film that grapples with the ugly and oversimplified violence of his earlier work, not to mention the genre as a whole.

Understanding the overlaps between the western and the urban crime drama can help us formulate questions concerning shifts in the cultural conversations and the social worlds of the 1960s and 1970s, which in turn can help us think about how genre makes cultural meaning. That particular social / political / economic moment was often figured around the powerful fear of an "urban crisis." Unsurprisingly, then, viewers flocked to movies in which poor black people replaced Indians, lone-wolf psychos replaced black-hatted gunslingers, corrupt city officials replaced corrupt railroad barons, and the dangerous wilderness of the western was supplanted by the wild dangers of the urban grid. These conventions no more reflected the complicated origins of the urban crisis—a story involving things like restrictive covenants, redlining, police violence, white flight, and more—than the western reflected settler colonialism. But they remained recognizable as generic siblings nonetheless.

To this day, the fading western has not stopped looking around for new genres to colonize (figures 29–32). The multigenerational franchise spawned by the original *Star Wars* (1977) has amalgamated conventions from science fiction, fantasy, romance—and the western. The black-hatted villain of the old westerns turned into the black-cloaked Darth Vader, and heroes Luke Skywalker and Princess Leia were outfitted in white robes. The character

FIGURE 29. *Star Wars* (1977).

FIGURE 30. *Brokeback Mountain* (2005).

FIGURE 31. *Pale Rider* (1985).

FIGURE 32. *Rango* (2011).

Han Solo wore a cool black vest like the sheriffs of old. He was quick with his guns, and he had a cranky Wookie sidekick who was something like a wild Indian, unable to speak very well, but good in a fight. A saloon scene was full of familiar conventions lifted straight from the western (down to the western dance hall music), and there was a crusty but wise old cowboy figure, Obi-wan Kenobi, as a sidekick and mentor for the hero.

Even as the western genre faded through the 1970s, 1980s, and 1990s, film-makers continued reworking the genre conventions of the old cowboy films, shifting them into new contexts, reversing them, challenging them, refiguring them, and borrowing their capacity to evoke—through generic elements—a rich array of shared cultural meaning. In each case, these films invite interpretations that put genre shifts into dialogue with new social and historical contexts. In the 1970s, for example, the western cross-pollinated with the blaxploitation film (*Buck and the Preacher*, 1971) to make arguments about black power and agency. It was inverted (*Unforgiven*, 1992), racialized (*Posse*, 1975), gender-transformed (*The Quick and the Dead*, 1995; *Bad Girls*, 1994), and satirized (*Blazing Saddles*, 1974). Later it was placed in the context of gang violence (*Tombstone*, 1993), gay sexuality (*Brokeback Mountain*, 2005), kung-fu comedy (*Shanghai Noon*, 2000), feminism (*Thelma & Louise*, 1991), environmental crisis (*Rango*, 2011), urban manliness (*City Slickers*, 1991), financial exploitation (*Hell or High Water*, 2016), and transnational imperialism (*The Last Samurai*, 2003). It was reread in terms of slavery (*Django Unchained*, 2012), crossed with the genre of apocalyptic space invasion (*Cowboys and Aliens*, 2011), and reshaped around cross-cultural Iranian vampirism (*A Girl Walks Home Alone at Night*, 2014). And this is only the tip of the iceberg. We haven't even touched how these genre-crossings played out on television, in examples such as the short-lived sci-fi western, *Firefly* (2002–03), which has maintained a cult following online ever since its cancellation.

Analysis of the fluidity and portability of generic conventions allows the interpreter to locate cultural meanings in particular times and places. You couldn't have made *Brokeback Mountain*, which deals with gay cowboys, in 1955, but social and cultural transformations made it a powerful and evocative text in 2005. Likewise *A Girl Walks Home Alone at Night*—a mashup of vampires, horror, and the western—surely seems an artifact of a moment characterized by both the global transit of (multi)cultural meaning and the popularity of recombinant texts such as *Pride and Prejudice and Zombies,* a novel published in 2009 that was adapted into film in 2016.

All of the categories we have surveyed—trope, form, and genre—allow us to find meaning by bundling texts together. Each has a key phrase that might help explain their distinct (but overlapping) mechanics:

Trope: repetition of figure

Form: pattern of rules

Genre: conventional elements open to recombination

These categories are evident in the expressions and organizations of a culture (they made sense to the people who created them) *and* are useful as analytical categories for you. They are useful because those categories—and the conventions that define them—are themselves amenable to close and distant readings and to thick descriptions. Name the *categories* (not simply individual texts) as objects of analysis, and you will find yourself using these kinds of *bundling tools* to manage multiple texts across time, space, and cultural production. Those tools also reveal the analytical power that comes with the curation of a project archive. That archive establishes the grounds on which we move our work from single-text interpretation through the category-analysis of generic meanings to richer layers of contextualization. Let's consider one more example, aimed at revealing the very close relation between interpretation, curation, and analysis, and pointing us toward our next gear shift, into *contextualization.*

Dime Novels

We mentioned that the genre of "the western" had its origins in the dime novels of the nineteenth century. Dime novel analysis is almost its own scholarly genre, and may, in fact, be the most frequently invoked example of American Studies practice in the entire history of the field. Here's a capsule version: Dime novels were cheap books (thus the "dime") aimed at a mass audience, primarily workers, who often passed the books among themselves, thereby increasing circulation even further. They offer us an excellent example of generic elements that become visible through curation and analysis. Let's take, for example, the figure of Buffalo Bill Cody, a frontier scout and dime novel hero (and an actual historical figure) who would later go on to produce Buffalo Bill's Wild West, one of the first great mass cultural spectacles in the United States. Not only did the Wild West show become an influential cultural export—touring Britain, France, and Germany—but the dime novels themselves had a broad global readership that shaped perceptions of American culture for years to come.

So let's consider how we might go about making sense of all this. An American Studies scholar interprets multiple texts (in this case, dime novels), identifying a set of generic elements that the texts hold in common. Out of those elements, we identify tropes and forms—as well as characters, structures, styles, and other figures—that repeat across all or most of the texts in our archive. What are some of the generic elements that emerge from a survey of Buffalo Bill novels? For one, Buffalo Bill is preternaturally talented in the skills of the outdoors. He does not hesitate to use violence against Indians and against "wild" men—the criminals that populate the border. He both dominates nature and is at one with it. He frequently encounters less-experienced people—women and settlers—whom he invariably saves. Often, rich or royal people are trapped in the roles and identities of poor people, orphans, or adoptees; their intrinsic natures will eventually reveal them to be of a "higher type." The plots in these novels are simple. Good and evil forces are clearly portrayed. The thrill comes from action (figure 33).

But as is always the case with analysis, we also want to complicate and interrogate our own archive. You might, for example, build a comparative archive around dime novels featuring female characters. The heroine Leonie Locke and the "working girl" dime novel, for example, would open up new analytical questions concerning gender and class. Or you might build an archive that is less centered on written texts. It might include the open-air performances of Buffalo Bill's Wild West show—the massive popular entertainment that opened in 1884 and ran for three decades. On this track, you might consider the many posters that advertised the show, both in the United States and abroad (figure 34). But you might also consider other visual representations of Buffalo Bill Cody, ranging from paintings (such as Rosa Bonheur's 1889 portrait of him on his horse) to film (such as Robert Altman's satire, *Buffalo Bill and the Indians, or Sitting Bull's History Lesson*, 1976). You might even consider the musical analogue to the dime novel—popular songs such as "Ragtime Cowboy Joe" (1912). As we've discussed, our goal in assembling such archives is to track shared cultural meanings—we can think of them as *discourses* or *ideologies,* which we will explore in the next chapter—and grapple with their complexities.

This is a good moment to return to historiography and see what others have written about dime novels. Remember the "anchor book" in the American Spaces mixtape? It was Henry Nash Smith's *Virgin Land: The American West as Symbol and Myth* (1950), a foundational text in the field of American Studies. Smith extracted generic elements from a literary-folk-

FIGURE 33. *Buffalo Bill's Cold Trail* (1905). Image courtesy of University of Missouri Special Collections.

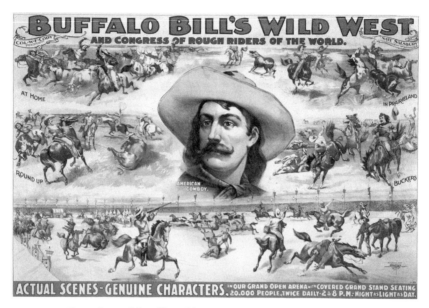

FIGURE 34. Poster for Buffalo Bill's Wild West show, ca. 1910. Image courtesy of McCracken Research Library, Buffalo Bill Center of the West.

popular archive that used dime novels and western scouts (among other figures) to reveal an ideological formation: an agrarian myth of agricultural settlement in the West. Another critical book to consider is Michael Denning's *Mechanic Accents: Dime Novels and Working-Class Culture in America* (1987). Denning's archive focused attention not on western scouts and pioneers, as Smith did, but rather on urban settings and the workers, or "mechanics," who lived there. Denning's genres included the detective story, the working girl story, the "mysteries of the city," the tramp, and the criminal, and from these he identified other kinds of genres, tropes, and forms.

But Denning—deeply influenced by Marxist class analysis—was equally committed to understanding the workers who *read* dime novels and the workers who *wrote* them. He created and brought other archives to bear, ones that demanded attention to the actual, historical lives of workers and the material conditions under which dime novels were produced. Denning paid attention to the ways that dime novels functioned as a part of working-class cultures. Through attention to both readers and writers, Denning identified how dime novels channeled the vernaculars (the "accents") of the nineteenth-century American working class. In 1999, Nan Enstad's *Ladies of Labor,*

Girls of Adventure: Working Women, Popular Culture, and Labor Politics at the Turn of the Twentieth Century drew from the same well, assembling archives and analyzing tropes and genre conventions in order to answer questions concerning working-class women, consumer culture, and labor politics. And there have been many others.

Let's summarize: *tropes, forms,* and *genres* all share the same basic function. They bundle together individual units into categories that reflect shared cultural meanings, the way these meanings are created, and the way they change over time. Tropes and forms are usefully considered as preexisting categories—that is, you, the American Studies practitioner, do not create them so much as identify them as bundles of shared cultural meaning. But whether looking at texts individually or in bundles, we are still operating in the realm of representation, even though much of the analytical work in American Studies is also concerned with the material dimensions of social and economic justice. Accordingly, we will now turn our attention to some strategies for contextualization that allow us to *expand* our work with texts into other historical and sociological domains.

INSTITUTIONS AND FORMATIONS

Why were the plots of dime novels so similar? In part, because they drew upon, and then amplified, tropic meanings and generic conventions. Writers wrote stories that were familiar to them, and that they knew would be familiar to their audiences. But there are other explanations, too. It turns out that the *context* in which those writers produced their dime novels matters a lot. Denning, for one, emphasizes that these writers were not freelancers—they were (mostly) employed by publishers, worked in "fiction factories," and paid in relation to the books they completed. Like the mechanics who read their words, the writers operated on an industrial "speed up" model in which they churned out a book every four or five days. Working at that pace, it made good sense for writers to recycle plots, characters, tropes, and devices. They drew upon, created, and reaffirmed generic conventions—and they did so precisely *because* of the institutional conditions under which they labored.

That fact points us to another change in gears. We've worked through the methods of interpretation, curation, and analysis, and can now shift more fully into *contextualization.*

Method	Object	Action
Interpretation	*Text*	*Perceive*
Curation	Archive	Collect
Analysis	Genre	Categorize
Contextualization	Formation	Expand
Generalization	Power	Connect

Along the way, our objects have changed as well. We've moved from text to archive to genre, and will now turn to what we are calling the *formation,* a key aspect of which is the *institution.* We'll linger on both terms for a moment. Having worked our way through *perception, collection,* and *categorization,* we'll now try to *expand* from texts (and bundles of texts) into the institutions and networks that shape cultural production and move it across political, social, and global boundaries.

Institutions

Let's begin with *institution,* which is one of those words that capture a range of linked meanings. We might talk of a new policy that is being "instituted." Or we might think of the institution of marriage; that is, a social practice, authorized by both custom and law, which has "rules," and is governed by both formal and informal structures. But most often we are referring to social, political, and economic institutions—the state, the corporation, the bank, the church, the university. One of the most important ways to make sense of cultural archives is to contextualize them in light of different kinds of institutions. An institutional focus shifts our analytical path from a kind of vertical axis to a horizontal one, as we "follow the money" through the processes of production, distribution, and consumption.

Text
Archive
Genre
Creation—*Production*—Formation—*Distribution*—*Consumption*
Power

Tracking institutions and cultural formations allows American Studies writers to make critical connections between their archives and larger social questions of domination, subordination, resistance, co-optation, emergence, residuality—in other words, to questions of *power*.

Let's continue the earlier example for just a moment longer. Imagine that we've done interpretive work on five dime novels, located generic themes, and confirmed them through a survey of additional texts. We might now ask: what were the institutional structures that produced dime novels with such generic commonality? Who organized the capital to buy presses and hire writers? Where and how were dime novels sold? Was it an industry in the same sense as, say, the railroad? How wide was the dime novel publishing world? Were publishers concentrated in a particular city? Did they have an overarching trade organization? Did they sell primarily to rural or urban readers? How many times were these books read? Did they pass from hand to hand, like some newspapers? How much money did a dime novel generate? Who captured that value? These are contextual questions that begin to point us to the structures, interrelationships, economics, and transformations of institutions.

For purposes of illustration, what follows is a brief summary of some of the conventional answers to these questions. Prominent publisher Erastus Beadle and other dime novel publishers served as journeymen in the printing trade just as technological innovations in the 1830s and 1840s were displacing older craft practices and putting many pressmen and newspapers out of business. Beadle and his cohort survived by bringing their entrepreneurial skills to bear on an uncertain industry, buying up failing newspapers, turning them into story papers, and ultimately producing cheap novels that they sold for a nickel or dime. A few found lasting success, but most dime novel publishers experienced the dizzying business cycle fluctuations of boom and bust. The financial panics that periodically produced economic depressions offered opportunities for business success owing to low costs for materials and for labor. Beadle's trade in dime novels took off after the Panic of 1857, and another boom period for dime novels occurred just after the Panic of 1873. Many of these publishers came out of the very class of small artisanal producers whose republican vision faced threats from the tremendous economic forces of mid-nineteenth-century industrial capitalism.

We are less sure about the origins and situations of the *authors* of dime novels. Most seem to have written for the genre for a short period of time; only those like Edward Wheeler and Laura Libbey, whose star characters commanded repeated exposure, enjoyed a whole career as dime novelists. Fewer still made a lot of money at it. In fact, authors hardly mattered in this industry; instead, their characters, like Deadwood Dick or Leonie Locke, were the stars. They were commodities that could be produced by almost anyone with a half-decent hand and that, most importantly, could be copyrighted and protected in court by a publishing house. In other words, dime novel authors were a dime a dozen, utterly replaceable cogs in a literary machine.

Indeed, writing dime novels reproduced something of the working conditions found in industrial production: an emphasis on uniformity, quantity, speed, and cost control. Beadle author Albert Aiken, for example, used to "grind out dime novels day after day with the steadiness of a machine" in "a little den on an upper floor."[1] Likewise, the audience for dime novels came largely, though not exclusively, from the working classes—factory hands, livery stable employees, domestic servants, and sweatshop workers residing in the cities and mill towns of northern and western America. By far the bulk of them were young. You might have found them reading dime novel stories at home, on the job, and on the trains and trolleys that carried them to work. Irish and German immigrants comprised a significant part of the dime novel reading public. The industry benefited from the high literacy rates extant among the working classes in the United States, and especially from the ability to distribute its wares far and wide by means of the American News Company, whose monopoly on distribution after the Civil War turned the dime novel from a localized to a national phenomenon. Hundreds of thousands of volumes were sold.

This kind of contextualizing work focuses attention on producers, audiences, distribution, industrial structures, and economic histories. It takes us a long way toward producing a history of popular culture in the second half of the nineteenth century. In America's shift from a society of small producers to one in which, by today's parlance, the "1%" dominated a class of dependent wage-earners, the country experienced not only economic and social conflicts but a cultural struggle as well.

What did that struggle look like? Despite the fact that readers from the middle classes—clerks, shopkeepers, and others—formed part of the reading public for dime novels, bourgeois reformers strove to do away with the books. They regarded them as an evil to be eliminated or controlled and replaced by more genteel, uplifting reading. Public libraries, and their corporate sponsors such as Andrew Carnegie; moral reformers like Anthony Comstock, who established the Society for the Suppression of Vice; and cultural elites at places like the *Atlantic Monthly,* who fancied themselves the true discerners of culture in the tradition of Matthew Arnold—all these sought to replace the sensational fiction of the dime novel with more serious, didactic, high-brow literature. But just as workers resisted industrial capitalism through strikes and other activity, so too did they strive to develop and sustain their own cultures in the face of middle-class attempts to reform them. Although this struggle has been interpreted as resistance to change, the dime novels were thoroughly *modern* cultural products—a fact that was not lost on readers. Charles Postel's *The Populist Vision* (2007) argues that working-class politics and reading practices were deeply intertwined. Attention to context, or *contextualization,* can help us see that resistance to the economic injustices of industrial capitalism was not the same thing as resistance to modernity.

To put it another way: working-class culture has never been monolithic. Rather, it has been marked by divisions between rough and respectable; immigrant and native; male and female; saloons and temperance meetings; cooperative associations and an ethos of individual self-improvement; and many more. All these examples reveal a multifaceted working-class culture that emerged in opposition to the politics and norms put forth by "middle-class culture." Rejecting the stereotypes of an immoral, violent, and savage proletariat espoused by bourgeois reformers, literary archetypes like the "honest mechanic" and "virtuous working-girl" helped draw distinctions between, on the one hand, the industrious, hard-working laborer—perhaps down-on-his-luck but far from lazy—and, on the other, the parasitic, greedy capitalist living off the sweat and blood of his employees.

This contextual narrative of the history of dime novels raises a series of themes that we might pursue, through further exploration of *institutions,* to address larger questions. Here's our list:

- The role of technology—its invention, dissemination, and consequences for any number of industries, and for the nature of work itself.
- The historical development of institutions such as the newspaper and the publishing house during the nineteenth century.
- The transition from artisanal to industrial wage labor; or, from widespread ownership of the institutions of production to their concentration in the hands of a small ownership elite.
- The place of authors within these transitions, as independent producers and as wage workers.

- The courts and legal institutions that protected property rights, not simply in land, but in intellectual goods such as copyright.

- The rise of industrial standardization, regulation, and mass production that emphasized commodities and created a kind of alienating "distance" between the points of purchase and the making of saleable goods.

- The structural failures of nineteenth-century capitalism that produced a series of panics and depressions.

- The schools and educational organizations that drove literacy rates among workers.

- The laws and regulations that enabled and supported particular forms of immigration, as well as the social self-organization of immigrants around nationality, jobs, and class.

- The rise of monopolies, particularly in commodity distribution, which forced a transition from local and regional business to the national model in which dime novels were embedded.

- Institutions that defined and enabled middle-class reformers: the library, literary magazine, and reform organization.

- Institutions that consolidated working-class culture: improvement organizations, labor unions, saloon, and immigrant organizations.

One might delve more deeply into each of these themes. In every case, what will become apparent is a new analytical register, one in which the wider world of *context*—historical, economic, social, and legal—opens up new questions. Those questions point us to social theory: how is power configured among humans in specific situations, and how do those configurations help clarify power relations in other times and places? In other words, we pin down institutional specifics in order to take our arguments to the point of generalization.

But what about the flows of production—*circuits, social networks,* and *communities*—that can't be pinned down in specific institutions? These might exist in relation to institutional structures (from barbershops to Facebook) but they do so in ways that exceed those structures, creating new connective threads of mobility and meaning built and used by people. Particularly in the digital world, where the spatial dimension of cultural production and consumption is increasingly elusive, it is clear that we need another analytical location for generalization besides institution. We propose *formation*.

Formations

Formation is a word that simultaneously evokes the verb-y process of *becoming* (the formation of a new online community, for example) and a noun-based sense of underlying *structure* (notice that the word "form" is nested within it). Like institution, *formation* captures both the creation of new configurations and the recognition of existing orders or patterns. It is at once stable and fluid, an apt description of not only culture itself but also the mechanics of its production, consumption, transmission, and retransmission, which can proliferate *into* and *out of* any cultural text.

When we move from seeing Buffalo Bill as a western scout in dime novels to considering the Wild West show—including its elaborate publicity apparatus of images, texts, and testimonies; its engagements with other cultural structures; its emergence as a subject of early film; and its frequent recurrence as a cultural icon over the following century—we see institutions combining and interacting to create a *formation,* a tangled complex of networks and circuits.

Take, for example, the song "Formation" (2016), by Beyoncé Knowles-Carter. "Formation" is itself a formation; that is, a networked thing that offered an open set of possibilities, a loose structure for the large-scale shaping of unanticipated meanings. Start with the song, which offers a hyper-loaded text, weaving together musical samples, references to specific song texts, personal history, public relationships, genealogy, and identity. Now add the video. An even richer pool of images multiplies the song's references: New Orleans and Hurricane Katrina, Southern black women's culture and history, vodoun, black queer performance, Black Lives Matter and police violence, Mardi Gras, and dance line formations. Now add the rich accompanying cultural infrastructure: full video album, Super Bowl performance, world tour, website, and hashtags. Finally, add the proliferation of online commentary, interpretation, and debate that sent the meanings and contexts of "Formation" far beyond the bounds of institution.

To be sure, there are institutional structures to be considered. No celebrity of Beyoncé's stature can avoid the mediating influence of institutions, even if they try. A musician who creates his or her own label still ends up working with corporations such as web hosting services that circumscribe the possibilities of experimentation in ways that don't generate a lot of attention. The *Lemonade* album that includes "Formation" proved the anchor for Tidal, the music streaming service owned by Jay-Z, who also happens to be Beyoncé's husband. Money flowed through "Formation," and an institutional tracing of that cash would offer valuable insights into questions surrounding gender, race, class, and power in a world still focused on production, distribution, and consumption.

But the nature of that consumption proved far more complicated than the "purchase, read, and pass along" quality of the dime novel. Listening to the album, many consumers saw "Formation" as part of a personal statement focused on Jay-Z's supposed infidelity. Early viewers of the video confessed that, even if they liked it, they didn't really understand it. Viewers of the Super Bowl performance—on February 7, 2016—thought differently: most understood it as a cultural-political intervention in the discourse on police violence against African American people, and it immediately set off a fierce online debate. Soon after the performance, Alicia Garza—one of the early leaders of the #BlackLivesMatter movement (itself a formation rather than institution)—published an article in *Rolling Stone* on whether the song might be considered a Black Lives Matter "anthem." She closed the piece with the words, "Welcome to the movement."[2] The touring "Formation" show invites yet another reading: it was visually stunning and self-consciously theatrical. One viewer described it as "more like a Vegas show than a concert," noting that its politics were "gestures rather than statements."

The Beyoncé Facebook page—and we might choose any number of other sites or platforms—featured millions of "likes" (as of this writing) and innumerable comments, so many that you cannot really get your interpretive or analytical head around the totality. Indeed, to make sense of this formation, the reader almost immediately begins to create categories: "loved the show," "don't let the haters get you down," "this is what this line means," "#BlackLivesMatter," "other statements of political support or debate," and so on. Each category is populated by a huge archive, and the challenge of curatorial excess might overwhelm the whole process.

For starters, what kind of text is "Formation" anyway? Is it political, personal, performative, commodified, Southern, Vegas, something else, all of the above, or beyond capture? It was created in a network context of authorial multiplicity, sampling, quotation, citation, and collaborative writing. Its distribution overflowed all existing channels in the worlds of music, video, performance, and online. And its reception was marked by a proliferation of commentary. From the perspective of interpretation, how do we even know where to start?

Politically focused observers pointed out that the release date—nested between the birthdays of Trayvon Martin and Sandra Bland, both victims of anti-black violence—suggested Beyoncé's intent to situate the song in the context of critical black response to the structures and histories of white racism. For others, Beyoncé was reclaiming regional identities and practices, through lyrics (referencing Alabama, Louisiana, and Texas), sartorial choices, and more. This interpretation was further supported when Beyoncé performed her feminist anthem, "Daddy Lessons," with the Dixie Chicks in Nashville at the Country Music Association Awards—an organization that the Dixie Chicks had avoided for years due to the fallout over their criticism of the impending invasion of Iraq in 2003. Still other critics embarked on a line-by-line exegesis, explaining the complex networks of meaning and citation embedded in each reference. (We can't do so ourselves, since we could not obtain permission from Beyoncé's legal team to quote lines from the lyrics—one of the hazards of writing about texts that are still in the process of making a lot of money.)

The video was immediately met with institutional critiques: filmmaker Chris Black suggested that the video had used images from one of his films without attribution or compensation. The medium for his accusation was Twitter, creating an immediate explosion of claim, counterclaim, and conversation. While technically drawing on organized structures of copyright law, the February 6, 2016 tweet (which used one of Beyoncé's nicknames, "Melina") was also about power: "Why Melina gotta use clips from our doc?!? Was the budget not big enough to spend a week in New Orleans and actually build with the people." Beyoncé's team tried to shut down the conversation quickly, and posted a statement insisting that the legal, institutional matters had indeed been taken care of. And they were right—a complex series of ownership transitions had apparently ended with a licensing payment being made to Microsoft. The Twitter conversation ended, more or less, but it continued to have an afterlife in tweets and retweets, screenshots, and meta-discussion of the controversy itself—which now became its *own* object of proliferating circuits of text and tweet.

One reason why "Formation" can mean so many things to so many different people is that it has no single argument; rather, it offers a series of conversational entry points. Its meaning is not generated by a narrative but rather a series of overarching gestures to larger issues. We might then gather up an archive—of Beyoncé songs, for example, or of similar big name, multi-platform "event" releases. Out of those, we might identify generic qualities: citation and sampling, the mingling of personal and political, multi-platform media strategies, and deeply engaged communities of critical commentators.

"Formation" bears the traces of the institutions with which it intersected—but institutional analysis does not fully capture the sheer polyvalence of its production, distribution, and reception. "Formation," in other words, is best understood as a formation.

A FINAL NOTE

We began by drawing a distinction—useful in laying out the issues, but hardly ironclad—between *interpretation* (the reading of textual evidence) and *analysis* (the reading of textual categories and connections). Our *analytical* toolkit has sought to make sense of the complicated experience that lies at the crossroads of *trope, form,* and *genre.* As we assemble collections of texts, we create analytical archives that serve the needs of our projects. We then move to *contextualize* and deepen our analysis by looking to *institutions* and *formations*—the social, political, economic, and legal structures that shape how texts are created, distributed, consumed, sampled, and critiqued. As we follow the money and the movement of thought and people, we can start to see the workings of power: those who have it; those who don't; those who struggle to acquire, hold, or resist it; and those who are shaped by it into individuals living within culture.

To get to this question of power, we'll now turn to the methodological strategy of *generalization,* seeking to connect our work to broader arguments made by others. In doing so, we'll practice working with *theory,* or abstract ideas that seek to produce useful general suppositions about power and the world of culture. We'll focus on four particular bodies of theory: theories about *the subject,* which focus on the positioning of the individual in relation to social power; theories of *identity,* which address how social categories and performances complicate that positioning; theories of the *state,* which aim to explain how political institutions utilize culture and ideology; and finally, theories of *the market,* which locate economic inequality as a primary determinant of the production of cultural texts and, as we've glimpsed already, the culture industry.

EIGHT

Power

A THEORETICAL TOOLKIT

LET'S TAKE STOCK FOR A MOMENT. We have built ourselves a toolkit, and we've loaded up the compartments. In one are strategies for the interpretation of texts; in another, strategies for creating archives; and in another, ways of understanding the categories and contexts through which texts spread across networks. In treating the registers analytically—as text, archive, genre, and formation—we have gone a long way toward understanding the interdisciplinary practices of American Studies. In thinking about these registers as disciplines, however, we used a different metaphor: not the toolkit, but the car and, in particular, the shifting of gears on a manual transmission. We have now worked through the first four gears, arriving at that moment when we shift into fifth. We've been literary critics, curators, and contextualizers; now is our chance to become *social theorists*.

Theory, we must emphasize, is *not* the end of a linear process of analysis, the highest "level" of intellectual work. When driving a car, remember, each gear is indexed to a specific situation: hills require different gears than highways, starting requires a different gear than cruising. So too with the American Studies toolkit. The skilled interpreter of texts is always informed by theories and contexts, and is constantly moving between these different registers of analysis.

In American Studies, "theory" has a certain cachet (it's considered by many to be a high-status activity), but it can also instill terror. The abstract language of "theory" is difficult to understand. Theories often speak to other theories, and it can get pretty dense, pretty quickly. Indeed, there are people who work *only* in the realm of theory, exchanging abstract ideas with other theoreticians through highly technical vocabularies. Insiders seem to swim in theory like water; outsiders drown, and feel humiliated about it. And there's more: our writing is always open to the criticism that we have failed to use this particular theorist or failed to understand that one—and many critics focus on exactly such "failures" when they read a paper or a thesis or a book. Likewise, many American Studies writers seek to produce their *own* highly significant theories, a noble aspiration not always realized.

We don't believe in theory for theory's sake. But we do believe that good American Studies writing should work inductively and reflexively to engage the widest possible audience of readers and thinkers. In this book, we've emphasized a relatively simple process: theory, for us, has been an act of *generalization,* the extraction of a broad claim from a specific case. This process helps establish principles—call them "rules"—that can be used to make sense of other cases in other times and places. To do *that,* our proposed "rules" have to rest at a relatively high level of abstraction, lest they fail to carry relevance beyond the particular cases used to develop them. With all that in mind, here is our definition:

Theory: A set or system of general principles that can be used to explain a number of specific cases, but which occupies an abstract location distinct from any individual case to be explained.

Let's illustrate this with an example: back in chapter 6, when we were piecing together our archival toolkit, we mentioned something called *structuralism,* and we attached it to a trio of specific scholars—Ferdinand de Saussure, Charles Peirce, and Claude Levi-Strauss—who had proposed the key theories of structuralism. Structuralist theory offers a series of abstract generalizations; "rules," if you will. Here are a few: humans are hardwired to see the world through language; the brain is structured to produce language; languages establish meaning through relations among their constituent parts; oppositions and dualisms are critical structures of the human mind and human experience. There are many more such "rules," but these should suffice as illustrations.

Notice how this set of general claims is in fact *abstract;* that is, nothing in these statements speaks to a specific language, society, or culture. Rather, they operate at a very high level of generalization. Theories of structuralism were derived from detailed investigations into specific languages and experiences; those investigations were assembled into an archive of cases; from those cases, structuralist thinkers such as Saussure and Peirce proposed general *theoretical* principles. Levi-Strauss advanced those principles, moving them from the domain of language to that of narrative, kinship, and culture. The theories became *portable:* they could be picked up and applied to different cases. They also had a life span. Structuralism had a rise, a moment of intense influence, and a slow move toward quasi-obsolescence.

Over the last forty years, theory has had an increasingly powerful resonance in American Studies. Why? We think it stems from the continual efforts to define the field, and the ways that culture emerged as a central concern across the humanities. That concern dovetailed with what was called, in the 1980s and 1990s, "the linguistic turn," an engagement with high-level critical theory that shifted many disciplines toward cultural studies approaches. You'll no doubt recall our efforts, in the Introduction to this book, to situate American Studies around four linked concepts—social, interdisciplinary, America, and culture. All of them matter. But *culture*, we suggested, offered the most useful grounding for the field—making it ripe for an engagement with theory. Here's how we defined it:

Culture is the word we use to describe the ways we think about (1) the transmission and transformation of meanings, (2) the practices that situate those meanings in the world, and (3) the full range of consequences surrounding those meanings: how they structure our senses of self, group, and world; how they both delimit and open up possibilities for being and becoming; how they cross social, political, and other kinds of boundaries; how they change through creative activity; and how they serve as sites of contest and consent.

Theory is the critical tool that allows us to engage the third part of that definition, and it's the one that lets us make strong (interdisciplinary) connections to both the social world and to the questions surrounding "America." Theory helps American Studies writers think about "the full range of consequences" and how "they structure our senses of self, group, and world." Indeed, you can't really explain these things without moving to the level of abstraction found in theory.

One final note of introduction: there is a bit of tension between the *use* of theory and the *creation* of theory. The use of theory suggests learning it, transferring it, transforming it, and elaborating it, each of which rests on a shared set of understandings. In this sense, *doing theory* is akin to knowing and using historiography; both are social practices that allow you to connect with a wider intellectual community. Doing theory is about familiarizing ourselves with positions and conversations. The *creation* of theory suggests that we also make our *own* moves toward high-level significance as we answer the "so what?" questions of our projects. It requires us to frame our specific studies in terms of general understandings that can be learned, transported, and transformed by those who come after us. The creation of theory usually means we push the conversation to new locations—though for some it means inventing a *brand new conversation*. To be in a theoretical conversation is to do both things: to derive from others and to advance positions from which others will derive.

This fundamental dynamic—between old and new, familiar and emergent—poses a problem for us, and for this book. If American Studies is a field built around the production of new "theory" at the level of individual books—and this, remember, is the explicit goal of many writers—then we can't really have a comprehensive discussion of American Studies "theory": the universe is simply too large. On the other hand, if we select out only a few theories, then we leave out huge sectors of writing in the field. Our answer to this dilemma is simply to do what we've already recommended: build, illustrate, and populate categories in order to make certain things visible, while insisting that those categories are *heuristic*—temporary, contingent, open to question, useful for learning, and inviting contest and elaboration down the road.

So we've tried to build a discussion around four large *categories* of theoretical interest, each one using a specific theorist's work as a springboard. There are a number of scholars that one might choose as the entry points into these categories. Others will no doubt make other choices, and we make no claim that ours are in any way inevitable. They're suggestive and, in the end, heuristic. But we think the following four are a good place to start: Michel Foucault, Judith Butler, Angela Davis, and Antonio Gramsci. All share an interest in the relation that individuals and groups have to larger social structures, particularly as those relations are mediated, imagined, built, and constrained through the meaning-making activities of culture. All four bodies of theory are threaded together in various ways—which is exactly what one would expect at a high level of abstraction. Here's a short summary of where we're headed:

- Subject (Foucault): *social-psychological ideas* surrounding individuals and how they are formed into *subjects* by, against, and in relation to social *institutions*. We often think of ourselves as independent agents moving through life on the basis of free choices, but this line of work has emphasized the ways our worlds are circumscribed by time, place, and culture. We can live in opposition to, but never completely independent from, the structures of power that surround us and discipline the way we live our lives.

- Identity (Butler): *ontological ideas* about how people are positioned in relation to one another, and how they challenge, change, or embrace these categorizations. A focus on the constitution of the *individual* offers the opportunity to consider issues such as intersectional feminism, performance, gender and sexuality, disability, toxic masculinity, and a range of identity categories that place human subjects in relation to structures of power. This line of theory has drawn attention to new kinds of freedom (and new insights on oppression) that might otherwise seem to be foreclosed by a strictly Foucauldian approach.

- State (Davis): *political ideas* having to do with the ways social life and cultural meaning have been created in groups through the practices of collective governance. Humans agree (mostly) to be governed, and the forms to which they consent range from participatory democracy to dictatorship to the global complex of the contemporary nation-state. A focus on *the state* offers the opportunity to consider such theoretical concepts as ideology, liberalism, neoliberalism, settler colonialism, imperialism, claims to exception, imprisonment, administrative and regulatory structures, law, and many others. The state offers a framework for contemplating both the formation of subjects and the exercise of power—from the subtle and discursive to the brute force of military action.

- Market (Gramsci): *economic ideas* having to do with the ways that relations of exchange, value, property, labor, and capital have also created social relations, shaped individuals, worked in partnership or opposition to the state, and established powerful systems of cultural meaning. A focus on the *market* offers the opportunity to "follow the money," to see the structures of self and state in relation to economic systems that operate both through abstract logics and through the precise actions of individuals. Markets—defined broadly—distance individuals from both work and work's products, require cultural explanation and the reproduction of social categories, and operate as complex systems that routinely transcend human control.

We recognize that there are other theoretical traditions. We also recognize that, as thinkers, Foucault, Butler, Davis, and Gramsci cannot be reduced to subject, identity, state, and market, respectively. And that each of these four categories blurs into the others. Within the diverse library of books of "theory," though, we think you can find a useful organizing thread for these four by contemplating the meaning of *power*. What is it? How does it shape institutions? What is the relationship between knowledge and power? How is power distributed? How does it function? What are its different modes? "Power" is for this chapter what "text," "archive," "genre," and "formation" have been for the previous chapters—an object of analytical attention. And so the first question to ponder is this: How does "power" work through culture to establish us as *subjects* with particular identities and particular interests?

POWER, CULTURE, AND THE SUBJECT

We have conventionally—and not incorrectly—understood power to emanate from a few central entities that seem to dominate our society. When we name "the state" as an agency of power, for instance, we might think of legislative, judicial, military, and executive bureaucracies. The state is a whole apparatus of people and institutions that takes on a life of its own. When we say "capitalism," we are thinking of another set of institutions and people—banks, industries, multinational corporations, CEOs, and Wall Street. But to think of power only in these ways is to miss other possibilities concerning the nature of power and how it operates.

Our first task, then, is to consider this thing called "power." To do so, we begin with the theories put forward by the French philosopher Michel Foucault. In a series of books, articles, and lectures, Foucault argued that power in modern society (by which he meant Europe and the Western world since the turn of the nineteenth century) inheres in a variety of practices and institutions through which the human subject is constituted. The human subject? That's *you*. And it's everyone around you. Each of us is a subject. Each of us has an *internal* sense of ourselves. We know who we are. We hear our own voice thinking inside our heads. We might think of that voice as our *subjectivity,* and we might wonder where it comes from.

Foucault suggested that the human subject was made through a proliferation of practices, institutions, and techniques that together constitute what he calls *discourse*. Discourse is a sophisticated term for something as seemingly simple as conversation, discussion, and communication. It often connotes serious speech, writing, or conversation, distinguishing it from the casual speech of everyday language. In particular, Foucault used the term to refer to technical speech used by "experts" in the fields of the social and human sciences—physicians, scientists, prison administrators, educators, psychiatrists, and the like.

But Foucault used the term "discourse" to mean more than simply speech. It incorporated the *institutions* inhabited by such experts and all the things that they did there. Discourses about crime, madness, and sexuality, for instance, involved the ways prisons, asylums, and hospitals were conceptualized and operated. For Foucault, discourses enabled the exercise of power through the creation and mobilization of expert knowledge. When a medical doctor at an asylum created knowledge, that doctor also created *power*. When a school headmaster figured out ways to gather statistics about the school's students, that headmaster was creating knowledge—and creating a kind of *power* that could be put to work upon the students. If you are a student, you have surely experienced such things yourself: automated grading systems, standardized texts, online paper submission systems, and surveillance cameras, for example. Or Big Data systems that aggregate test scores and locate you precisely in relation to an enormous cohort of others. Scientists, educators, physicians, psychologists, and the institutions within which they worked created knowledge and used it to "normalize," and thereby police, behavior. In doing so, they created and wielded power.

In this sense, power did not emanate from some central location. Indeed, Foucault made his argument by drawing a distinction between the old days, when people thought that power *was* centralized. Power came from God, passed through the figure of the king, and then spread through a hierarchy of officials across the land. The "new" kind of power that Foucault hoped to explain was not like that at all. It was made over and over again, in small ways, and differently, in every school and prison and hospital and military training ground (these were the institutions that interested Foucault most, but we can imagine others).

Foucault conceived of power not simply as decentralized; he also saw it as *diffuse*. Power in pre-modern Western regimes derived from the king's authority—that is, the authority of the state—to punish by taking human life. In this sense, it had a lot to do with *force*. Power in the modern world, he suggested, operates at the farthest reaches of society, and it does not rely (primarily at least) on the threat of death. Using the metaphor of the human heart and circulatory system, Foucault describes this new power as "capillary" power, a working of power at the farthest remove from the heart and the center. Capillary power affects people in the living of their everyday lives, in the practices they participate in as they go about the business of living. Moreover, this kind of power operates continuously—24/7—and in this way it is also different from the pre-modern power of the king. The king's power was imposed through an agent of the state, who was usually not around. Rather than being *continuous,* then, the king's power was occasional and intermittent, exercised when one of his lords or sheriffs dropped by for the annual visit.

This modern power, you will have observed, is both more difficult to grasp and to understand—and more effective than that of the monarch. The king's power was, in essence, a *negative* force, denying or censoring the expressions, needs, wishes, and desires of people. This new modern kind of power actually *produces* those expressions, needs, wishes, and desires. It is a productive power, in other words, rather than a repressive or prohibiting power. Because it operates at such a local level—diffuse, decentralized, and omnipresent— Foucault's power can be thought of as being both broad *and* intimate. It is as large as the world itself, and as small as a gesture made by a particular individual on a particular second of a particular day. It is everywhere in what he referred to as "micro-practices," or the social practices that make up everyday life. And it is this kind of power—micro, capillary, ordinary, working through discourses—that produces us all as individual subjects.

DISCIPLINE AND SUBJECTIVITY

We are "disciplined" and made "normal," Foucault argues, through various techniques, among the most important of which is surveillance, or the use of the *gaze* to make visible large numbers of people, and then to control and manage them as individuals. We have just suggested that Foucault's conception of power works both broadly and with fine precision. The *gaze* functions in a similar way. It is capable of bringing into view a large population—of prisoners, patients, or students, for instance. It does this through the collecting of mass quantities of information and the assembling of this information into categories that produce knowledge. Think, for example, of the United States census, Google analytics, Amazon algorithms, election polling, and pretty much all forms of statistics. These things create knowledge about large categories of people: Who and how many people live where? How are they distributed racially? What do they buy and watch? What do they search for? Who are they going to vote for? This kind of surveillance *unifies* and organizes an otherwise random mass of data.

We should emphasize that such surveillance is different from the kind of data mapping that we described in chapter 5 in relation to Franco Moretti's concept of "distant reading." For example, the University of Virginia's Cooper Center for Public Service produced a racial dot map of the United

States based on the 2010 census, with a single color-coded dot for each of the country's 308.7 million people based on reported race and address.[1] This tool enables researchers to visualize the racial segregation of housing in cities like Chicago, Birmingham, and Los Angeles, over forty years after the passage of the Fair Housing Act. Such tools are less about controlling subjects (no individuals are identified in the racial dot map) than making patterns visible. An example of data mining that better captures the kind of surveillance power that Foucault is talking about might involve political parties sending voter registration cards to some citizens but not others based on race, gender, purchasing records, and partisan reading habits. In other words, the gaze also *divides* and individualizes. Surveillance creates specific, precise, detailed, and intimate information about a particular person. Experts such as physicians or psychiatrists extract from patients the most minute details of their lives, turning people into "cases" about whom these experts amass a great deal of knowledge. A student file, for example, records your supposed potential (test scores) and how well you may or may not have brought that potential to fruition (grades). It records absences from class (which suggests level of effort). It will contain other specific data concerning your socioeconomic status (visible in your address), your social world (through the names and addresses of parents), and your relative degree of obedience and participation (through notations on suspensions or academic probation).

Your record raises a question: Are you outside the range of what is *normal?* Are you, perhaps, in need of some form of correction? The record provides the information necessary to make that decision. At the same time, the broad technical knowledge produced through a proliferation of student records actually creates the discourse through which your correction will be understood. Those proliferating records *produce* the expertise and power that will make your correction possible. So you are simultaneously subject to both a very specific understanding of *you* and a universal knowledge that will be used to *discipline* you, to bring you into a state of *normal.*

These can be depressing ideas. But Foucault went still further. It is not simply the case that these discourses and techniques, institutions and knowledges are slamming you down, forcing you into social conformity. That's true, in part. But it is equally true that you are *made*—and, to some extent, make yourself—in relation to the broad gaze of a collection of institutions: credit reporting bureaus, your bank, your phone records, and all that data you create every time you post on Twitter, Instagram, or Snapchat, or buy something online.

FIGURE 35. Panoptic prison, Presidio Modelo, Isla de la Juventud, Cuba.

To help think about the ways that surveillance, knowledge, and discourse expand beyond institutions and come to permeate the entirety of social life, Foucault uses a concrete example as a metaphor for how power and subjectivity work in the modern world. The example is a prison, imagined by Jeremy Bentham (an eighteenth-century social theorist) in 1785, called the "panopticon"—an architectural device designed to render large numbers of people visible from a single, central viewpoint and then providing organizational plans that categorize them (figure 35).

Think of inmates of a prison whose cells ring the walls of the building, observable from a tower in the middle of the space. The warden or guard can observe all of the prisoners, while remaining virtually invisible to them, even as they are denied the chance to see one another. Or think of hospital wards organized according to the diseases presented by patients, or a classroom arranged according to the age or ability of the students. Or think of our dime novel readers, working on a factory floor under the surveillance of managers who can look down upon them from second-floor observation points— otherwise known as "offices."

Because the inmates of the prison cannot see into the central tower, they don't know when they are being watched. But the very possibility that their every move is being observed leads them to police *themselves,* to behave in a particular way just in case a guard is looking at them. Workers carry out tedious, repetitive tasks on the assembly line, aware that supervisors *could be* watching their every move. Or not. But that's the point: we don't know if we're being watched, but we sure do act as if we are. We *internalize* the gaze, in other words, and perform self-surveillance. No one has to enforce discipline on you, because you enforce it upon yourself, well aware of the continuous, diffuse, productive functions of power. As you do, you create yourself—and are created—as a *subject*. In this sense, society itself is like one giant panopticon. Jeremy Bentham's model prison becomes a way of thinking about the entire social world. The result, Foucault argued, was the "disciplining" of populations, a process through which society produces "docile" and "useful" bodies.[2]

One classic example of Foucault's formulations concerns sexuality. He noted that during the nineteenth century the discussion of sex and sexuality, far from being censored and silenced, actually flourished; that the era witnessed what he described as "the great process of transforming sex into discourse."[3] Physicians played a major role in the expression of discourses concerning sex; they took it upon themselves to discover and guard "the truth of sex," to act as arbiters in formulating sexual norms and the sexual identity of individuals. In the hands of doctors, sexuality became transformed from one element of individual identity to a major determinant of personal identity. So, in the eighteenth century, for example, a man might be a husband, father, American, Bostonian, merchant or craftsman, and lover of men. In the course of the nineteenth century, that multifaceted individual became, in the hands of physicians employing discourses about sexuality, a "homosexual."

One component of identity now stood in for the whole person, superseding all other attributes and constituting that individual as "perverse" or outside of "the normal." Doctors defined sexuality as particularly susceptible to unhealthy, even pathological developments, and therefore an area that called for their intervention. That intervention—an act of *power*—was made possible through the production of *knowledge*. These dynamics were particularly salient for white, middle-class women, whose bodies were, in the hands of physicians, turned into vessels of disease and hysteria. Regarded as "thoroughly saturated with sexuality" and inherently pathological, women's bodies became the object of much medical pronouncement and practice.[4] The constitution of a person as a particular kind of sexual individual—and the categorization by experts of that sexuality as normal or abnormal—compelled men, women, and children to live in relation to those internalized norms. They policed themselves. They became subjects.

Discourses make, classify, and order people in the world. They are inherently political; that is to say, they involve relations of power. And because the operations of power occur at the everyday level of social practices, power is everywhere, inherent in every relationship. It is *not* simply located in state or economic institutions, though it pulses through these larger structures. Perhaps the most recognized example of the large-scale utility of an analysis of discourse is Edward Said's formative book, *Orientalism* (1978), which demonstrates through textual examples and genres the formation and maintenance of a Western discourse concerning the Orient. For Said, this pervasive and powerful discourse has real material consequences in the form of European militarism, conquest, and colonialism. It underpins and justifies the many interventions and management plans enforced by Western powers over the Middle East. And it carries consequences for individuals.

We are all on the receiving end of operations of power simply by virtue of living our lives within systems that seek to name the "normative" and bring individuals and social groups into its boundaries. But perhaps all is not lost. For, crucially, discourses that establish the knowledge and power mechanisms in society can also be seized by individuals or groups to resist the operations of power. Foucault called these "reverse" discourses, or discourses of resistance; he thought of them as ways that people might incorporate the vocabulary and categories of the dominant discourse to assert alternative claims to power. Many critics, however, have suggested that these possibilities remain underdeveloped in Foucault's theoretical writings.

The possibility of oppositional discourses points to other important theoretical models. It gestures, for example, to a long-standing model of *structure and agency*—that is, the relation between the mechanisms of domination and the possibilities for resistance. The ways in which knowledge is constituted through the creation of categories such as sexuality might point us to others such as *race, class, and gender*. In these (and other) cases, one sees theoretical traditions colliding, crossing, and conversing. Consider, for example, a transformative piece of writing, Joan Wallach Scott's article "Gender: A Useful Category of Historical Analysis" (1986), which emerged from multiple theoretical and disciplinary genealogies, including labor history, French history, women's studies, sexuality studies, historiography, and Foucauldian discourse analysis. Scott argued that "gender" was not simply a different way of saying "women's history," but was in fact relevant to both women *and* men, and was an unstable, discursive category in any case. Gender is something constantly being made and remade, which required a tracing of its history, and it is a vector of power that demanded new theoretical frameworks that went beyond those developed by Foucault.

IDENTITY AND PERFORMANCE

Perhaps the most influential feminist alternative to Foucault was developed by Judith Butler in *Gender Trouble: Feminism and the Subversion of Identity* (1990), which decoupled the categories of gender and sex from the biological characteristics of individual bodies. According to Butler, the notion that biological sex could be cleanly divided into "male" and "female" was a product of discursive forces invested in treating sex as an essential status, which in turn determined one's fixed gender identity. In fact, Butler argued, there is no such thing as a fixed sex-gender identity; rather, these things are continuously constituted through *performance*. Gender is better understood as a script—much like a script to a play—that individuals spend their lives trying to master. Moreover, gender scripts vary dramatically across time and place; there is no single set of gender norms, or scripts—even in the most repressive regimes, and no matter how much effort people put into convincing themselves that masculinity and femininity are innate. Precisely because there is nothing natural about gender norms, their compulsive repetition opens the door to performances that go "off-script" and reveal the underlying contingency of the norms themselves.

We can illustrate Butler's theory of gender performativity through *Moonlight* (2016), a film which follows the coming of age of a young black man in Miami. The film is organized around three parts—"Little," "Chiron," and "Black"—each of which follows a different moment in the protagonist's life. His given name is Chiron, but he is called Little by his peers in school, who incessantly bully him and call him "soft" and "faggot." Every step of the way, he is bombarded with messages about what it means to be "a real man." One night on the beach, however, the normative script breaks down and Chiron has sex with his best friend, Kevin. For all its profundity, this shared experience does not protect either of them from ongoing violence. After a series of betrayals, Chiron becomes a drug dealer in Atlanta, where he lifts weights, buys expensive jewelry, and retreats into a persona of being "hard." Nevertheless, it is the underlying fluidity of gender as a *performance* that proves to be its undoing in the film. Through the sheer effort that Chiron puts into his transformation, we see that "hard" is just as much a performance as "soft." It follows a script—"toxic masculinity"—that emphasizes violence, power, aggression, predatory sexuality, and emotional disconnect. And we see that Chiron is never fully comfortable with this script. This discomfort ultimately leads him on a road trip back to Miami, where he rekindles his connection with Kevin, who paves the way with vulnerability, cooking, and "grandma rules" (which is itself a script: "You eat, you talk!"). In a culture that casts gay sexuality as a failure of heterosexuality, the power of their friendship to disrupt Chiron's downward spiral shows that the real failure lies with toxic masculinity, which pretends to be natural but clearly is not.

These slippages and disruptions are why we characterize Butler's theoretical position as *ontological*. By that, we mean that it concerns being and becoming, especially in relation to the categories established through social practices surrounding sex and gender. Here's one familiar way to think about it: most of us assume that there is an essential *you* that exists in a material form—an actual body of flesh, blood, and bone—and as a distinct subject; that is, you are a being who acts in the world. Your actions are supposedly authentic in that they emanate from that deep, core *you*. This central script of Western modernity is encapsulated by the advice of Polonius in *Hamlet*: "This above all: to thine own self be true." But Butler points us in the opposite direction: there is no essential *you*—only a collection of events and performances. These are given shape by social scripts, but not necessarily dictated by them. In other words, it is your *actions* in the world that create the thing that is you.

The analogy of script and performance suggests a theoretical relation between the concepts of subjectivity and identity. In Foucault's terms, power works through institutions, knowledge, and surveillance to constitute *you* as a subject. Your subjectivity is an interiority, even though it is produced by external forces. Foucault has referred to it, for example, as a redefined sense of a soul. Identity, on the other hand, is a complex ontological label that crosses and confounds the categories of the *interior* (think psychological) and *exterior* (think social). It takes social shape through practices of *identification* (in which you align yourself with certain scripts) and *ascription* (in which others see you as being aligned with certain scripts). Both practices locate you in social categories such as sex, gender, and race. But identity also takes social shape through your performances—the actions you take in the world that constitute you. In this sense, the relationship between *who we are* and *what we do* is opened up in ways that admit both oppression and active choice. Identity, in this sense, is a complicated theoretical location. It is *contextual:*

identity is scripted and performed differently in different moments. It concerns *power:* others insist on seeing you through the expectations found in particular scripts. And it takes seriously *agency:* you can go off-script, write new parts, and craft a new play altogether—or maybe even start a new theater company!

Identity is frequently seen in political terms. The term "identity politics," for example, is used to describe—and often critique—political activity that focuses on the interests of a particular group. The #BlackLivesMatter movement is dismissed by its detractors as black identity politics. The followers of Donald Trump are seen to exemplify white identity politics. In theoretical terms, *identity* does have political consequences—but these consequences do not stem from ascriptive categories, so much as from performances that go off-script, changing the nature of their contexts and thus challenging the power of expectations and norms.

By cracking open the inexorability of such expectations, Butler opened the door to considering the possibilities for what scholars have come to call *queering* the discourse: not simply claiming rights—civil or otherwise—for identities constituted as different, but opposing, fragmenting, and questioning everything that appeared to be normative. Butler imagined an oppositional politics that opened up new possibilities for theories of *performativity,* in which subjectivities—and their social face, *identities*—were recognized as being constituted in particular actions and contexts that could be made anarchic and chaotic. And these theoretical concepts—performativity, queerness, and anarchy relative to the normative—have always been linked (as is so often the case with American Studies scholarship) with equally complex social movements. Theorists such as Michael Warner, Jack Halberstam, José Esteban Muñoz, and Roderick Ferguson (among many others) have expanded these possibilities even further.

Indeed, some of the most critical of those expansions have come in relation not simply to gender, sexuality, and social norms, but also race, ethnicity, and social class. Earlier, we noted the ways Foucault led readers to consider the impact of the discourses of sexuality on white middle-class women. Those same mechanics of knowledge and power were applied as thoroughly, and more brutally, to other men and women. Consider the relationship between racial profiling and police violence, and how it contributes to a pervasive sense that black lives simply do not matter. Or the explicitly Foucauldian enterprises of the American Indian reservation system, which counted, measured, and "normalized" Native American gender roles and sexual practices—

and did so on the basis of theories of knowledge and power focused on race and social evolution. Both cases (and they are only two obvious ones) complicate Foucault's sense of the quiet, productive workings of power on a population. While black and Indian subjectivities are produced out of discursive relationships of power and knowledge, they are also the subjects of (gendered and raced) forms of physical violence: death, torture, rape, and the destruction of families. One might well argue that it was not continuous surveillance but rather continuous violence that defined these histories. They bid to open up both a *critical race theory* approach, and what we now think of as *queer of color* critique. If some of the most pointed critiques of queer theory—and of Foucault himself—have focused on its cultural location in *discourse,* its intersections with critical race theory have served as a strong reminder of material, social, and historical contexts.

Likewise, even as theories of discourse and power take us to key categories of social analysis—race, class, gender, disability, and more—they also point to the insufficiencies of those categories in making full sense of individual identities. Patricia Hill Collins has famously argued for the critical importance of *intersectionality*—the understanding that different social categories reflect different structures of oppressions and thus different kinds of subjectivities that engage multiple identity positions and categories. A person who is black, female, and gay confronts distinct and overlapping discourses and practices of power. Or perhaps even that hypothetical subject is too categorized. What kinds of transgressive possibilities and oppressions come with a more complex subject: not black, but multiracial; not cis female or cis male, but intersex or transgender; not gay, but bisexual, pansexual, or asexual? Intersectional analysis works particularly well when the object of analysis is a single individual, with both subjectivity and identity shaped out of cultural discourses, social practices, and individual agency. And performativity offers a useful theoretical tool for seeing how that individual might craft an identity in relation, and in opposition, to the world.

IDEOLOGY AND INTERPELLATION

In *Gender Trouble,* Butler's theoretical interlocutors included not only Foucault, but the mid-twentieth-century Marxist critic Louis Althusser. All three theorists shared a number of premises. For one, Butler, Foucault, and Althusser all saw subjectivity as a twofold process: of *acquiring* a sense of self as a subject, on the one hand, and of being *made* a subject through operations of power, on the other. Foucault located the process in discursive practices associated with institutional forces. For Althusser, the process involved not discourses, but *ideologies*. He defined these as systems of belief within which we move, often unconsciously, and through which we make sense of the world, usually without even thinking about them.

The word "ideology" is often taken to mean a body of beliefs that are somehow false or deceptive. But that is far from the case. Ideologies might be political, economic, or social—they are the "isms" that seem to explain how the world works, or should work. Liberalism, socialism, fascism, capitalism, feminism—these (and many others) are systems of meaning we use to organize our view of the world, to understand our relationships to others in the world, to make claims about our places in the world, and to argue for changing the world in which we live (or keeping it the same). Yet, if we as humans develop ideological systems, they also take on their own structural life, creating subjects that reflect not essential humanistic qualities (say, human rights, humanist values, individualism, or collectivity) but the ideological system itself. As such, ideologies structure the ways we think; they become "real," in the sense that we act upon them and thus create the actual situations in which we live our lives.

How is ideology different from discourse? One particularly useful illustration can help demonstrate this distinction. Think of the social custom of monogamy, or the expectations that couples will remain sexually exclusive to one another. There are a whole series of ancillary practices that regulate and sustain monogamous relationships, including marriage, mortgages, dating websites, reality shows valorizing monogamy, social rules around who can attend Thanksgiving dinners, and more. We might think of all this as the *discourse* of monogamy. In and of itself, monogamy doesn't necessarily carry any social meaning. Largely self-regulating, it merely limits the range of sexual arrangements that most people imagine for themselves. But if we place the practice, the discourse, within the *ideological* system of beliefs in which gender inequalities are naturalized—patriarchy—it speaks profoundly of relations of power. The expectation of monogamy starts to seem more pernicious, something unevenly enforced for men and women through "slut-shaming" or worse. It takes place within a heteronormative ideological structure that subordinates women to men and positions a range of alternative sexual worlds, such as bathhouses or sex clubs, as deviant. And this discourse serves to obscure unequal relations of power, to mystify them, to make them invisible or natural, even as it serves to reinforce and reproduce those social relations. In this way discourses and ideologies work together, and within one another. They create individual subjectivities in relation to *social beliefs.* Few people stop to think about why, exactly, they believe so strongly in monogamy. Instead, such beliefs become *social realities* as human beings live them in the everyday world. And these belief systems carry a kind of weight and direction to them: they are both pictures of the world *as it is* and templates for how the world *ought to be.* And here's the thing: those templates are *not* of an ideal world of human equality and prosperity. They favor certain groups of people over other groups, and they make these inequalities seem right and natural.

Ideology functions as the "common sense" with which we approach daily life. We don't question it. It seems to be entirely natural. For Althusser, ideology is what calls us into being as subjects, as a combination of subjectivity (sense of self) and subjection. His fundamental contribution to this question is the idea of *interpellation,* which Butler drew on to explain how something best characterized as a performance—gender—came to be understood as natural. Ideological expectations call out your name in the most intimate way, and you respond. This begins at the very moment of birth, when the parents or doctors check genitalia and exclaim, "It's a boy!" or "It's a girl!" This act of *hailing* (Althusser used the example of a police officer shouting "Hey, you!") sets off a cascade of additional ways of talking and acting that seek to assign a particular cultural script on the basis of that snap exclamation of biological classification at birth. This hailing is the essence of "interpellation." A constellation of multiple acts of interpellation come together to form the *ideological state apparatus,* or the practices that educate citizens *into* belief. Conveyed through schools, family, churches, and a host of other civil institutions, the ideological apparatus offered, in Althusser's words, "the imaginary relationship of individuals to their real conditions of existence."[5]

Consider the public service announcement on a Metro train in Washington, DC (figure 36). The image depicts a woman standing on an empty train in daylight, her head resting on her right hand in a contemplative pose not unlike Rodin's famous sculpture *The Thinker* (1902). What is the object of her gaze? A gallon of milk on a seat. The text of the announcement offers emphatic (and counterintuitive) interpretive instructions to the viewer: "Don't *assume* it's *just* a gallon of milk." The message, never explicitly spelled out, is that the gallon of milk might actually be an explosive. As part of the ideological state apparatus, this PSA works to train (no pun intended) Metro

FIGURE 36. Advertisement on a Metro train in Washington, DC, June 2016. Photograph by Alexander Olson.

riders to stay vigilant against terrorism by watching for potential danger all around them. But dig a little deeper, and it is easy to see how "Don't trust what you see!" can morph into psychological preparation for practices like racial profiling. Classifications ranging from gender to race to nationality impact the way a person is treated (or the way a particular "Hey, you!" is shouted), which over time makes it difficult to avoid internalizing—and in so doing, reinforcing and reproducing—the dominant relations of power in one's society.

As you can see in the case of both discourse and ideology, it's easy—perhaps too easy—to focus on the practices that exert power to create subjectivities and to see them as totalizing, or nearly so. Theoretical genealogies emerging out of, and intersecting with, Butler's work have sought to shift that focus, recognizing not only the power of interpellation, but also the possibilities for off-script performance, contradictory identities, and contextual complications. A theoretical position resting not on essential identity but on constitutive performance asks us—through its very nature—to contemplate the intersections of various other theoretical platforms. Queer theory, for example, critiqued the identities presumed by various ethnic studies traditions. Critical race theory critiqued the whiteness that centered much queer theory. Queer of color theory then engaged with feminist and Marxist questions centered on gender and class. New identities—personal, social, intellectual, and institutional—were performed and consolidated, as was a new theoretical field. And that field proved to be interested in many other forms and questions of power, including those figured around the state.

The state poses unique challenges for social theory. If you recall the definition we proposed earlier in this chapter, theory occupies *an abstract location distinct from any individual case to be explained.* If your theoretical position cannot be separated from the particular examples from which it is derived, you might have a useful observation on your hands, but not theory. This is a problem when dealing with social change in the living, breathing world of everyday experience. The power of the state in this domain is messy and tenuous; this is why Foucault's panopticon hinged on the *possibility* that authorities might be watching, not the reality. In practice, there simply isn't enough attention to go around. Most of what actually takes place in a panopticon slips past even the peripheral vision of the guard in the center tower.

The state's vision, in other words, is incomplete. And yet, it is able, when needed, to mobilize guards and guns, since it holds a legal monopoly on violence. Paradoxically, it is apart from its citizens, while drawing at least some of its authority from them. The state is a fundamental concept in *politics,* which frames our third body of theoretical work. Politics describes the wide range of practices through which groups of human beings reach *collective decisions.* Such decisions concern courses of action to be taken by (or on behalf of) the group, to be sure, but more fundamentally they concern the *governing structures* used to make those decisions and the *delegations of authority* necessary to implement them.

Among such decisions, structures, and delegations rest a host of theories about the individual and the group, about coercion and persuasion, about intergroup relations, and about general principles for organizing, governing, and contesting the affairs of everyday life—all the stuff that happens in relation to a guard tower that is imperfectly occupied. Theoretical generalization in a realm as multivariable as everyday life can be challenging, and scholars often end up circumscribing the universe of examples from which they draw in order to reach conclusions that can actually matter in the world. And let's be honest: most social theory is written with an eye toward social change.

There is even a term for this, *praxis,* which refers to the application of theory to practice. Indeed, to a striking degree, the methodological conversation in American Studies—always concerned with the politics underpinning social organization and cultural meaning—has moved ever more decisively into the realm of praxis. We even contemplated adding an extra toolkit on "engagement" to this book, in light of the range of American Studies work being done on the practical challenges of community organizing and social justice activism.

Despite its important role in American Studies today, activism presents social theory with very real challenges. Among the vulnerabilities of praxis-oriented work is the charge that one's prescriptions work "better in theory than practice." We've all heard this line a thousand times, often unfairly. It can be a quick and easy way to try to delegitimize scholarship that unsettles the status quo. However, we think it is worth considering some of the reasons behind its resonance. In the complicated back-and-forth between theory and praxis, sometimes scholars can find themselves working backward from pre-determined political positions. Instead of starting with observations, developing hypotheses, and seeking to *disprove* your predictions (as would be the case in the scientific method), it is tempting—especially when dealing with political issues—to start with a desired outcome and then seek out the best case studies for affirming it. Indeed, Russ Castronovo and Susan Gillman identify the desire "to make our objects of study coincide with our political goals or objects" as a central element of contemporary American Studies.[6] From the earliest days of the field, as we saw in chapter 3, these political goals have largely (but not exclusively) revolved around a critique of American state power.

So what, exactly, do we mean by *the state?* One way to answer the question is to turn to the Montevideo Convention of 1933, which offered an internationally accepted definition of states in terms of *sovereignty.* A state has these characteristics: a permanent population; a defined territory; a central government; and the capacity to be recognized by, and to enter into relations with, other states. These norms can be traced back even further, to the Peace of Westphalia in 1648, which settled the Thirty Years War in Europe through mutual recognition of territorial integrity by the various warring parties. Another way would be to compare different forms of statehood. A Greek *city-state* based itself—population, territory, government, and diplomatic standing—on a particular city and its political and productive hinterland. A *nation-state* fuses together the governmental apparatus of the state with the cultural apparatus of nationalism: a sense of shared identity, ethnicity, memory, and aspiration. A *multinational state* might have two (or more) "national" cultures operating under a single geopolitical entity. Nations, in other words, do not inevitably mirror states. As Benedict Anderson suggested, nations are "imagined communities," or entities so large that individuals could not actually *know* the community, even though they could conceive of it through print culture, museums, monuments, and other unifying cultural practices.

We could add to this list the models of state power offered by Foucault, Althusser, and many, many others. But this is where it's worth giving *praxis* another look. As cultural theory flourished in American universities between the 1970s and 1990s, a lot was happening in the world that was making some of the models seem, well, theoretical—and not in a good way. To explain this problem, and find a way out, we now turn to our third guide through the world of social theory: the feminist scholar-activist Angela Davis. As Foucault and Althusser were theorizing about the state, Davis was battling directly with state authorities through her involvement in the black freedom movement in ways that unsettled the narratives that were starting to coalesce around mid-century American liberalism. From a distance, it appeared that the state apparatus of the Jim Crow South was being dismantled in the courtroom, culture, and halls of Congress. But it was clear to communities of color that structural racism was only shifting to new forms, most notably barriers to black homeownership and the rise of mass incarceration. Davis worked with the Black Panthers to address these issues, which brought her to the attention of the FBI. Her advocacy on behalf of prisoners led to her indictment on conspiracy and murder charges. Despite being acquitted of all charges in 1972, Davis spent almost two years in jail. This only further galvanized her work for systemic change, even as it underscored the difficulty of such work. Theory is one thing; praxis can get you thrown in jail. In 2012, the American Studies Association established the Angela Davis Prize for Public Scholarship to recognize "work that explicitly aims to educate the public, influence policies, or in other ways seeks to address inequalities in imaginative, practical, and applicable forms."

Davis's work has been a guiding force in developing two models of state power that have become central to American Studies: the *carceral state* (or the massive shifts in resource allocation toward prisons and criminal supervision) and the *neoliberal state* (the privatization of public goods and the outsourcing of once-collective obligations onto the generally unprepared individual). In her landmark book, *Are Prisons Obsolete?* (2003), Davis sought to unsettle the assumption that prisons are a natural and inevitable part of the American social order. The growth of the carceral state seemed unremarkable because it seemed natural (or what Althusser would call an ideology). But for many black Americans, mass incarceration represented merely a shift in the experience of oppression from one kind of interpellation to another. Instead of being treated as citizens and full participants in democracy in the wake of civil rights legislation, as liberals imagined, people of color found themselves still marked as criminals and objects of largesse, with racial profiling and racialized welfare rhetoric replacing the terrorism of lynching. The consequences of this shift, Davis argues, extend far beyond the concrete archipelago of correctional institutions that have "prisonized" the American landscape. The lack of voting rights for prisoners means that rural areas with large prisons (the inhabitants of which are included in the census) are overrepresented in legislatures. Building on Foucault's description of the shift from corporal (and capital) punishment to imprisonment, Davis argues that the illusion of a more humane system masked, among other things, the persistence of multiple forms of violence.

Davis's advocacy for prison abolition and contributions to intersectional feminism can obscure her significance as a theorist of the neoliberal state. Neoliberalism refers to the privatization of public goods in all facets of political and economic life since the 1980s. This included the devolution of basic governmental functions to entities like charter schools, for-profit prisons, and treaty organizations designed to serve the interests of multinational corporations. In *Freedom Is a Constant Struggle* (2016), Davis points to the transnational security firm G4S (Group 4 Security), one of the largest privately held corporations in the world, as an example of how the even the state's monopoly on violence can be offloaded and privatized—much as it was during American military actions in Iraq and Afghanistan. The services offered by G4S range from mercenary soldiers in Africa to security guards in American elementary schools. Unlike state actors, corporations like G4S have an incentive to encourage violence or the threat of violence, since their business models are not viable without it. In effect, such private firms have replaced the state monopoly on violence with a situation that cannot be easily captured by metaphors like the panopticon.

It is no coincidence that these neoliberal changes—organized for and benefiting economic elites—have been accompanied by aggressive state oversight of non-elites. Indeed, while theorists of the carceral state such as Ruth Wilson

Gilmore, Elizabeth Hinton, Kelly Lytle Hernández, Khalil Gibran Muhammad, and Heather Ann Thompson point to increased policing and the growth of a "prison-industrial complex," they also suggest that the *carceral* reflects a broader social *formation*. That formation includes probation, parole, and community service (or sanction in the form of offender lists). It encompasses the arguments for longer sentences and harsher punishment, including the arguably torturous conditions of solitary confinement, a penal strategy in widespread use. It recognizes and accepts that certain racialized groups— African Americans, Latinxs, and American Indians, among others—will be disproportionately represented among the incarcerated and will be subjected to differential attention from police. It accepts the militarization of police, and locates police violence in the context of the individual and anecdotal rather than the structural. It positions citizens in the position of "civil death"—unable to vote, drive, work, or otherwise make a life for themselves due to an encounter with the law. It adopts the neoliberal position of privatizing what began as a public responsibility. And it both underfunds and extends new harshness into the legal system, removing and attenuating long-standing constitutional safeguards. In all these ways, the prison-police-legal complex has become a semi-autonomous force of its own, capable of shaping the very nature of the state itself and the social and cultural relations of its citizens.

The discourses and ideologies that underpin this radical shift in state power are often based on what theorist Giorgio Agamben called a "state of exception," a special emergency claim that justifies removing citizens from civil law and noncitizens from human rights discourse entirely. Such a state reduces the individual from the human to simply a biological life-form (a situation that some theorists refer to as *biopolitics*). It is not difficult to see— in slavery, warfare, or debates on criminality, for example—that states of exception can quite rapidly become the status quo. The United States, some would argue, far from being *exceptional,* has *always* been in a state of exception.

A number of theoretical doors can open when you view the United States *not* simply as "America"—a nationalist idea with a history—but as a *state.* For example, James Scott's *Seeing Like a State: How Certain Schemes to Improve the Human Condition Have Failed* (1998) examined modernist social planning as a key location for the imposition of an administrative order over the notoriously unruly domains of nature and society. Writing from an anarchist perspective, Scott replaces Foucault's metaphor of the panopticon with the *map*—a necessarily imperfect document that is legible only to the extent that it *fails to see things.* To be useful to the central state administrator, a map needs to omit unnecessary details and standardize whatever remains into a coherent system of signs. Passports, social security numbers, and time zones are all technologies of mapping through which modern states exercise power. The resulting top-down schemes can have catastrophic practical consequences (such as crop failure and mass starvation) precisely because of all the local knowledge that is edited out in the process of mapping. Scott later explored the practice of state evasion as a response to state power, publishing his findings in *The Art of Not Being Governed: An Anarchist History of Upland Southeast Asia* (2009).

Both Davis and Scott suggest the importance of investigating models of state power that look beyond clearly bounded territories. Indeed, perhaps the most frequently invoked theoretical word in American Studies over the last decades has been "empire" in all its permutations: imperialism, neo-imperialism, transnationalism, and colonialism. Empires can take many forms. Some are contiguous, others global; some require constant force, others are ruled indirectly through an indigenous elite; some verge on being confederations of multiple polities, others colonize indigenous people; some focus on territory and tribute, others on land and resource extraction. The nature of old and new imperialisms, the ways domestic state apparatuses have been put to work offshore, and the relation between state power and economic power—all these have been theoretical questions preoccupying American Studies scholars. Amy Kaplan and Donald Pease's foundational edited collection, *Cultures of United States Imperialism* (1993), included twenty-six essays that raised exactly these questions, and both Kaplan and Pease then proceeded to continue writing in ways that helped press forward the study of empire as a new theoretical field. Since then, countless papers and presidential addresses at the American Studies Association annual meeting have taken up this theme. It sits as the primary global location for state-focused work in American Studies.

Here, though, one can also see variations in the fabric of American Studies. Where scholars of immigration, the state, and global capitalism have turned to the question of imperialism, writers in aligned fields—take, for example, Native American and Indigenous Studies—have considered imperialism and American military conquest as a given and turned instead to concepts such as *settler colonialism,* which places a theoretical emphasis on colonial settlement over political empire and posits a series of distinctions that make it different from the "regular" colonialism so often associated with empire. *Settler* colonialism emphasizes land over labor, and *conquest* over migration, sojourn, or diaspora. It suggests a logic that demands elimination of the indigenous rather than the conversion of them into a docile labor force, and explores a dominating majority that seeks to "become indigenous" rather than a dominating minority that remains proudly imperial and linked back to the metropole. In these ways, settler colonial nations—such as the United States, South Africa, Australia, and Israel—found new political orders, rather than simply moving people back and forth across existing imperial political frames.

Settler colonialism has been a powerful theoretical tool for thinking about the very foundations of the American state as an empire, and for making certain that pressing discussions of slavery, class warfare, and ethnic labor discrimination do not elide the basic fact of the conquest of the North American continent. It entered American Studies through Native American Studies, but looked for some of its earliest theoretical articulations to global scholars such as Patrick Wolfe (Australia), Linda Tuhiwai Smith (Aotearoa / New Zealand), and Lorenzo Veracini (Australia, studying Israel). Indeed, it is striking to consider the number of useful theoretical contributions made to American Studies by scholars located in other disciplines, fields, and geographies. Whether you work in a state or a nonstate, or are aspirational or resistant to state structures, the question of power in the contemporary world is inextricably linked to the question of the state and its relation to its subjects, citizens, and others.

HEGEMONY: THE RETURN TO CULTURE

Even though we opened this chapter by positing that the turn to theory in American Studies can be attributed, in part, to the heightened interest in culture across the humanities in the 1980s and 1990s, our discussion of Foucault, Butler, and Davis has largely pushed culture to the sidelines. Likewise we only briefly touched on economics, that mysterious, hard-to-figure "invisible hand" that accompanies the gloved fist of the state. Our final discussion will seek to unify these by putting culture (the place where inequality, social relations, and human subjectivities are understood, formed, justified, explained, fought over, and made into common sense) in dialogue with economics (that social science concerned with the production, distribution, and consumption of goods and services that, in turn, produce, transfer, and maintain wealth).

Our guide will be the Italian social theorist Antonio Gramsci, imprisoned by fascist dictator Benito Mussolini under a "state of emergency" for a decade beginning in 1926, and the author of a trove of writings known as *The Prison Notebooks*. Among his many insights, let's begin with these: Gramsci recognized that, contrary to the predictions of Marx and Lenin, socialist revolutions were not taking place in capitalist societies. Dominating force did not wholly account for the failure, he argued, nor did the economic power of elites. Ideology mattered, but it was not simply a question of false consciousness or an imposed belief system. How should one explain the failure?

Classical Marxism located power in a complicated set of structural relations that characterized industrial economies. Workers produced value through their labor, earning wages. Employers—those who owned the factories and equipment that constituted the means of production—established a market in which labor was sold and purchased, thus establishing a price for the worker's time, energy, and skill. That price—defined by a labor market, not by the worker's output—was less than the value of the commodities that the worker made. The owner thus extracted from the worker the difference between the value and price of the labor, which was called surplus value. Owners came out ahead; workers failed to perceive the value of their own labor. Owning capital, which enabled control over the means of production, produced for the capitalist more capital, a return on investment in equipment and labor. Workers, on the other hand, became alienated from their work, failing to understand the value embedded in either their labor or the commodities it produced.

Likewise, both workers and owners occupied positions as consumers of commodities; these too became mystified in the process. Commodities functioned like fetishes, magical talismans out of which one could read market values and fashion, but *not* the production chain that took raw material, transported it to factories, reshaped it through labor, then packaged, marketed, and sold it. Commodities seemingly appeared out of nowhere, as consumers failed to remember their origins in nature and labor.

This system could not succeed without an apparatus that insured and supported a common understanding of property, the ability to say, "This is mine!" and back up the claim. In other words, capitalism required a state structure, with a functional legal system and the threat of force for those who refused to comply. Karl Marx was thus interested in state systems, theorizing the transition from feudalism (an older system in which property rights inhered in the Crown, passed to nobility, who might in turn grant some part of them to vassals, while peasants labored at the bottom of the social scale) to capitalism. It will not be lost on you that Michel Foucault's vision of power—though not Marxist—drew on the same kind of transition from monarchy to modern power.

In recounting the transition to capitalism, Marx suggested a history of primitive accumulation, in which force was mobilized to build stores of capital. One recent scholar renames this moment one of "war capitalism."[7] The greatest primitive accumulation in world history was likely the transfer of New World wealth, in the form of Aztec and Inca gold and silver, into Old World economies moving from feudalism to capitalism. In England, and elsewhere, primitive accumulation often took the form of land enclosures, during which individuals and families were forced off what had been commonly held lands (the *commons*), so that—under new ownership regimes— those lands could be turned to pasture. In that moment, new capitalist elites were able to claim the land as their own. This land would now produce rent, another way in which capital generated income.

As Marx observed, there was a fundamental structural inequality built into a system in which capital produced interest, land produced rent, and labor produced wages, or so it seemed. Each generated value in relation to a market, but workers were subjected not only to competition in a wage labor market (which drove down their wages by making them a commodity), but also to the extraction of value from their work for the benefit of someone else. To say that labor *produced* wages, then, was not wholly accurate. The wage system, according to Marx, organized and controlled labor in order that capital might produce more capital.

The distinction between workers and capitalists (and we might add to that, managers) is easily visible in the relative amount of wealth that each controlled and passed to the next generation. Those distinctions, which take on weight and heft over time, we name as *class*. Workers are able to create and save little wealth and so they pass down little. Capitalists can create and pass down a great deal of wealth, thus reproducing themselves as a cross-generational elite. The inclusion of a managerial class that splits the difference is, it turns out, vital to a belief in class mobility—that you can start as a worker, pass through management, and end as an owner.

Perhaps the greatest signifier of the distance between the production of raw materials and the consumption of commodities is *money*. Imagine a barter economy, in which individuals swap concrete things for other concrete things or (in terms of labor) for discrete tasks. Value, in such cases, is visibly equivalent; it is determined by the individuals involved in the act of trading. Money makes both labor and commodity abstract. "I give you a fish in return for a sack of grain" is quite different from "I give you a fish for a coin, which you got for some fraction of grain I don't know, and with which I might—or might not—be able to get a goose from that guy over there." This process of abstraction has grown increasingly complex: sacks of grain gave way to massive grain elevators, which mystified the products of every farmer involved and opened the way to price speculation.[8] The basic dynamic behind the manipulation of *abstract value* has underpinned every speculation and crash, from the panics of the nineteenth century to the Great Depression and, more recently, the Great Recession.

Marxist analysis has had an interesting career in American Studies. In 1986, Michael Denning suggested that American Studies, as a form of "radical cultural critique," had served as something of a substitute for an American Marxism, which had never really materialized.[9] Denning was one of several scholars who were developing and exchanging theoretical tools in Marxist cultural studies around the same time. These included three of our favorite pieces, each of which helped to create what you might call a "usable Gramsci." They reframed key sections of *The Prison Notebooks* in ways that moved his concept of *cultural hegemony* to the center of the field. Each is worth close study: T. J. Jackson Lears, "The Concept of Cultural Hegemony: Problems and Possibilities" (1985), Raymond Williams, "Base and Superstructure in Marxist Cultural Theory" (1973), and Stuart Hall, "Gramsci's Relevance for the Study of Race and Ethnicity" (1986). We encourage you to track them down.

Karl Marx worked in the tradition of *political economy*, which we might think of as the meeting point of economics, political science, history, and philosophy. This field helped inspire the rise of American Studies through the interdisciplinary work of Thorstein Veblen and lesser-known scholars such as Max Handman in the early twentieth century. Subsequent thinking in the field of economics went in very different directions, though, asking technical questions about the supply of money, the power and utility of modeling, the role of the state in regulating markets, the capitalization necessary to take on appropriate amounts of risk, and the place of a Federal Reserve in backing money, among many, many others. Such questions tend to ignore the role of culture in economic behavior, often assuming that human beings act in terms of rational self-interest. This assumption (the intellectual backbone of both *neoclassical economics* and *neoliberalism*) has created a bias for abstract models over empirical historical data in economic thought. Only recently, with the Occupy Wall Street movement and books such as Thomas Piketty's best-selling *Capital in the Twenty-First Century* (2013), has political economy started to make a comeback. This renewed interest in the cultural dimensions of global markets has strongly influenced work in transnational American Studies.

Antonio Gramsci was concerned with why humans sometimes act against their self-interest, how we willingly consent to our own domination, how we internalize ideologies that uphold a particular set of social relations (those pertaining, say, to industrial capitalism), and how these shape our behavior. In that sense, you can see strong resonances with Michel Foucault, Judith Butler, and Angela Davis, as well as the contemporary field of behavioral economics, which dispenses with the assumption that people always act rationally. Like them, Gramsci was particularly interested in the question of "common sense," the ways that unexamined understandings become inscribed in our consciousness. Why, for example, do workers go to work every day to make a product that is sold by the capitalist for far more than the worker's wage? It's not that the industrial bourgeoisie, possessing brute economic power, imposes its views, interests, and values on the hapless working classes, which have no choice but to accept them. Working people have all kinds of ways of making their own worlds rich with meanings, and they are often acutely aware of the inequities of the system.

Rather, in the exercise of what Gramsci calls *cultural hegemony,* the dominant social group *persuades* subordinate groups of the social and cultural rightness of a given ideology. Through this persuasion, dominant groups establish a kind of cultural and moral—as well as political and economic—unity among people possessing wildly disparate interests, who might be expected (according to Marx) to espouse different, if not antagonistic, ideologies. But these disparate interests do not often get in the way of ideological alignment. Why is that? According to Gramsci, the dominant social class, by offering concessions and compromises to subordinate groups, manages to coordinate its cultural interests with those of subordinate groups. They *lead* society by establishing alliances within the realm of cultural meaning, often leaving economic and political differences intact.

Marx focused more on economics than culture, which for him was a kind of *superstructure,* the consequence of particular forms of the economic and social organization that were primary to his analysis. By contrast, Gramsci argued that *culture* was a distinct arena, a kind of battlefield of its own. It was hardly disconnected from economic organization or the state, but it was also partially autonomous. In other words, you could imagine an economic struggle between Main Street and Wall Street taking place at the same time that a struggle in the cultural arena looked very different—say a fight over patriotism or gay marriage, or the meaning of stardom or religious belief or love. Culture, in this sense, was *anything but* a distraction that took people away from the economic or political things that really mattered. Rather, it was a critical part of the entire social system. When a leading class was able to create a cultural consensus among many contesting groups, the moment of consent was special and powerful. Gramsci called this dynamic *hegemony*.

In a sense, almost every moment in time is a moment of hegemony, in one way or another. There will always be a group that seeks to persuade (not just impose or dominate) all other groups of the rightness of its ideological belief systems. And there will always be groups that oppose that dominant group. Gramsci called these groups *counterhegemonic,* since their ideologies ran counter to that of the leaders or the society as a whole. And here's the thing. No group—and no individual—is defined consistently by a single ideology or interest. Dominant groups seek to find common ground and to persuade others to align their interests—even if it means subordinating other struggles about which they care. The result is a complex system of cultural negotiation and tension.

The American 1960s provide a good example. Coming out of the 1950s, the United States might have been described—in the terms of cultural hegemony—as a culture of progress, scientific expertise, state-corporate power, and global reach. A dominant group consolidated cultural meanings around themes of prosperity, consumerism, technical prowess, and anticommunism. Under this umbrella, however, was a roiling sea of counterhegemonic currents. The black freedom movement was developing the tools it would use to try to delegitimize segregation as abnormal and establish equal rights as a dominant common sense around which most Americans could agree. As the Vietnam War heated up, a counterhegemonic movement formed in opposition, and it too developed modes and means of persuasion that it hoped would convince others to follow its antiwar lead. Countercultural groups, disenchanted with the cultural logics of conformity, began offering new systems of belief that emphasized freedom and communitarianism. They, too, sought to persuade others to follow their leadership. All of these movements—and of course there were others—sought to persuade a range of other groups to throw in their lot with a new hegemonic consensus.

Women were active in all these movements, and many of them found that their contributions did not receive the respect they deserved. Building on a long history of feminist thought, a new counterhegemonic movement—the women's liberation movement—emerged in the late 1960s and early 1970s. This example underscores the complexity of Gramsci's picture of the social world. You might imagine women who subordinated their feminist interests to what they perceived as the greater cause of the black freedom movement or peace movement. Such women would have been making a consensual deal within the framework of hegemony and counterhegemony. They perceived their strongest interests to lie not in feminism, but in other movements and were thus willing to join a social group that did not always honor their interests as women. They gave consent, in a manner of speaking, to patriarchy—even while laying the groundwork for a more wholesale social revolution to overthrow that patriarchy.

As particular goals were achieved such as ending direct U.S. involvement in the Vietnam War, some women active in these movements changed their cultural alignments, joining different counterhegemonic groups based *primarily* on feminism. Many of those groups were formed among white, middle-class women, and the cultural logic of their feminism represented *those* particular interests, those particular subjectivities. When Helen Reddy sang in 1972, "I am woman, hear me roar! In numbers too big to ignore!" she was not really including a lot of women in her count. Part of the significance of Angela Davis's intersectional feminism rested in her refusal to accede to the pragmatic logic of hegemony—her refusal to divide the global struggle for freedom and justice into a series of localized identities and interests.

This counterhegemonic challenge to white, middle-class feminism from women of color compelled feminist academics to examine a number of assumptions from which they operated as both political activists and scholars. Clearly, one of the fundamentals of Western feminist thinking—that women, as both subject and object of feminism's program, share common natures, common needs, common wants, common desires, and a common oppression—could no longer be held so determinedly. Women of color had made it clear that differences in race, sexuality, class, nationality, culture, religion, age, and ethnicity must undermine any such notions of an essential femininity or womanliness upon which feminism might rest. In short, when women of color began to subject the categories of the white middle-class feminist movement to scrutiny and criticism, feminist scholars sought alternative ways of thinking about identity, subjectivity, culture, and power.

This is what it means to think, theoretically, in terms of *hegemony:* a nuanced, complex, holistic theoretical picture. It's not simply about subjectivity . . . or ideology . . . or the power of the state . . . or of the economic system. It's about all of these things at once. Gramsci encourages us to view the cultural realm as interconnected with the social, political, and economic worlds in a system full of inputs, contingencies, and unpredictable outcomes. Consent must be won more often than it is imposed, and everything that seems counterhegemonic and oppositional is at the same time also working, in some way, in the interests of the dominant hegemonic cultural ideologies and discourses through which individuals make sense of the world. In this sense, Gramsci helps make a *different* kind of sense of Foucault's assertion that power is not simply domination from above, but is rather an almost infinite negotiation that flows through an unimaginably complicated *cultural* system. In many ways, the root of that system rests with the popular culture that is visible through texts, and created and consumed through the institutions and formations American Studies so often takes as its objects of study.

When the police or the army comes out shooting (as they have on many occasions in the United States), you can bet that the organizing power of cultural hegemony has broken down, and cultural consensus has been unable to neutralize real grievance. When that happens, the forces of the state and the market will have lost their authority—at least with the people being shot at—and it may well take both additional force *and* concessions on the part of the leading class to restore *hegemonic* consensus. But when crude and violent force proves unnecessary (which has *also* been true for much of United States history), you can also bet that the mechanisms found in cultural meaning, production, and consumption have created sufficient consensus for the society to function and for individuals to make lives and meanings in relation to social power. When we interpret individual texts, assemble them into project archives, and seek to put those things into context, we're trying to figure out how individual human beings negotiated their social and cultural worlds—how they made sense of hegemonic consensus and counterhegemonic opposition.

In this light, it is perhaps useful to revisit one more time the metaphor of the car and the shifting of gears across different registers of interpretation and analysis. These kinds of theoretical insights offer new possibilities for the very first steps of interpretation, the close reading of texts. It is easy to find in texts either evidence of domination from above or resistance from below. Most texts, however, when read deeply and complexly, will yield up moments of *each,* and will often demonstrate complex negotiations among would-be dominations and wistful resistances. They are both hegemonic and counter-hegemonic, in Gramsci's terms—and thus complex cultural statements of larger social dynamics. Similar complications are usually visible in our archives as well, which we read *both* for generic similarity (perhaps hegemonic) and for curious exceptions (perhaps counterhegemonic). And the same complications permeate institutions and formations. Dime novels demonstrate exactly this kind of complexity. So too do blues tunes, advertisements, photographs, movies, WPA archives, and even *carceral* formations. In this sense, we hope that the chart we keep offering as a reference now makes a new kind of sense.

Method	Object	Action
Interpretation	Text	Perceive
Curation	Archive	Collect
Analysis	Genre	Categorize
Contextualization	Formation	Expand
Generalization	Power	Connect

We haven't touched the full world of theory. Not even. We didn't say much about psychoanalysis, for example, or deconstruction. We left out one of our favorite theorists, Walter Benjamin. Oh, and another, Lauren Berlant. And another, Pierre Bourdieu. And we skipped various traditions from ethnic studies, the social sciences, and social psychology. We missed Mel Chen, and Lisa Lowe, and many, many others, all of whom we hope you'll investigate (our theory mixtape at the end of chapter 2 only scratches the surface!). What we *have* tried to do, however, is weave together four useful clusters of theory. Each allows us to consider the possibilities, limitations, and strategies of *praxis,* the linkage between theory and action. Each offers historical and diagnostic contexts, structural critiques of complex power relations, and possibilities for personal and collective action. The gradualism implicit in Gramsci's theory sometimes proves frustrating to those wishing to drive rapid social change. And yet, *hegemony* offers useful ways of thinking through both barriers to change *and* the occasional moment of rapid cultural and social transformation. It serves, for many, as the intellectual grounding for praxis, which draws on the integrations of critical, activist, and performative possibility.

Four clusters, we think, are probably more than enough for now. We've picked integrating threads—subjectivity, power, culture—that have strong connections to one another. They allow us to triangulate theoretical traditions focused on subject, identity, state, and market in such a way that—we hope—forms a useful base for further exploration. It's an idiosyncratic version of an American Studies Theory 101, we grant that. But we hope that you take the next course, and the course after that, with other books and other authors.

PART THREE

From Jotting It Down to Writing It Up

NINE

———

A Few Thoughts on Ideas and Arguments

THIS BOOK HAS TRIED TO PULL together a range of techniques, strategies, and theories that can serve as a springboard for work in American Studies. In each case, we have distilled large bodies of work down to a few pages. We hope that you now have a better sense of how to read texts, build archives, follow cultural change through institutions and formations, and join a theoretical conversation. We also hope you feel comfortable situating ideas within the history and historiography of American Studies—and maybe even making your own mixtapes. One final challenge, then: to craft your work into some form of communicative expression, one worthy of your talents in close reading, curation, contextualization, and theory.

There are many different ways of sharing work, from video to the spoken word. But for all the expressive possibilities opened up by new media, *narration* continues to lie at the core of academic communication, particularly the ability to think systematically about *written* expression. Our closing discussions, therefore, focus on how to organize, revise, and put the finishing touches on your writing. We recognize, of course, that you can turn to any number of writing guides out there for detailed advice on questions of style and composition. They range from classics like *The Elements of Style,* by E. B. White and William Strunk, Jr., to the array of digital guides published by various university writing centers. The following notes and examples will be aimed specifically at writing in the American Studies tradition.

INSPIRATION

So how do you come up with a project in the first place? Everyone has ideas about ideas, and here are two of ours: direct *problem solving* and indirect *creative observation.* Despite the names, they are both avenues into creative thinking. In the former, one identifies a problem that emerges out of a topic you care about. Let's take sports, for example. There are some standard ways to identify such a problem:

- Contradiction ("Why was Marla suspended for five games and Trudy only for one when both were caught using the same performance enhancing drugs?")
- Correction of Claim ("You say that Jim Thorpe was the only important American Indian athlete of the early twentieth century . . . and I think you're wrong.")
- Anomaly ("During the Cold War, why didn't the United States and USSR push to dominate soccer—the most popular sport in the world—with the same time and resources they devoted to victories in the Olympics?")
- Constellation ("Novak Djokovic, Ana Ivanovic, Jelena Jankovic, Janko Tipsarevic, Jelena Dokic, and Viktor Troicki—why are there so many good Serbian tennis players?")
- Comparison ("Why doesn't the WNBA receive as much attention as the NBA?")

We could keep going with problems, each with different avenues for solutions. Get the easy and obvious ones out of the way first. Next, keep chewing on the problem. Think about it a lot. Then misdirect your attention and *don't* think about it. Go for a walk. Take a long shower. Or wake up fifteen minutes early and just muse in a half-dream state. The most interesting solutions—the best ideas—are likely to emerge from your unconscious, in a process of directed creative thinking.

If "direct" methods begin with a problem in need of a solution, "indirect" methods often show up as a solution in search of a problem. Here, the central act of creative thinking comes not from a challenge, but from simply paying close attention to the world around you, and pulling oddities and anomalies out of the stream of existence. These are the *itchy* moments when something strikes you as just a little off.

("Yeah, playing baseball with a tennis ball is really a waste of time . . .")

Usually, we shrug those moments off and keep on doing what we're doing. But if we slow down, grab onto the weirdness and scratch at it a bit, we'll often find that we have a new idea.

("... because each kind of ball is built to match the court, field, alley, course, or pitch where the sport is played. And each carries certain kinds of meanings: spin and speed; power and control; unpredictability. And the combination of ball, field, and action creates additional meanings: strategic management of time, for example, or aggressive conquest of space.")

Suddenly, you're in American Studies terrain! When you find yourself saying, "huh ... that's strange," pay close attention. You could have an idea on your hands.

PROJECT GATEWAYS

So maybe you have an idea? How do you develop it further? We have suggested that there are (at least) *four* main pathways into an American Studies analysis. The first pathway is to begin with an evocative *text*. Perhaps you are taken by a building, or a film, or a blog. You might wonder, for example, about *Atanarjuat: The Fast Runner* (2001), a film made entirely in the Inuktitut language in Nunavut, the northernmost territory of Canada, by an Inuit cast and crew. The film's cinematography included innovations in color balance for dealing with the snowy, white-saturated landscape. From that single text as a starting point, you can build a kind of archive. You might consider film as a vehicle of language preservation. Or you might compare it to other films that push the limits of lighting, including *Moonlight* (2016), which uses extreme color contrasts to evoke the humid, gleaming darkness of night in Miami, and *The Exiles* (1961), which does the same with smoke and steam to represent the atmosphere of Los Angeles overnight. All three of these films, in turn, could lead you to larger theoretical questions around gender scripts across spatial and racial lines, or how the technologies of color in film contribute to perceptions of race. But whatever direction you take your investigation, your point of entry would be a single specific text, which you would then surround with other texts, building your archive and moving from context to formations, and then to theory, and then back and forth across all of the different registers. This sequence matches the structure that we have explored in this book, but it's certainly not the only way to think about a project.

Second, your project could originate in an *archive,* either a preexisting collection or one you constitute yourself. Consider the case of James Edward Deeds, Jr., a longtime resident at Missouri State Hospital No. 3, who bound a collection of 283 drawings for his mother, which was then accidentally thrown into the trash, where it was rescued by a young boy, who kept the album for forty years before it entered the world of dealers and exhibitions of so-called outsider art in 2006. That's a fantastic ready-made archive, to which you might add additional texts: details on Deeds's treatment at the Missouri State Hospital, information about his family, and other examples of outsider art. In such a case, your project originates not from a single text, but a collection.

The third pathway would be to begin with *context*. You might be curious about a particular moment, cultural location, or category of texts. One example might be the rise of "mixed race" as a category in the late twentieth century. Rather than starting with a specific text, such a topic might begin with cultural and social context. Your questions would arise out of the context, but you would then go in search of texts (that is, evidence) that would answer your questions and provide the basis for your argument. Such texts might include the U.S. Census, but also magazines and organizations aimed at serving the parents of mixed-race children, images of mixed-race celebrities, and so on. The creation of social, political, and economic structures around the category of "mixed race" would prove critical to your analysis, raising questions of institutions and formations. And since race is a key location for theoretical work, a project on mixed-race identity would be engaged with social theory from the beginning.

Another example of a research topic rooted in context is the digital asset and payment system bitcoin. While the bitcoin world is full of texts (from glib manifestos to speculations on the identity of its mysterious founder, "Satoshi Nakamoto"), bitcoin itself is not really a text. Rather, it is a formation—a circuit or network. You might locate secondary sources and archives—there's an entire genre of "death of bitcoin" writing, for instance— and you might engage any number of theoretical possibilities. But your analysis might also focus on bitcoin in relation to *other* formations and institutions. You might compare or contextualize it in relation to earlier systems, such as Digicash, Open Coin, b-money, or Bit Gold. You might analyze it in terms of the qualities that make it a formation: things like decentralization, encryption, peer-to-peer, finite systems, core organization, and the complexities of transactional inputs and outputs. You might place it in dialogue with institutional structures such as national banks, online vendors, and bitcoin exchanges. To track these things, you would still find yourself building an archive of texts (descriptive, technical, operational, and economic). And these could move you toward theoretical questions. Is bitcoin is really a currency? Is it yet another speculative bubble . . . or something new? Is it a critique of neoliberal economic institutions . . . or the ultimate manifestation of neoliberalism's logic?

Fourth, and finally, you might conceptualize a project in terms of *theory*. You might be interested in understanding why small towns—especially very small towns—seem to be more politically conservative. Is social change perceived as more disruptive in sparsely populated areas? If so, why? And are such places *actually* more conservative, or is your intuition wrong? These are broad questions, and to answer them, you would need to move across the methodological spectrum of text, context, and, of course, theory. A question rooted in theory opens the possibility of enormous, almost unmanageable, archives; the challenge will lie in narrowing rather than locating. Will you focus exclusively on rural areas? What about conservative pockets within cities? Theoretical questions also pose distinct challenges—and opportunities—when it comes to engaging with existing scholarship. Have you been inspired by a particular theorist? How might their writings illuminate your research? Have other writers offered competing theoretical frameworks for understanding resistance to social change? You might find that your topic has mostly been explored through ethnographic methods. Why do you think that is? Is there something about the rural that screams "anthropology!" and the urban that screams "history!" . . . or is this one of those itchy contradictions that demands a whole separate project?

The common denominator across all these questions and gateways is the necessity of paying close attention to method. That attention will likely move in several directions at once as you engage the actual process of analysis, which is full of dips and turns, false starts, and do-overs. As your analysis becomes more detailed, and as genuinely interesting bits and pieces of knowledge begin to emerge, you'll want to think about how these elements will take shape in an actual piece of writing.

WHAT NOT TO DO

Let's start by pointing out three strategies that you *don't* want to use. The first structures a narrative focused not on your actual subject, but on your own process of research and thinking. Perhaps you discovered an extremely interesting text, then thought hard about it, then consulted secondary sources, and then had a revealing conversation with a friend. These events can offer a storyline—"first, this happened, then that happened!"—but they center on your experience, not on your analysis. Unless your own experience is spell-binding (and sometimes, these kinds of *quest* narratives can be exactly that, though the bar is high), it's not likely to hold a reader.

A second strategy will likely be familiar to you—the standard five-paragraph structure that American schools have drilled into students for generations. In that form, you have an introductory paragraph and a concluding paragraph. The first will establish context and state a thesis. That last will summarize the argument and restate the thesis. In between, three (or more) body paragraphs will each argue a distinct point. In other words (as the form is often framed): "tell them what you're going to tell them; tell them; and then tell them what you told them." This form isn't *evil* or anything. It's great for an essay exam, for instance. But when you finish summarizing your argument in your fourth or fifth sentence, a reader has to be as interested in *the way you make the argument* as the actual argument itself. After all, if you've read the first paragraph, you already know the argument. This form is an example of what we might think of as a simplistic form of persuasion. We can—and must—be more subtle.

The third trap is to jump directly into complicated theoretical terms such as *neoliberalism, biopolitics, settler colonialism,* or *homonationalism.* Or worse yet: pack four or five of them into your title. These terms are important but complicated concepts, which means you should work up to them slowly—especially if you're interested in reaching readers who are not already steeped in the literature of American Studies. This doesn't mean ignoring specialized vocabularies. One need only spend a few minutes with Randall Munroe's brilliant but comical book, *Thing Explainer: Complicated Stuff in Simple Words* (2015)—which tries to explain phenomena like tectonic plates using only the thousand most common words in the English language—to see that abandoning jargon would be a disaster. But all too often, students feel pressured to demonstrate expertise by *starting* with difficult and fashionable keywords rather than developing sound research questions.

WHAT TO DO

How *should* you think about organizing your project? Let's begin with two large categories: narrative and analysis, which function as distinct organizing strategies for a paper, article, or book. Narrative refers to the telling of stories that offer descriptions, introduce characters and settings, and build the sense of drama that makes for compelling writing. Analysis refers to breaking down a complicated issue into smaller parts and then building them back up into an argument. The five-paragraph form emphasizes analysis ("Here is my thesis. Here are my main points. They add up to an argument."). It does so, however, at the expense of storytelling, which is notably absent. The "showing-my-process" approach, by contrast, emphasizes narrative ("I did this, then this, then that."). It tells a story—but it does so at the expense of analysis, which often can make for a pretty boring and uninspired story.

The challenge, then, is to find ways to integrate the two organizing registers. Underpinning everything is your analysis and argument. Floating above and generating interest is your narrative, which should gradually build in intensity. Here are three basic principles that can help you navigate the relation.

- Establish a rhythm of *beats* and *stepbacks* that takes a reader through the two connected registers—narrative and analysis—that make up your story.
- Build small arguments, and from them move to larger arguments in a hierarchy of questions and answers.
- Begin not with a thesis statement, but with a question or conundrum driven by a story or character.

Our highest aspiration—the Holy Grail of American Studies writing—should be to produce descriptive and narrative writing that *also* functions analytically. Such synergy, though, is hard to come by. More likely, you'll need to think about how you toggle readers back and forth between narrative and analysis. Think of developing little snippets of storyline or description—anecdotes, accounts, testimonies, and the like. Call these *beats*. You might assemble one or two beats in a sequence—that is, one or two discrete pieces of narrative storyline. If you've done it well, these beats should raise a question. To answer that question requires a different kind of writing, one in which you *step back* from your position as narrator and assume a new position as interpreter or analyst. Think about your writing, then, as an ordered sequence of *beats* and *stepbacks* that lead a reader through both a storyline and an analysis.[1]

This kind of rhythm is not easy to describe, so let's turn to a brief example. What follows is our humble attempt at an introductory *beat*—a narrative sketch of a historical event (one that you've likely heard about many times before).

On a hot June day in 1876, Lt. Colonel George Armstrong Custer led his men down a ravine in what would later become part of the state of Montana. They crossed a meandering river. Indians called it the Greasy Grass; white explorers, the Little Bighorn. On the other side lay an enormous village of Lakota Sioux, Cheyennes, and Arapahos. The men of the village met Custer's troops—some say in the water, some say at the edge of the village—and pushed them back. Some soldiers retreated to a deep ravine, where they died. Others made their way back across the river and to higher ground, the site of the archetypal "last stand."

Note the ways this paragraph tells a story through a series of events, almost like a plot. Custer leads his men across a river into a village. The Indians resist, pushing Custer's men back. The battle will conclude with the deaths of the soldiers. Note also the ways that the story offers descriptive details: *who* (Custer, Lakotas, Cheyennes, and Arapahos), *where* (a river in Montana called either the Little Bighorn or the Greasy Grass), *when* (June 1876), and *what* (a battle that ends in the death of Custer and his men). Finally, the story also tries to set a certain emotional tone: we see differences in perspective (Indians and non-Indians have different names for the river) and interpretation (was the turning point of the battle in the water or at the village?), reminding us of ambiguities still at the heart of the story.

We'll follow that beat with a second one, this time engaging the painting that represents the battle we've just narrated (figure 37). Here, we'll offer *only* the descriptive details necessary to support the interpretation that is to come.

This image, painted by Cassilly Adams in 1885 and later elaborated as a chromolithograph by Otto Becker, purports to show what happened that day. The enormous painting measures over nine by sixteen feet and is rich with detail. A series of subtle "pointers" leads one's eye to the figure of Custer, who stands, sword upraised, in the left center of the image. Two contour lines just below the horizon join together in a gentle "v" above Custer's head. Immediately behind Custer, a row of three Indians on horseback points to him as well. Below him, and to the right, a wounded soldier forms a blue line that also leads to Custer, and to the left a dying Indian—slightly more brown than the surroundings—fills out the frame that surrounds the general. These framings are important, because Custer is portrayed wearing light brown buckskin clothing, which blends and blurs into the landscape—a curious way of neutralizing, through color and tone, the hero of the last stand.

The paragraph begins by reinforcing the sense of ambiguity we sought to evoke in the first paragraph ("purports to show what happened that day"). Next we offer two forms of description: first, the enormous size of the

FIGURE 37. Otto Becker, *Custer's Last Fight* (1894), chromolithograph after a painting by
Cassilly Adams (1885).

painting; second, a quick unpacking of the image, organized around a series
of lines, forms, frames, and shapes that point the viewer's eye to the figure of
Custer. The paragraph closes with an implicit question, couched in additional description: why is Custer, the subject of the painting, muted to the
point that one has to follow formal pointers and work hard to see him? Why
isn't he a more obvious focal point?

Through a narrative beat and a descriptive beat, we've established—without ever saying so explicitly—a sense of ambiguity that characterizes the
event and the image. It's time for a stepback that will move us from storytelling elements into analytical ones:

*Perhaps this ambivalent portrayal has something to do with the ambiguity
of the last stand itself. Last stands and Indian surrounds have long been evocative tropes in the cultural atmosphere of the American frontier, and it is not
hard to imagine a generic image: Indians circle a wagon, brave but doomed
frontiersmen stand back to back, white men go down fighting but take plenty of
Indians with them. This iconography served the ideological agenda of westward
expansion, but it took on a very different resonance in the aftermath of the*

Custer fight. The Little Bighorn was at once a triumph for Indian people and a harbinger of the almost immediate defeat of the Lakota people on the plains. The United States Army waged a brutal winter campaign in 1877 and forced most Lakota people onto reservations. In Adams's painting, then, both sides function as underdogs. Custer and his men will lose out against overwhelming odds; so too will the Indians. In the late nineteenth century, Americans began feeling the first pangs of nostalgic regret about the end of the Indian Wars, and it is not hard to imagine a viewer feeling an odd kind of sympathy—simultaneous and ambivalent—for both sets of combatants.

It should come as no surprise that the stepback paragraph is more complex than the narratives. In this example, you can see a number of analytical strategies at work. There is a descriptive account of the *generic* qualities of "the last stand." There is the invocation of an *archive* of similar stories of last stands and Indian "surrounds." That archive is flagged with words that insure we are thinking analytically: "trope," "cultural," "iconography," and "ideological agenda." Words such as these ask readers to make connections between the text and broader cultural contexts. A key analytical moment then follows, as the paragraph turns to the question of change over time (the iconography of the last stand "took on a very different resonance in the aftermath of the Custer fight"). Here's a very specific analytical claim, with a cause and an effect: the Custer fight *causes* a shift in cultural meanings. And the analysis builds in the following sentence, laying out a seeming paradox: the victory at the Little Bighorn led to a rapid defeat. This dynamic—contradictory and thus ambiguous—will, we anticipate, *explain* the nature of the shift in cultural meaning. The next sentence gives us, quickly, the facts of the rapid Indian defeat. And the two sentences that follow elaborate, clarify, and summarize the argument: as Americans became nostalgic about the closing of the frontier, it became possible, perhaps for the first time, to see *both* Indians and soldiers as sympathetic figures, a complex *structure of feeling* that made both the event and the painting compelling and evocative.

You can see how the stepback does a significant amount of analytical work. That work is connected to the earlier *beats,* but goes on to establish a sequence of linked analytical claims:

· The Last Stand is a trope, with an archive, and is thus representative of larger cultural forms.

· The Custer defeat changed the meanings of the Last Stand trope in American culture.

- This cultural change was also linked to the rapid defeat of Indian people, which was spurred by the Custer defeat.
- The nature of that change can be captured by the word "nostalgia," which motivated a complex emotional structure of feeling in which both Indians and soldiers could be celebrated and mourned simultaneously.
- Those complex meanings have made Custer's Last Stand a powerful trope of the ambiguity of conquest—and so it is not surprising that an artist would paint an enormous image, characterized by . . . ambiguity.

The stepback requires energy and attention from the reader, who now deserves the pleasures of another beat or two. Here's one that both *describes* and offers a bit of additional *analysis.*

It turns out that a tremendous number of Americans actually saw the painting—or a version of it. Shortly after its completion, the Anheuser-Busch Brewing Company acquired the copyright and produced tens of thousands of lithographs of the image. Though not as large as the original, they were of substantial proportion, and, as a promotional gift from the brewer, they ended up gracing the walls of saloons and bars across the nation.

And we could keep going. You can see how a paper that begins with this painting might unfold in a series of beats and stepbacks, each advancing argument or narrative—or both. And if you look closely, you'll see that such a paper would probably come back again and again to the painting for descriptive beats that open up analytical stepbacks. Who is that *other* figure in buckskin, standing at the bottom of the image? And who is the man in the red shirt to his right, taking aim at Custer with a rifle? (They are a *very* ambiguous pair!) Why are some of the Indian warriors carrying what look like African shields? These little descriptive snippets demand further analysis. You can imagine other story elements as well: details from the life of Custer; accounts of the battle from the many Indian participants; details from the life of Cassilly Adams; more information on the lithographs and the role of the company in distributing the image.

Out of these beats, you can also imagine a second, connected series of analytical stepbacks. These might include a discussion of the meaning of the apparently treacherous white frontiersmen. Or of the gender politics of American drinkers contemplating Custer's fall in the homosocial environment of the turn-of-the century saloon. Or of the goals of the Anheuser-Busch Brewing Company in establishing a distribution network, not solely for beer, but also for art. Or of the global networks of primitivist symbols that would allow a lithographer to imagine African shields in Montana. It turns out this final question has already been tackled at length by a number of scholars. Historian Paul Andrew Hutton noted the African shields; James O. Gump directly compared conflicts involving the Sioux and the Zulu.[2] James Clifford, in *The Predicament of Culture: Twentieth-Century Ethnography, Literature, and Art* (1988) and *Routes: Travel and Translation in the Late Twentieth Century* (1997), explored how global networks helped build tropes of primitivism. And the Last Stand itself was used in the title of one of the landmark books of the twentieth century, Vine Deloria, Jr.'s *Custer Died for Your Sins: An Indian Manifesto* (1969). Our sample paragraphs do not tackle this kind of historiography, but soon enough they would if we were to turn our investigation into a full-blown essay.

The result of the beats / stepbacks strategy is a creative fusion of description, interpretation, and storytelling with a structured analytical trajectory. It is not the only approach available in American Studies, but remember— this is a user's guide, not an owner's manual.

HIERARCHIES OF QUESTIONS AND ANSWERS

Whatever specific approach you choose, your writing project's argument will build to a final conclusion in which you do, in fact, state a central thesis. That thesis will likely be the answer to the *one overarching question* that powers the entire project. Our view is that, while any project will attempt to answer a number of big questions, the best organized and most coherent work is able to be framed around a *single* large question. If your project is a book, your question must be complex and significant enough to demand hundreds of pages of organized evidence and argument—no easy task. If the project is an article or paper, then the question will be more tightly focused. An example: Phil's 1998 book, *Playing Indian,* is framed around a single question: Why have white Americans so often dressed up, played, and performed as American Indians?

Here's the thing: the single overarching question cannot be answered by turning directly to evidence. The details of the Boston Tea Party, for instance, are not enough. Rather, we must turn to the analytical connections drawn among several *other* big questions that the overarching question raises. Who, exactly, dressed up, played, and performed as American Indians, and when? How often did these things happen? What was the nature of the performances? Was it only white Americans? What did Indians think about the practice? Let's call the overarching question the *first order question,* and let's call those others *second order questions.* The second order questions, in turn, require another register of analytical connections drawn among *third order questions.* And we could go on. As you move down the hierarchy from first order to lower order questions, you'll find yourself also moving across a spectrum from the abstract to the concrete, from large generalizable claims to specific pieces of evidence. You'll quite likely move from *why* and *how* questions, which are interpretive and analytical, to *who, what, where, when* questions, which tend to be evidentiary.

Here, *hierarchy* is an organizing principle for prose and analysis. A hierarchy does not have to devalue its lower reaches. Indeed, if we return to the question of beats and stepbacks, we'll see that *who, what, where, when* questions are critical to our writing because they provide the valuable tools that make narrative possible. As we sift to the level of the paragraph and the sentence—*sixth, seventh, eighth* order questions—we'll be working with the stuff that readers *like* to read: stories of people doing things in specific times and places. The first order question is critical; so are all the others. They work together, and if you fail to give each one the care it deserves, your writing will be the worse for it.

When beginning a project (or when you need a reboot, as often happens), it's extremely useful to take some time, clear your head, and write down all the possible questions that your project generates. It should be a long list that runs from the very concrete to the ill-formed and abstract. Share that list with a friend and see what the two of you can add by thinking together. Sift your list into *how* and *why* questions, on the one hand, and *who, what, where,* and *when* questions, on the other. Try to arrange them in an organizational tree. Then think about a linear arrangement for your hierarchy. What questions have to be answered first, before you can answer others? Doing this will give you a rough sense of your *analytical structure.* On top of that, you can now overlay your *narrative structure.* And then, you'll be well positioned to start writing. You'll craft a sequence of beats and stepbacks—a set of "lower order" beats that tell stories, offer detail, establish character and setting, followed by "higher order" stepbacks that offer interpretation and analysis.

CONUNDRUMS

If beats and stepbacks can come in handy through the middle section of your writing project, there is still the question of how to get in and get out. Our advice, again, is to begin not with a thesis, but with a question. So your introductory paragraph should not lay out the context of your argument. Rather, it should narrate a small story or an intriguing description, one that produces a *teaser question*. That teaser question is probably not your primary research question; that will come later in your introduction. Rather, it pulls readers in with narrative, pushing them forward through the framing of a *conundrum:* a small mystery that they must have answered.

Think of the conundrum paragraph as being analogous to the opening scene in one of the many police procedurals that have appeared on American televisions over the last decades. Innocent tourists stroll through Central Park, only to peer under a tree and discover . . . a dead body. Who is he? Who killed him? How did he get there? These are the questions that power viewers through the commercial break and into the first segment of the show. Your conundrum paragraph, when well executed, should do something similar, enticing readers with unanswered questions rather than pummeling them with (as yet) unproven assertions. Here's an example from the opening pages of Jennifer Price's book, *Flight Maps: Adventures with Nature in Modern America* (1999). Notice how the chain of details pulls you in. It's then followed by an extremely quick story (four short punchy sentences), and then the conundrum.

> They say that when a flock of passenger pigeons flew across the countryside, the sky grew dark. The air rumbled and turned cold. Bird dung fell like hail. Horses stopped and trembled in their tracks, and chickens went in to roost. . . . We know the exact day of the extinction: the last passenger pigeon died on September 1, 1914, in the Cincinnati Zoo. The last of seven captive birds, she was named Martha. In the wild, however, the species was effectively extinct by 1900. The number of birds had declined rapidly, almost in an instant, from billions in the 1870s to dozens in the 1890s. *What happened?*

In the conclusion, your writing project (particularly if it is a shorter form) might well return to your opening conundrum to pull readers back in, reminding them of how the journey began. This closing of the circle, when done well, can be both satisfying in a narrative sense, and extremely useful as an occasion for summary. Price, for example, ends her chapter this way, answering the *what happened* question quite precisely—and then raising another question, this time more poetic than analytical.

> As the market hunter H. Clay Merritt proposed, what really happened was "progress": the transition to a more urban, long-distance, economically

expanding high-technology world. In the 1870s, progress in America meant shooting the wild pigeons by the millions for profit. But it also meant the removal of the pigeon feet from the pigeon pie. After that happens, how do we know what kind of pie it is?

Conundrums are not simply useful for introductions and conclusions. You can see the ways that they have affinities with the beat / stepback strategy. Indeed, you can narrate lots of conundrums throughout a writing project as a way of hooking your readers, getting them to follow you for pages and pages. The next time you read a piece of writing that pulls you along, stop and break it down. Odds are that you'll find a series of conundrums, a rhythm of beats and stepbacks, and a well-ordered analytical framework.

FINAL THOUGHTS

There's much more to be said about writing. Read novels—not just academic writing—to stay grounded in the craft of beautiful prose. Don't try to edit a whole paper on your computer screen. Print it out and lay it out on a big table so you can literally see your argument. Be relentless in editing yourself (no easy task!). And so on. The bottom line? You could do worse than to keep in mind the advice offered by Carlo Rotella in the epigraph to this book: "Follow the money, and tell good stories."

What does Rotella mean by this? *Follow the money* means tracking the mechanisms of culture—which are so often driven by markets and exchanges—through the institutions and formations of their production, distribution, and consumption to the point at which you can see the visible workings of power. But *good stories* are also critical. That means finding good textual evidence and interpreting it well, always hunting for larger significance and possibility. And just as important is *telling*. For us, that means, in the end, putting your work into careful and powerful prose that speaks with purpose, intent, and awareness to an audience. Find the story, make sense of the story, and then tell the story well.

TEN

Dispenser

A CASE STUDY

IN THE FIRST SECTION OF THIS BOOK, we set out to define the field of American Studies in terms of its *historiography*—multiple genealogies of scholarly writing that have explored American vernacular expression, framed social and intellectual problems, and engaged other disciplines. These genealogies have unfolded in relation to both a changing array of institutional constraints and a powerful history of agenda-setting social movements. Next, we sought to define American Studies in terms of *methodology,* which we framed as a flexible set of interpretive, analytical, and theoretical possibilities. Trying to put a bit of structure on those possibilities, we suggested thinking across five distinct methodological registers, each with an object of inquiry and a way of approaching it:

Method	*Object*	*Action*
Interpretation	Text	Perceive
Curation	Archive	Collect
Analysis	Genre	Categorize
Contextualization	Formation	Expand
Generalization	Power	Connect

Along the way, we have discussed a number of books that, we think, offer useful—though widely divergent—examples of American Studies writing that capture both its methodological breadth and its historiographical sensibilities. Now, we'd like to give you a concrete example of American Studies work in practice.

We'll begin with a *text,* an object pulled out of the slipstream of everyday life, something so mundane it would not seem to have much to say. The

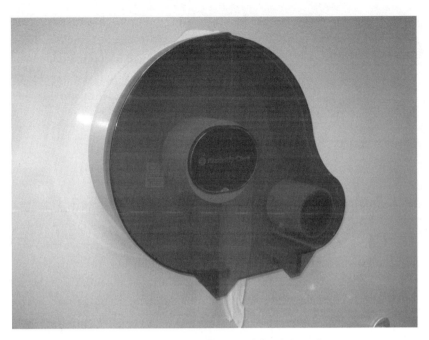

FIGURE 38. Mysterious Unknown Object. Photograph by Philip Deloria.

analysis moves through stages roughly aligned with the five registers outlined in this book, so it should feel familiar to you. We want to be clear about one thing: we are *not* writing up the case study as if it were a polished final draft, drawing on the advice we've given you about structuring and writing; rather, we're walking you through the guts of the analysis itself in order to slow down the record—as we did with Parton's "Jolene" at the outset—and show you some of the stops and starts, the missed opportunities later reclaimed, and the shifts back and forth across analytical registers.

INTRODUCTION: THE CONUNDRUM

One day a few years ago, Phil found himself in the restroom in the hallway near his office, on the third floor of Haven Hall, on the University of Michigan campus, in Ann Arbor, Michigan. It was a day like any other— except that, for some reason, he found himself staring curiously at the toilet paper dispenser, noticing, as if for the first time, its extremely odd shape (figure 38). It was a moment of "itchiness," one of those momentary experiences that sometimes produce interesting questions. Best to pay attention and scratch the itch! Like many dispensers, this one was roughly circular—but it had an odd rounded protrusion bursting out of one side, which completely destroyed the symmetry of the circle. "Why?" he wondered. "Why ruin the perfectly good circular wheel of toilet paper by putting this ugly bulge on the side?"

DEFAMILIARIZATION AND CLOSE READING

To answer this seemingly trivial question, we might begin by looking methodically, and in detail, at the object. In other words, we'll start with a close reading of it as a *text*. First, though, we've got to try to remove from our heads any sense that we *know* that we're talking about a toilet paper dispenser. We'll try to make the object as unfamiliar as possible, in order to force ourselves to make a thorough description and not simply to look, but to *see*. So get it *out* of your head that this object has a name or a function. Imagine it instead as something dropped here from an alternate universe.

We'll begin by observing some basic empirical facts about the object:

- There are two other protrusions from the smooth circular sides, both on what one might call the "bottom" of the object. These are bluntly triangular in shape.
- From the bottom of the triangular protrusion on the left to the top of the circle measures 16 1/4 inches. From the upper left of the circle to the farthest edge of the smooth circular protrusion measures 19 1/4 inches. The diameter of the large circle, from left to right, measures 14 3/4 inches. The diameter of the small protruding circular area—let's call it "the bulge" as a descriptive shorthand—measures 8 inches. The flat section on the bottom, between the two blunt triangles, measures 5 inches.
- The "front" of the object is made of a smoky gray, partially translucent, plastic substance. The "back" of the object is also plastic, but tan, opaque, and different in texture from the "front."
- These are two different pieces, and they can be detached from one another. The "back" piece is firmly attached to the wall by means of five screws. The very top of the object contains a small hole, near the seam between the "front" and "back" pieces. At this point, the tan "back" piece loses its smooth circular feel and flares out.

- The center of the object has a darker-colored circular pattern, in which one can read the words "Kimberly-Clark." Inside the object, one can barely see a white square of paper that contains several lines of text. It is difficult to read this through the front of the object; it would be easier to read if the front was detached.

- Inside the object, one can see two cardboard rolls, with white gauzy material wrapped around them. One of these rolls sits in the center of the large circle; the other sits in the center of the bulge. They measure 3 1/4 inches in diameter. From one of the rolls, a strand of this gauzy material dangles down and out of the object.

- At the object's "bottom," where the blunt triangles protrude, are three sets of jagged edges cut into the plastic.

Let's look at the object from a couple of other vantage points, above and below. From these angles, we can continue our close reading on slightly different terms, moving from *description* toward the steps of *deduction* and *speculation:*

- The hole at the bottom of the object is like a passageway for the white gauzy material. Presumably one grabs the material and pulls it, thus unwinding it from the roll on which it is stored. On three sides of the hole, the jagged edged plastic functions as a kind of serrated knife, allowing one to cut the material as it is pulled from the roll (the fourth side is that which abuts the wall). This setup suggests that one selects a certain amount of material, pulls it from the object, and tears it off.

- Because there are two rolls of material, there is plenty of it on hand. We might speculate that one roll serves as an extra or backup. Perhaps each roll contains different types of the material. There is also the possibility that material from both rolls will be dangling from the opening in the bottom of the object, in which case one might grab not one, but *two* strands of material. So one might imagine a situation in which one needs a single strand—or perhaps another situation in which one needs both. Maybe the two rolls are placed here to give the user different options, either in terms of kind (different material) or quantity (single or double shot).

- The small hole at the top of the object is circular, with an elongated slot on "top" and "bottom." It looks something like a cross or a keyhole. If a keyhole, it suggests that even though one can see through the translucent front of this object, one cannot gain access to the interior without possession of a key.

- This fact, in turn, suggests that, while one person or group of people has a key (and thus access), other people (who do *not* have access) might also be interested in getting inside the object. It is built to be secure—though not radically so. The plastic can be broken relatively easily, and the "keyhole and lock" do not seem particularly formidable. If one really wished to get inside the object, one could easily break it or pick the lock. The object is not a safe or a lockbox, which suggests that the rolls of white material inside are only marginally valuable. The measures here are meant to *inconvenience,* but not absolutely prevent, a person from opening the object. The white material is thus protected in proportion to its *value;* it is not worthless, but it is not particularly valuable either. If it were, the object would have real locks and would be made of steel or thick plastic.

- We can deduce that there are two modes of access to the white rolled material: one involves unlocking the object and removing the front cover; the other involves reaching up into the hole in the bottom—or perhaps simply grasping the material as it dangles out of the hole—and pulling. With this action in mind—the pulling of unwinding material through a hole—the jagged teeth at the edges of the hole have a new functional meaning. Set well below the location of the cylinders holding the white material, they cut the material as it is pulled in such a way that the remaining material will dangle near the edge of the hole. This suggests that one user will be followed by another user . . . and another after that, each one pulling and tearing in such a way that the material dangles easily for the next person to come along.

- So we could speculate that the object was built to be used in two different ways. One can pull the material out of the object and then tear it off. Or one can open the object with a key. From this inference, one might speculate further that two kinds of users interact differently in relation to the white material. Since a group of "Pull and Tear" users will invariably use up the material (which is finite), the second group of users might be called "Replacers." Replacers remove the front cover in order to replace the rolls, which are being diminished by use (that little white sticker that is so difficult to read from outside may be some kind of direction or notes for these Replacers). But . . . the Replacers do not want the Pull-and-Tear users to have access to the rolls themselves. The Pull-and-Tear users *might* break the object and gain direct access to the cylinder rolls themselves, but the rolls themselves seem to be not worth the effort.

- Replacers, we could speculate, interact with *rolls* of material. Pull-and-Tear users interact with discrete *pieces* of the material. Both groups have access to the totality of the material—but for Replacers that totality is compact and neatly rolled. Pull-and-Tear users would have to unwind the entire roll, thus creating a huge mess. We might further speculate that, simply because it looks like a lot of trouble, this unwinding doesn't happen very often.

The object, then, might be described as a dispensing machine, one that is periodically recharged with rolls of white material, which are then dispensed in variable amounts, according to the needs and wishes of the Pull-and-Tear user. Many dispensers (think of a candy machine) do not allow this kind of user-defined flexibility. Although Pull-and-Tear users cannot access the rolls directly without effort and mess, they can unspool as much of the white material as they wish. This machine is user friendly, in that sense, and it suggests a feeling of abundance. The white material must be abundant, and it must be so inexpensive that the Replacers see no need to put limits on the Pull-and-Tear people. It's just that, if the Pull-and-Tear users want the entire roll, they will have to pull it from the machine, bit by bit. At that point, it will no longer be a roll, but a really long strip of white gauzy material.

We might also conjecture that the name on the object—Kimberly-Clark—is that of the company that makes the dispenser. Next to the name is a small logo image. Along with the molded plastic parts, this name and logo suggest that the object is not hand-made, but rather mass-produced by a corporation. Already, we can begin making a few notes about the social relations surrounding this object—a first step toward thinking at the registers of *formations* and *social theory*. There seem to be at least three broad categories of people who interact with this thing: Makers, Replacers, and Users. To that, we might easily add Installers (remember the five screws?) and Distributors (how else would it get from the Maker to the Replacer or Installer?). As we dig further into the context surrounding the object, we will undoubtedly see other groups of people become visible, and we'll wonder about the networks that put them in relation to one another, generating wages, investments, and other flows of money and meaning.

These speculations raise questions for further research, which we might conduct through archives, comparisons, or perhaps ethnographic observation and interviews. Pursuing an ethnographic method, for instance, we might locate and talk to people in each of the categories. What matters most immediately, though, is to look for other examples of the object—let's call it a *Pull-and-Tear Machine*—and situate it in its immediate contexts. In other

FIGURE 39. Pull-and-tear machine in context. Photograph by Philip Deloria.

words, we will start building a *project archive*. We've pushed in the clutch, as we prepare to shift gears from an *interpretive* register to the *curatorial* and *analytical*.

Here's a moment to talk about process. We might conduct the same kind of exercise of defamiliarization and close reading of the space in which our object resides. That would certainly offer up an additional round of new insights, for there is much to be said about the tile, the porcelain bowl, the fittings, the handrails, and the other features of the space (figure 39). But we might also decide simply to embrace the context and admit that the *Pull-and-Tear Machine* is a toilet paper dispenser. Fine. We'll give up the stance of *defamiliarization*. Before we move on, though, it's worth summarizing the insights that have been produced out of our close reading. Note the ways that these claims can be easily reframed as *why* or *how* questions.

- The dispenser gives users unusual flexibility.

- There is some curious type of value attached to the toilet paper via this dispenser. This value takes shape around security and protection measures.

- At least two groups of people interact with the dispenser as it is put to use, and they have very different relations to it.

- One group focuses on taking paper; the other on its resupply. It is possible that those groups have different interests, and perhaps even an antithetical relation to one another—at least in terms of the machine and its use. More groups are likely involved in its institutional and market life, particularly people connected to the words "Kimberly-Clark" printed on the front.

BUILDING AN ARCHIVE

Once we name the device a "toilet paper dispenser," we find that our analysis moves in two different directions. We'll build a *project archive* of other, similar (or not so similar?) devices. And we'll begin making a thick description of not simply the object itself, but the varying *contexts* surrounding toilet paper dispensers in general. One of the things that might strike us immediately is that this particular dispenser is *big*. Maybe it's just the picture (it's not), but the thing looks larger than the toilet itself! Indeed, 19 1/4 inches (the dispenser's longest dimension) is pretty substantial for a toilet paper dispenser. In addition to the specific issues of value, user flexibility, and relations between Users and Replacers, then, we'll be chasing two additional analytical questions:

- First, why is the thing so darn big?
- Second, because it is so darn big, you have to wonder why the dispenser needs to have that second roll—and the unsightly, asymmetrical bulge that it creates?

The latter question comes out of an aesthetic response to the object. It just doesn't look quite right. The former question comes out of our experiences with toilet paper, and in particular, with an *archive* of familiar toilet paper dispensers. Most of them look something like the dispensers shown in figure 40. Note the significant differences between these dispensers and our original dispenser:

- Whereas the *big* dispenser was solidly attached to the wall in five places, these dispensers are attached at only one or two points. They are relatively fragile, in that regard.

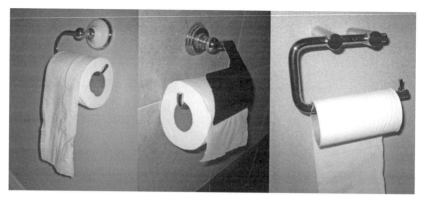

FIGURE 40. Toilet paper dispensers. Photograph by Philip Deloria.

- There are no locking mechanisms or protective plastic covers on these dispensers. A user has equal access to strands of paper *and* to the roll itself. Indeed, unlike many similar models, which have a spring-driven, two-piece central core that locks the roll in place, the dispensers in this picture simply require sliding the roll over a hook and onto an arm. The roll rests against the wall and is very easily replaced. You are almost *invited* to walk off with the roll.

- The cardboard tube rolls used in these dispensers are of a standard size (about 1 3/4 inches in diameter, as it turns out), and that size is much smaller than the 3 1/4 inch diameter cardboard cylinder rolls used in the first dispenser. These tubes are thinner as well, made from lighter, less sturdy cardboard.

- The easy access to these rolls makes it clear that we have forgotten something: we need to look at the paper itself! (Note: this is how this kind of analysis often works: you miss things the first time around, but then something else reminds you of a question and you go back to your original texts.)

It turns out that the paper in most toilet paper rolls is larger than that found in Haven Hall. Most paper is about four inches in width and has a very different character. Go ahead and unroll some: every four inches one finds a series of subtle perforations, forming a long roll of perfect squares. One may reasonably deduce that these perforations are built into the roll in order to help tear off pieces of paper. But what does that mean? That the paper is designed to be used only in square segments of 4 × 4 inches? Hmmm . . . that doesn't seem quite right. Perhaps, we speculate, this measurement is simply the product of the design of the roll: since you cannot tell *which* perforation you will use to tear your piece, they are arranged in a regular pattern. You can tear at any point on the roll, but you'll almost certainly end up tearing at *one* of these perforations.

The dispenser in Haven Hall, on the other hand, offers you a single, unperforated sheet (thus the "teeth," which help you tear off a piece) that is only 3 1/2 inches in width. The nature of the paper is different as well. The paper in the original large dispenser is thinner and coarser than that found in the smaller dispensers we examined. The paper in these smaller dispensers has a richer, softer texture, with many more dimples and a very subtle pattern of flowers imprinted into the paper. In some cases, there is a distinctly perfumed smell emanating from the paper itself. If we continued to investigate papers, we would find more varieties, including some that are thick and "quilted." But we're getting ahead of ourselves; there are still some additional questions raised by the smaller dispensers.

- Only one of the devices pictured above (the middle one) has a piece—a steel shield of sorts—that seems designed to assist in tearing off a piece of toilet paper. Is that indeed its function? Or is it meant to protect the paper from stray splashes and keep it dry?

- Hmm. Keeping it dry? That makes us think of something else, and sends us back again to the original dispenser, which not only locks up its toilet paper, but *seals* it from almost any water. Go back and look at that restroom. It is tile from floor to ceiling, with a ceramic fixture and glossy painted or stainless steel. We might deduce that this place was designed to be easily washed down. You could go in here with a hose, and spray the whole thing, slosh some antibacterial soap around with a mop, then rinse the thing down again. Your dispenser might not withstand a direct and prolonged hit with the hose, but it would take only minimal caution to keep your paper dry. Compare this process with the far more delicate cleaning necessary to protect the paper and walls and fixtures in the three dispensers shown in figure 40.

- The need to keep toilet paper dry raises another issue: could one speculate that toilet paper—because it is meant to be flushed down a toilet and into a sewage or septic system—is designed to change its character when it gets wet? Yes. Empirical experiment will demonstrate that toilet paper tends to start dissolving when wet—so keeping it dry turns out to be an important activity.

All of these things suggest that the mini-archive above is incomplete, that we are dealing with at least *two* different categories of toilet paper dispensers:

A public, industrial category.
A private, domestic category.

Dispensers in the first category, we might say, are designed for durability, protection, and security. Their paper is smaller, rougher, and cheaper than that used in domestic dispensers. The industrial context suggests that the people interacting with this particular toilet space are basically strangers to it: either casual users or hired employees. Neither can be expected to *care* very much about the restroom or its dispensers (although one can indeed imagine a situation in which the person cleaning the toilet comes to care a great deal about the way the area is treated by users). In the end, the dispenser is built to compensate for the relative emotional detachment of all who use this space. Indeed, its molded plastic frames, simple interchangeable parts, basic strategies for wall attachment, and security systems all suggest that it not only *serves* an industrial function, but that it was itself *produced* out of an equally industrial setting.

Dispensers in the second, domestic category are quite different. They are not particularly durable—but they do not receive particularly hard use. There is no impetus to secure the toilet paper—since there is presumably no one interested (even in a minimal way) in walking off with it. There is no need to seal the paper in for cleaning—since cleaning will be intimate and detailed, not the efficient spray of a hose. In a domestic situation, the User, Cleaner, Owner, and Replacer may well be the same person. This means the User has excellent reasons not to make a mess, steal the paper, get it wet, or rip the dispenser out of the wall. This *caring* about the toilet allows and encourages the Replacer to buy a better grade of paper (after all, his or her friends and family will be the primary users). Indeed, in some places, we might imagine, the grade of paper will carry a kind of social and cultural currency. When guests arrive, will they find soft, thick, perfumed, patterned, and quilted toilet paper? What will that say about the homeowner? Since the number of users will be small, the frequency that the paper will need to be replenished will be relatively low—thus the smaller, more easily handled rolls and the possibility of "fine" toilet paper.

What we've just been articulating is an analysis based in *generic* evidence, produced out of engagement with an *archive*. And we needed only a tiny

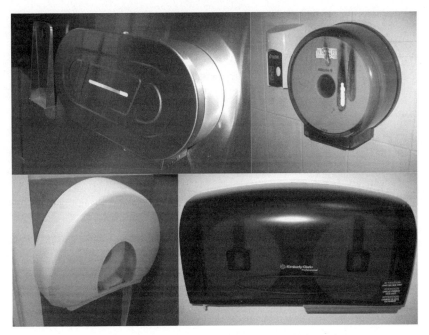

FIGURE 41. Industrial toilet paper dispensers. Photograph by Philip Deloria.

archive—four total dispensers—to be able to identify shared characteristics that define at least two genres of toilet paper dispenser, *public* and *private*. We've used the contrasts between those genres to sharpen our questions and firm up the lines that define the two categories. To build our case further, we'll want to assemble a better, more comprehensive archive, one that clarifies and sharpens the distinctions between public and private, and that convinces the reader through a larger collection of evidence. We've got a small archive of private dispensers. But only one example of the public category. Thankfully, Phil has curated a much more comprehensive archive over the course of a decade. Figure 41 provides a very small sampling.

All these dispensers can be seen as "industrial" and "public." That is, they fit within the parameters we have defined for this particular category of dispenser. They are large. They secure and seal their paper. All are located in public restrooms rather than private homes. Indeed, all live in tiled and painted restrooms that can easily survive an industrial cleaning. All allow a Replacer to view the amount of paper left in the roll, and thus to calculate when replacement is necessary. All are standardized. That is, they represent not only an industrial approach to cleaning and manufacture, but also to supply. The toilet paper rolls they utilize are themselves standardized around a limited number of roll styles and sizes. We could speculate further and suggest that such dispensers appear most often in institutional or industrial settings, such as museums and airports, in which substantial numbers of people pass through a restroom. Note that the top-right dispenser has been burned.

Now we have two archives of generic examples—those delicate domestic dispensers and these standardized industrial ones. Our hope is that readers will be satisfied with these examples, and that, if we claim that there is a whole universe of similar dispensers out there that fit into these categories, we will be believed. After all, this is absolutely true!

ANALYTICAL WORK WITH THE ARCHIVE

We've toggled a bit between the first three of our methodological registers: close interpretive reading of an individual text, assembly of a project archive, and analytical reading of genres. In the process, we've actually gone a long way toward answering that question we asked a while back: "Why is this dispenser so darned big?" One primary reason is that it is serving the general public—not a small household, but a significant number of often-unpredictable users. Their numbers and unpredictability also help explain the public dispenser's durability and security.

Having established the categories of public and private dispensers, we can continue to move the analysis forward. One of the most useful things one can do with generic categories is to look for *anomalies* within them. Their difference might let us think more about the original question, "Why ruin the perfectly good circular wheel of toilet paper by putting this ugly bulge on the side?" As the photograph makes clear, the bulge allows room for a second, smaller roll of paper alongside the one in the middle. So stop and think: we're talking mostly about public restrooms and industrial dispensers. Run through your own long experiences with public restrooms. Right. Check. But . . .

"Wait a minute!" (you might be thinking). "I've seen plenty of public places without the big-roll mega-dispensers. What about those?"

Is it possible that we might need to name, curate, and analyze a *third* genre of toilet paper dispensers, one that is public, but perhaps somehow *less* (or differently) industrial? What about public dispensers, such as the ones in figure 42, that use those regular domestic rolls?

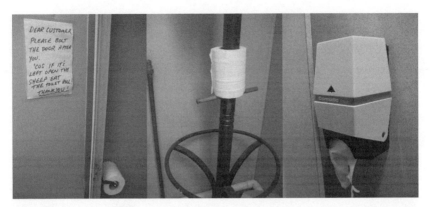

FIGURE 42. Public dispensers using domestic-sized rolls. Photograph by Philip Deloria.

Let's speculate some more. Imagine a moment in the dim mists of the past, in which there were *no* large standardized rolls of toilet paper, but only 4 1/2 inch rolls of domestic paper (the longtime standard). In that moment, even public and institutional toilets used the little rolls—which meant that users sometimes . . . um . . . ran out. It must not have taken very long for someone to come up with the bright idea of including an *extra* roll in the dispenser. Perhaps you've seen older toilet paper dispensers that hold two rolls side by side? Or dispensers that allow a second roll to drop down when the first roll was used up?

These kinds of dispensers were at one time extremely common. They are still around today, of course. In these dispensers, the domestic forms and the public forms were mixed together into a kind of hybrid. Figure 43 displays two great examples of this kind of public-domestic hybrid genre carried to extremes. Both have to determine ways to use small, short rolls for a large public usership, so both embrace the logic of *quantitative expansion:* keep the form, but increase the contents (in this case, toilet paper). And just to give you an idea of the wide-ranging nature of this particular genre—the public-domestic hybrid—the first can be found in an outhouse at Yellowstone National Park; the second in a restroom in the British Museum in London:

This new archive of dispensers leads us to yet another series of intriguing questions. Some of these questions surely cluster together around the history of toilet paper and hygienic practices:

- Prior to toilet paper, what kinds of products did people use for their hygiene needs? There is a folklore about nineteenth- and early twentieth-

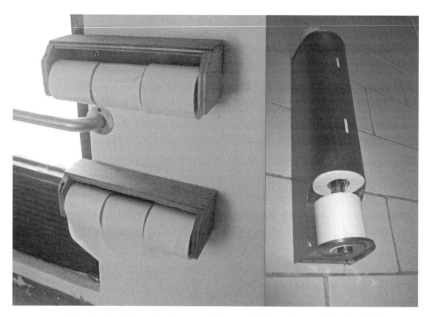

FIGURE 43. Rustic six-roller at Yellowstone National Park and vertical eight-roll dispenser (with extra on top) at the British Museum. Photograph by Philip Deloria.

century uses of the Sears Catalogue in old outhouses. Phil has actually used these, so for him, personally, the claim rises above the level of folklore. There is also folklore about corn cobs ("rough as a cob," as they say) and other waste and plant matter. So we might ask, "What kind of innovation *was* toilet paper?"

- When was toilet paper developed, and by whom? Did it originate in the small-roll form or were there other possibilities that were tried and rejected? Was it marketed and sold for domestic or institutional uses first? Or both at the same time? We might compare the toilet papers we know today with those in the past, or those in other countries. Public toilets in the United Kingdom, for instance, were long marked by individual sheets of very waxy (and very unsatisfying) paper. Does this indicate a different sense of obligation to the public? A different hygienic aesthetic?

- What kinds of raw materials are used in toilet paper, and from where do they come? Considering its transitory purpose, we might speculate that toilet paper is produced from the kind of scrap second-growth wood that springs up in the wake of logging. Thinking historically, one might ask if an entirely new industry developed out of the overexploitation of commercial timber. In that sense, knowing the *where* of toilet paper's origins becomes important. Logging moved roughly westward over time, from Maine and northern New England to the upper Midwest and the Southeast, and then to the Pacific Northwest. We might speculate that toilet paper at first seemed like a viable commercial product to logging companies in northern New England, since they might have seen scrappy, second-growth forests spring up first.

And of course, we can also ask similar questions about the dispensers:

- When were toilet paper dispensers first manufactured commercially? Did they develop in tandem with toilet paper? Which companies started this business? Was there an overlap between those making paper and those making dispensers? What did the first industrial or institutional dispensers look like? How much did they cost? What kinds of materials were used in their construction?

- Is toilet paper linked to the widespread use of flush toilets? If so, when did the indoor plumbing systems and municipal sewage facilities emerge that enabled the use of paper? Or was its rise linked not to technology (plumbing) but to hygienic convenience—in which case one might trace its relation to the outhouse?

- When did commercial / institutional / industrial dispensers begin to change and what was the nature of those changes? We've proposed a trajectory leading from single-roll dispensers, to double-roll, and then to multiple-roll dispensers. That's just a hypothesis, though. If we test it by returning to the historical record, how well does it hold up?

INSTITUTIONS AND FORMATIONS

We hope that you can see what's happening: we've generated questions out of our analysis of three toilet paper dispenser *archives,* and those questions point us to the register of *institutions and formations.* They deal with manufacture, distribution, and consumption patterns—the networks and systems through which money flows and social relations are created and maintained. And make no mistake: the question of toilets and paper offers a lot of opportunity to think about social categories, relations, and the question of power.

Many of these questions cannot be directly answered through these particular primary sources—a collection of dispensers—but they can be addressed by turning to secondary sources (that is, written histories and accounts) and, later, an expansion of our project archive to include primary sources: dispenser industry trade magazines, advertisements, patents, autobiographies, ethnographic interviews, and more. For the moment, our secondary research can give us a few basics:

- In the past (and present), people have used almost *everything* as toilet paper: seaweed, wet sponges, rocks, sand, leaves . . . you name it.
- The first paper seems to have been used in sixth-century China, inaugurating a long tradition of toilet paper manufacturing.
- The first flushing toilet was invented in the late sixteenth century by Sir John Harington, godson of Queen Elizabeth I of England.
- In 1857, the first factory-made toilet paper was produced in the United States.
- Between 1871 and 1883, Seth Wheeler of Albany invented and sold rolls of perforated paper, as well as the brackets to hold and dispense the paper. In the mid-1880s, Wheeler's company, the Albany Perforated Wrapping Paper Company, built a factory for making standardized toilet paper.
- In 1888, the *New York Times* first used the term "toilet paper."
- In 1894, the U.S. Supreme Court took up the question of toilet roll dispenser patent infringement in *Morgan Envelope Co. v. Albany Perforated Wrapping Paper Co.*, waxing eloquent for many pages on oval rolls, the tearing of paper, wastage, and restrictions on the amount of paper made available. Wheeler's company came out on top.
- By the early twentieth century, the dominant player in the toilet paper industry was the Scott Corporation. But it was no monopoly: Great Northern, Charmin, Kimberly-Clark, and others all pushed their way into the toilet paper market.
- In 1943, toilet paper was printed with pictures of Adolph Hitler.
- Toilet paper is widely considered unhygienic in India.
- Toilet paper consumption is lower in areas where bidets are popular, such as Southern Europe, East Asia, and the Middle East.
- Japan has pioneered the use of paperless bidet-toilets complete with dryers and seat warmers.

We might choose to pursue any one of these contexts in greater detail, perhaps through additional secondary or primary source research. But these are *hardly* the only questions to be considered.

- How did manufacturers market their products? Did they emphasize hygiene? Convenience? Technology? Modernization?
- What about domestic users? How did they respond to these messages? How did the reasons for buying toilet paper change over time?
- How did toilet paper change the calculus of domestic labor? Did toilet paper make housework more or less difficult? What meanings did it carry for the understanding of masculinity and femininity? How did such meanings change over time?
- And what about lower-class households? What was the economic threshold at which toilet paper could be considered a necessity as opposed to a luxury or an unaffordable indulgence?
- Were there other factors that led some groups to adopt toilet paper and not others? Could one imagine different uses of paper among different social groups, based upon economic status, cultural practice, religious belief, and ethnicity?
- And what about the Replacers of public toilet paper—janitors? How did they interact with the dispensers, and how did those interactions change over time as the nature of the dispensers changed? Who does this kind of work? Has that workforce changed?
- What about the explicitly cultural meanings that have been attached to toilet paper, from the tradition of imprinting images on paper to the practice, common among some high-school students, of TP-ing houses and trees, so wonderfully enabled through easily unwinding rolls that can be flung with joyous abandon?

All of these are interesting questions. And all make clear the interdisciplinary shifting of gears that takes place in an American Studies analysis. We began with a close reading of a single text (a toilet paper dispenser). We then assembled constellations of similar texts into three overlapping archives, and have gestured to the ways those archives might be expanded. The generic categories visible in these archives (public, private, and hybrid) allowed us to formulate a series of questions, many of which were historical or contextual in nature. Those questions focused on certain institutions and formations. We want to know about those who produced paper and dispensers, those who distributed them, those who marketed them, and those who ended up consuming them. We want to know what these folks said and thought about paper and dispensers. Indeed, though we began by positing two groups of people—Users and Replacers—we also noted other possibilities: Makers, Sellers, Distributors, and Owners.

Historically (and in the present), each of these activities and roles took (and takes) place in institutional frameworks: logging and paper companies, manufacturing corporations, advertising agencies, supermarkets, architectural firms, supply companies, public safety and hygiene committees, and perhaps local governments. Through these formations, economic power— that is, the power of money and exchange—has flowed. Tracing those flows will help make sense of a larger story, of toilet paper and dispensers as an interesting (and perhaps even important) window into the culture of the United States, broadly conceived.

THEORY AND THE SOCIAL WORLD

As we've framed a set of questions having to do with *people,* we turn in yet another direction—toward social analysis and a focus on the meanings and relationships among people that emerge from these objects and institutions. Following those questions might even lead us back to what now seems like an insignificant issue: that unsightly, asymmetrical bulge on the dispenser in the restroom in Haven Hall. To head in this direction, let's add to our archive, and consider a few more dispensers (figure 44).

Suddenly, the reason for the asymmetrical bulge becomes crystal clear. It has nothing to do with different kinds of paper or multiple combinations. It has everything to do with people, their work, and the delicate issue of timing. Here we can work, inductively, to *theorize a rule.*

Consider the situation in which public users had to deal with domestic-sized toilet paper rolls. Every Replacer has confronted the same problem: when a User enters the toilet stall, he or she needs to have toilet paper reliably available. So when and how does a Replacer replenish the rolls? Do you wait until the roll is completely used up, thus creating the risk that disgruntled users will be stranded without paper? You *could* do that if you spent a great deal of time in the restroom, checking frequently on the various rolls of toilet paper. In other words, the rhythm of your work would be based upon the actual toilet paper usage that took place in the restroom, which would mean

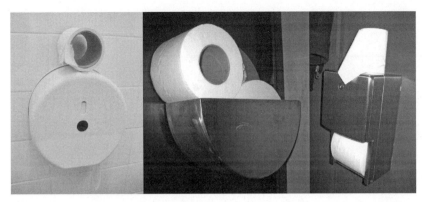

FIGURE 44. The problem of the paper. On the right, a fully stocked, multi-roll dispenser—with an extra remnant. Photograph by Philip Deloria.

that you would be tightly tied to that place. You can imagine, in other words, a *restroom attendant*, whose only job is to tend closely to a single restroom.

Alternatively, you could also consider a work rhythm that was based *not* on the particular space of a specific restroom, but upon a time schedule, one that had you visiting a round of restrooms at regular intervals. Perhaps you would check every restroom at 7:00 p.m., and replenish the paper so as to have things in order for the next day. You can imagine, in other words, a *janitor*, whose job is to maintain a number of restrooms, perhaps during "off hours."

These are two very different ways of thinking about the role of human beings as Replacers. In the first case, the attendant is meant to be extremely visible to Users. The institution that is able to afford to pay someone to tend a restroom is likely to be invested in making a public performance of its wealth and privilege. The attendant might be required, for instance, to wear a uniform, to sit at a certain place in the restroom, to interact with Users in certain prescribed ways. In other words, there are a range of cultural behaviors and belief systems that might govern this particular form of human labor.

In the second case, the janitor is perhaps meant to be largely *invisible*. His or her labor often takes place at night, when most Users have left the building. For those Users, the restroom can appear to be a magical thing. During the day, the toilet paper, the paper towels, and the soap are all used up in varying degrees. The trash can fills up, and careless Users leave newspapers on the floor and make all sorts of messes. The next morning, however, the restroom is clean and shiny again. The trash is emptied, the papers are gone, the soap scum is absent, and there are new toilet paper rolls in the dispensers. Of course, a human being did this work, which is so easily forgotten by the Users. The ability to forget about the Replacer is a mark of a particular set of social relations: mostly about class and money, but also about race (janitorial labor, in many places, has been traditionally the preserve of low-income people of color) and about gender (the act of cleaning up after others, for instance, has a particularly gendered set of meanings).

The janitor—rather than the attendant—confronts the most difficult issues having to do with toilet paper replacement. In some stalls, the toilet paper will have been used up and the roll can be replaced. In others, the paper is almost untouched and can be left for another day. But in many other stalls, the roll is neither empty nor full, but rather "halfway" used up. To replace such a roll would be wasteful (surely the supervisor, who watches the costs, would not approve). But to fail to replace the roll would mean that it would surely run out of paper sometime in the middle of next day, producing disgruntled Users, who might complain to the supervisor. The janitor seems to be in a no-win situation. Here is our rule, our theoretical framework. Call it *the Janitor's Dilemma,* a structure of labor, consumption, and management that functions at an abstract level capable of describing similar situations in which resource use, consumer demand, and managerial oversight place a worker in a difficult bind.

No doubt janitors all over the world applauded the brilliance of the person who invented the first multi-roll dispenser. Indeed, one might reasonably wonder if the inventor was not a janitor! The multi-roll dispenser must have solved the problem for janitors who cleaned and restocked their restrooms every night. Knowing you had a backup roll tucked securely in the dispenser, you could afford to let the half-used roll go another day. We could pursue further our new role as social theorists by thinking more about who these people were, and how their work may have been transformed by these new dispensers. Earlier, we noted that people in certain social groups—defined by class, race, gender, and immigration status—have disproportionately performed janitorial labor. In the mid-twentieth-century American city, for instance, many janitorial jobs were held by African American men. And, after working as janitors for some time, some of these men were promoted to supervisor, thus edging their way into something approximating a gateway to the middle class. One can ask if similar dynamics continue today, though across the wider spectrum of gender and race that characterize contemporary janitorial work. Are talented and experienced janitors still considered to be the best equipped to supervise janitorial labor? Or have new management philosophies closed down even this narrow avenue?

But back to the paper for a moment. Even as the multi-roll dispenser solved one issue—running out of toilet paper midday—it opened the door to other possibilities. If one were going to build dispensers with two rolls, then why not three? Or four? Or, as in the British Museum, eight rolls? Once you start down this road, it's not hard to reimagine the very nature of both paper *and* janitorial work. Why not create *big* dispensers, with heavy wheels of toilet paper? Such a dispenser (you can almost hear designers thinking out loud!) would not require frequent janitorial tending. Instead of changing out toilet paper rolls every night, maybe you could replace them once a week.

This matters. Because if you can hear designers thinking out loud, you can also hear supervisors doing the same, rethinking the work schedules of janitors. Perhaps those schedules could be rationalized so as to save labor costs. Janitors could be asked to clean more restrooms, but less frequently. One can speculate—and then go and investigate—an entire line of thought that has to do with the transformations of work, class position, economic possibility, and status. These are big and important questions that have everything to do with the humble toilet paper dispenser in Haven Hall. And this analysis of janitorial labor is only one of many possible directions.

There is, of course, an irony to the creation of the mega-roll toilet paper dispenser when we pair it with the (possible) transformations of janitorial labor. If a janitor comes to replace a roll only once a week, you still have the problem of the unforeseen shortfall in paper. Rolls, therefore, must be manufactured to last a period of time that is longer than the interval a janitor visits. If once a week, then the roll must last for eight or nine days. This eliminates one problem, but creates a situation in which waste will be almost certain. Two priorities are set clashing. On the one hand, there are efficiencies in janitorial labor—and thus increased profits. On the other hand, there is the possibility of waste—and thus decreased profits.

In other words, even the large rolls may not solve *the Janitor's Dilemma,* particularly if this is an example where technological innovation changes the nature and rhythm of work. You go ahead and change the roll and then you place the remainder of the old roll on top of the dispenser, where it serves as a kind of emergency roll, just in case the dispenser comes up short. It's pretty clear, though, that this is hardly a perfect solution, for reasons both practical and cultural. Users, one speculates, prefer the paper coming from the dispenser over the paper sitting on top of it. It's not simply that one must unspool the latter paper by hand, and tear it without the aid of perforation or jagged teeth. It's also that the remnant roll has a different character. It feels a bit unwanted. It's not "protected" by the dispenser, and therefore may be perceived as "dirty." It can get wet from the misty spray of the flush toilet. And the whole thing feels just a bit sloppy, doesn't it? Particularly when placed in relation to those gleaming, shiny plastic and steel dispensers. There's a theory here, too, about *purity and contamination*. Unprotected toilet paper rolls feel germy, dirty, and unsafe—okay in a pinch, but never the first choice.

With these issues in mind, we can return, at last, to our original dispenser and answer decisively the question: "Why ruin the perfectly good circular wheel of toilet paper by putting this ugly bulge on the side?" Once each week (or so), the janitor comes around to change the toilet paper rolls in the dispenser. He or she removes the roll that has been on the large diameter portion of the dispenser. There is some remnant paper on that roll, which should not go to waste. The janitor places the remnant roll into the "bulge" of the dispenser and then replaces the first roll with a very large, new wheel of toilet paper. With any luck, users will use up the remnant roll, even as they pull and tear paper from the large roll. As pieces of paper coming out of the opening at the bottom, the two rolls are, in effect, indistinguishable.

If it is aesthetically displeasing, then, the bulge on this dispenser actually serves a very functional purpose: it seeks to solve *the Janitor's Dilemma* by preventing waste and dealing with the remnant roll. The most mundane object thus offers us a story about human beings and labor, and about the cultural meanings that we take from things such as paper, hygiene, work, visibility, public and private, industrial production, value, security, efficiency, and a host of other ideas, all of which are connected to this simple device.

Of course, we have only scratched the surface of what is possible in an American Studies analysis. We might, for instance, get really serious about the materials. Where *does* this paper come from? What about the various ingredients that make up the plastic and steel parts? Almost certainly, many of these resources come from somewhere outside the continental United States. If we traced the flows of these materials, we could open ourselves up to a range of new questions: Who controls these networks? What are the geopolitics surrounding these forms of petrochemical, steel, and wood?

Or, we might pursue further the question of social relations. We would urge you to check out a gorgeous short film, *Sueña Despierto (Dreams Awake)* (2010), about an immigrant janitor at Stanford University who writes poetry and leads union meetings. In the film, the janitor reflects on his feelings of invisibility when walking around campus: "Sometimes we are working in the offices, and people almost run into us, and if they don't run into us, they don't even notice we are there."[1] Similar stories might be gleaned from the workers who make the dispensers. Where *are* the factories that produce Kimberly-Clark's paper and dispensers? Who works there? From what we gather, the company seems to have a major share of the dispenser market for college campuses. How did one company become so dominant? These questions might lead us to even larger questions about power, discipline, individual subjectivity, and cultural meaning.

But let's conclude by returning one last time to the thick context surrounding our toilet paper dispenser. We pursued some of these questions ethnographically, by talking with janitors and with a manufacturer's representative knowledgeable about janitorial supplies. They thought that some of our speculations needed a bit of adjustment. At Michigan, the big toilet paper dispensers changed the nature of the work, but they did not alter it substantially. Janitors *still* clean the restroom every day or so. It's a quick trip in, usually, to empty the trash, check on the rolls (which seem like they hardly ever need changing!), pick up the papers, and rinse out the sinks. Periodically, they swab the place down. Rather than worrying about carrying lots of small rolls around, and constantly changing out toilet paper, this part of the job has actually gotten easier. It seems that each category of restroom (high traffic, low traffic) has its own appropriate dispenser. It turns out, as well, that companies like Kimberly-Clark *lease* the dispensers for fixed periods of time. Paper rolls are proprietary to their dispensers, and the money flow centers on the paper, not the dispenser. Indeed, those leases include complicated pricing guarantees that offer stable rates should the toilet paper supply market turn volatile.

Earlier, we split our toilet paper world up into the three analytical categories of public, private, and hybrid. What the janitors suggest is that even these categories require a bit of complication and revision. It turns out, for instance, that the first two of our private dispensers (those that could easily be found in a private home) are, in fact, *public.* They can be found in the Hilton Hotel in Midtown Manhattan—and not in hotel rooms, but in public restrooms in public areas (figure 45).

The Hilton? That should tell us something about the very nature of "public," and about the different kinds of janitorial "narrowcasting" that comes with precision planning of public space and labor. The Hilton—because of its clientele and its self-image as a luxury hotel—wishes to offer to guests the illusion of comfortable private space. Indeed, such things as toilet paper dispensers, which so powerfully represent domestic private space, actually *create* a sense of luxury—for what is hotel luxury if not the sense that you are

FIGURE 45. New York Hilton Midtown restrooms (left) and private home (far right). Photograph by Philip Deloria.

in a controlled private space, among people who care for you and your needs? No generic comforter on your bed. This one is nicer than the one at home. No cheap little bottle of shampoo. These are super groovy Aveda products. And definitely no industrial toilet paper dispenser.

The Hilton bombards guests with cultural meanings surrounding luxury and class, which can be powerfully attached to even such a mundane thing as toilet paper. Surely we can assume that the Kimberly-Clark Corporation is equally astute. And indeed, just a few minutes perusing the Kimberly-Clark Professional brands website will demonstrate the wide range of possibilities KCP offers its customers. Here, one can find it all: single roll, multiple roll, jumbo roll, jumbo roll junior, and so on. No matter what the need, KCP has a dispenser, which is exactly what the janitors suggest has happened: *toilet paper narrowcasting.*

And although it seems that the Michigan dispenser has been replaced, it is not hard to find the new model equivalent. It is called the "JRT Jr. ESCORT Jumbo Roll Bathroom Tissue Dispenser with Stub Roll," and here is how it is listed in the catalogue:

> The JRT Jr. ESCORT Jumbo Roll Bathroom Tissue Dispenser with Stub Roll gives you a graceful look. It is curved and contemporary. Designed for easier access to bathroom tissue. Replaceable lock with push button option and stub roll. Spare parts attached to back wall.[2]

What are the differences between the old and new versions? If you're reloading the new machine, you can choose from four different grades of toilet paper. There is a "decorator strip" across the middle. The KCP website pushes new models clearly aimed at further reducing waste: a full roll of paper *without* the cardboard roll, and single-sheet dispensers that promise to limit the amount of paper taken by a User. Indeed, it turns out that the right paper / dispenser combination—installed in hundreds of restrooms—can let an institution such as a university claim points for LEED (Leadership in Energy and Environmental Design) or Green Globes certification for environmentally sensitive building design and operation. But these things are mostly behind the scenes. The most visible difference between new and old: the new dispenser has eliminated the aesthetically unpleasing, asymmetrical bulge on the side. Though it still allows one to save the "stub roll," the new dispenser takes the form of a simple, aesthetically pleasing rectangle.

A FEW FINAL WORDS

We hope this chapter has served as a leisurely walk together through methods, questions, and possible lines of research of an American Studies project. We've tried to read the dispenser as a text, assemble a series of archives that open up to analysis, identify generic commonalities, and frame a series of questions that lead us to consider institutions and formations—a contextualization that then allows us to build theories (about *the Janitor's Dilemma,* or *quantitative expansion strategy,* or *purity and contamination,* or *toilet paper narrowcasting*) that reach a level of abstraction that makes them useful beyond toilet paper. A mundane object, it turns out, can be read as a text in ways that let us see things we would not otherwise have noticed. It's the essence of American Studies analysis: to see the world with fresh eyes; to work through processes of description, interpretation, and contextualization; and then to consider our insights in terms that are generalizable in one way or another.

Conclusion

IN THE FIRST PAGES OF THIS BOOK, we invited you to hang out with us and listen to some tunes, suggesting that the world of American Studies was as big, diverse, and joyful as the world of music. We pulled out old 78s and 45s in order to share with you some classic vinyl from the early years of the field. We walked through the historiographical equivalent of eight-tracks and cassettes, compact discs and digital streaming services. Out of all that "music," we crafted a series of mixtapes, hoping to make sense of the field in many different ways. We built those mixtapes as examples of how fun and fruitful it can be to create an American Studies archive. But we were also playing you some greatest hits collections in order to *slow down the records* so that together we could inspect and learn individual notes. We closed the book by getting on stage (with writing) and playing you an original—our unfinished song about the curious interpretive routes in and out of a toilet paper dispenser.

In between, we tried to think systematically about the practices that make up some of the interpretive, analytical, and theoretical frameworks that power American Studies. We were, in that sense, curating a *methodological* mixtape, assembling a methods archive of our own. As we warned you, all archives are incomplete. Ours too. So we claim suggestiveness, not comprehensiveness. There are lots of other things for you to explore. It's impossible to do more than that—which means that a book like this is best understood as an invitation to further reading, writing, and exploring.

We learn a craft—in this case, American Studies—in order to draw on generations of knowledge, experiment, failure, and success. Knowing a craft is a good thing. We do it, not to replicate, but to create. The "rules," in this sense, are like the forms of the blues or the sonnet or the limerick. They are invitations to new creativity in relation to familiar forms and structures. Likewise, "the rules"—such as they are—also carry the more capacious meanings attached to genres: they invite us to expand our horizons into new areas, to carry the tropes and styles of hip hop into classical music, bluegrass into jazz, Chinese opera into the powwow drum.

That metaphor of crossing has something to do with the open interdisciplinarity that has characterized American Studies, but it is larger than that. Like all forms of intellectual life, American Studies method is a way of thinking—and we've tried here to think with you about *how we think.* Academic fields have their own distinct qualities in this regard. They pursue specific subjects, ask and answer questions in certain ways, consider particular phenomena as evidence, and communicate their findings according to idiosyncratic norms. American Studies is no different. It is its own thing; its own *think,* if you will. And yet, American Studies has also been particularly interested in exploring a relatively open-ended world of possibility that pushes boundaries. We work in categories and comparisons, analogies and metaphors—but also with microscopic attention to detail and a telescopic sweep of the universe of generalization and theory. We step outside the visible boundaries of nations, into the complexities of cultural and social circuits. We interrogate ourselves in order to arrive at common statements about the conditions and prospects of others. We disorient and defamiliarize in order to see the world as clearly as possible. We build rigorous archival collections that allow our projects to knit together the specific with the general, the text with the context, the individual with the social world.

And we bring an epistemological orientation that is directed toward that social world. Culture is our *object,* but so often our *goal* is rooted in the unjust, sometimes violent, and altogether human choices directed toward other people, toward the planet, and toward the very categories and structures we have created. American Studies—though our field is certainly not alone—has had unique relationships with social movements, and with concepts of social justice and equality. This does not make our field any nobler than any other. It does not *a priori* make our moral or ethical claims more convincing. But it does make the experience of doing American Studies powerful and compelling.

It might even make it a little addictive. The mix of complex intellectual challenge and human caring that so often fuels American Studies gives it a certain kind of music. For us, American Studies is that song that gets stuck in your head and just won't leave. That's why, in this book, we've tried to slow down its tune, dissect its harmonic and rhythmic structures, examine its lyrics and melody, consider its performance, put it in context, and write up some solid criticism. For us, American Studies is music worth listening to, playing, and understanding. You'll use your own understanding to play it with your own particular style, as you should. This book, we hope, is like a lead sheet for a jazz musician, a meaningful structure for your own creative exploration. To say it again, this is a user's guide, not an owner's manual.

Use it well. Do good. Be kind. Be smart. Have fun.

ACKNOWLEDGMENTS

This book has been a long time in the making, and has incurred substantial debts along the way. Our partnership began a decade ago at the University of Michigan, when Phil was working on his American Studies Association presidential address, and Alex was preparing for his field exams. Joining forces, we took on two tasks over the summer: reading several of the old American Studies classics, and gathering syllabi from graduate programs around the country. As the summer drew to a close, we noticed a pattern. American Studies seminars rarely assigned books like Constance Rourke's *American Humor* (1931) or Henry Nash Smith's *Virgin Land* (1950) anymore; instead, graduate students were presented with articles that framed these and other writers as supposedly offering a monolithic view of American culture. But while this conventional wisdom accurately described some writers, it failed to capture the nuances of others. Why the dissonance between much of this early scholarship and the origin stories that American Studies told about itself?

Another puzzle arose much earlier, when Phil was assigned to teach a graduate methods course at the University of Colorado in 1995. While he had a sense of "method" that seemed to work well enough, he had rarely given it any systematic attention. When pressed, he couldn't really offer a coherent description of American Studies methods or methodology. He was tempted to assign a collection of interesting books as case studies and guide students through a discussion of their methods, but what seemed missing in American Studies—unlike literary studies, or history, or anthropology—was a "how to" guide for reading evidence, making analytical connections, building arguments, and using context. In the absence of such a model, he was aided by generative conversations with three bold and creative colleagues at

Colorado—Susan K. Kent, Fred Anderson, and Steven Epstein. But the problem remained: Why did American Studies, as a field, seem constitutionally averse to anything that smacked of disciplinary consolidation?

In his 2008 ASA presidential address, Phil offered remarks on both of these puzzles—remarks that ultimately propelled us toward writing this book. He suggested that the apparent fracture between American Studies and Ethnic Studies (and other fields), while real, might be productively negotiated through a broad, open reading of both historiography and methodology. Formal comments on Phil's address in *American Quarterly* by Nikhil Singh and Jack Halberstam helped shape our view of the challenges and opportunities presented by contemporary American Studies. Informal responses from Matt Jacobson, Maria Cotera, Hsinya Huang, Paul Anderson, Robert Warrior, Carolyn Thomas, and a host of others proved equally helpful. The 2008 meeting also featured a presentation by James Brown, who won the Gene Wise–Warren Susman Prize for his archival reassessment of American Studies during the Cold War. Brown's startlingly original paper planted the seed for our work in the ASA Records at the Library of Congress, where many of our assumptions about the history of the field were laid to rest.

For the next several years, we continued to gather feedback from the wider American Studies community. In 2010, Alex met with Leo Marx, who generously shared stories from the early years of the field. The following year, we participated in roundtables at the ASA annual meeting in Baltimore, which generated valuable insights from all who contributed. In 2014, the project was jump-started by Niels Hooper of the University of California Press. We received extremely useful comments from three early reviewers—Julie Sze, Matthew Guterl, and Janet Davis—who helped shape and clarify our approach. In the final stretch, we were fortunate to have smart and helpful readings from Ann Fabian, Ramzi Fawaz, Kristin Hass, and an anonymous reviewer. We deeply appreciate their generosity, and we take this opportunity to note that, though we have been assisted substantially by these readers, any errors of commission or omission are our own.

This book owes a particular debt to three past collaborators: Michael Goldberg, Susan Kent, and Frank Kelderman. Over a decade ago, Phil joined forces with his forward-looking friend Michael Goldberg of the University of Washington–Bothell for what they thought would be an American Studies textbook, combining their material and looking toward a structure of online e-modules, frequently updated. Though that effort did not come to fruition, Phil's conversations with Michael—a brilliant, thoughtful, and charismatic teacher—refined the book as a serious exercise in pedagogy and opened up new possibilities for expanding it. We would like to think that Michael's passionate commitment to music, film, food, and life itself lingers in these pages. The book got a second injection of energy from Susan Kent, who sat together with Phil for a week, laptop to laptop, testing ideas for a more traditional textbook focused on cultural studies in general, replete with exercises, callout boxes, and sidebars. Susan is one of Phil's oldest and dearest colleagues, and has our deepest gratitude for her ideas, enthusiasm, friendship, and generosity, all of which have left their mark in this book. More recently, Alex teamed up with Frank Kelderman, then of Oberlin College, for a project on the history of American Studies in the Midwest that grew into a wider reassessment of the field. Their collaboration resulted in an article for *American Studies,* and their conception of the field as a series of "ad hoc" projects has carried over into this book. We are grateful to Frank for his generous and detailed feedback on our manuscript.

Along the way, we've been fortunate to cross paths with some of the most interesting scholars and teachers of American Studies. It's impossible to list all of those influences; you'll see them in the text, oftentimes explicitly listed. But here are a few people to whom we are particularly grateful. Carlo Rotella has long been a source of inspiration for all things concerning the method and craft of scholarship. In many of the practical details found in this book, from analytic structures to writing advice, we're channeling Carlo and riffing on some piece of advice he's given at one time or another. Likewise this book is indebted to Jay Cook's work on the genealogy of American cultural history. As a friend, colleague, and mentor, he strongly influenced the evolution of our thinking on this project.

Our colleagues at the University of Michigan have created a community of powerhouse scholars; every day is a clinic in the study of American culture. Over the course of this project, we have accumulated debts to Kristin Hass, Tiya Miles, Michael Witgen, Sara Blair, Julie Ellison, June Howard, Amy Sara Carroll, Kiara Vigil, and many others. At Western Kentucky University, we are grateful to Clay Motley, Gillian Knoll, Ted Hovet, Elizabeth Gish, Leila Watkins, and Judy Rohrer. Our book has drawn on the skills and energy of graduate and undergraduate students at both Michigan and WKU, including Nikki Roulo, Jordan Weinberg, Sophie Hunt, Annah MacKenzie, Noah Greco, and Maggie Sullivan.

This project has relied on the support of numerous curators, archivists, editors, and friends. We extend our gratitude to Mary Dougherty of

University of Massachusetts Press; Marsha Rooney and Anna Harbine of the Northwest Museum of Arts & Culture in Spokane; Katie Glaeser of Sweet Briar College; Wendy Hall of the Boulder Public Library's Carnegie Branch Library for Local History; Masumi Hayashi-Smith of Holy Names University; Timothy Perry of the University of Missouri; and Mary Robinson of the Buffalo Bill Center of the West. We thank Oxford University Press, University of North Carolina Press, Cambridge University Press, and W. W. Norton for permission to reproduce book covers. Thanks as well to Deb LaBelle and Flip Daly, for helping us understand the nuances of toilet paper.

We hope this book will reach many different publics: undergraduates learning the ropes, graduate students wanting to interrogate their practice, faculty members teaching American Studies or engaging with its interdisciplinary project, and even general readers interested in ways to think about the interpretation of culture. It was once a textbook that still aspires to be useful in the classroom—but also to participate in a wider scholarly conversation. That broad vision, commensurate with American Studies itself, has relied on our editor, Niels Hooper, at the University of California Press. We are grateful for his support and engagement as well as the excellent work of Bradley Depew, Paul Tyler, Jessica Moll, and Jolene Torr.

No writers work alone, but this project has deepened our appreciation for the rewards—both personal and intellectual—of co-authorship. Writing this book together has been a joyful experience. We kept each other motivated when energy flagged, spent hours hammering out ideas, and sent countless drafts back and forth. Most importantly, we embraced each other's enthusiasms, whether it was Phil's archive of toilet paper dispenser photographs— lovingly built up over a decade!—or Alex's endless tinkering with mixtapes. We hope our voices have come together as one.

Finally, this book would never have materialized without the support of our families. Phil thanks his wife, Peggy Burns, for tolerating wild-eyed sermons on the form of chairs and bowling shoes, and Jackson and Lacey, sure-handed guides to the world of contemporary popular music and culture. Alex thanks his wife, Nicolette Bruner, and his mother, Irene Olson, for their love, labor, and insights. During the writing of this book, Alex and Nicolette welcomed their son Igor into the world, and some of his earliest experiments with crayons used pages of this manuscript as a canvas. When we started this book, we hoped that it would inspire new avenues of creativity; crayon artwork is not exactly what we had in mind, but it's a start!

NOTES

INTRODUCTION. THE OBJECT OF AMERICAN STUDIES

1. Raymond Williams, "Film and the Dramatic Tradition," in Raymond Williams and Michael Orrom, *Preface to Film* (London: Film Drama, 1954), 22.

CHAPTER ONE. HISTORY AND HISTORIOGRAPHY

1. "The William Robertson Coe Program in American Studies, University of Wyoming," brochure, n.d., Box 26, Folder 11, ASA Records, Library of Congress, Washington, DC.

2. James Harvey Robinson, *The New History: Essays Illustrating the Modern Historical Outlook* (New York: Macmillan, 1912), 1.

3. This observation is from Ramzi Fawaz's reader report on our manuscript for University of California Press.

4. Deborah Gray White, "'Matter Out of Place': *Ar'n't I a Woman?* Black Female Scholars and the Academy," *Journal of African American History*, 92, no. 1 (Winter 2007): 9.

5. "Articles in American Studies, 1955," *American Quarterly* 8 (Summer 1956): 173, 179.

CHAPTER TWO. FOUR AMERICAN STUDIES MIXTAPES

1. Edwin Bowden, ed., *American Studies: Problems, Promises and Possibilities* (Austin: University of Texas, 1958), 22–23.

2. Richard White, "A Commemoration and a Historical Mediation," *Journal of American History* (March 2008): 1081.

3. Carl Becker, "Everyman His Own Historian," *American Historical Review* 37, no. 2 (January 1932): 231.

4. Robert Spiller, "American Studies, Past, Present, and Future," in Joseph G. Kwait and Mary C. Turpie, eds., *Studies in American Culture: Dominant Ideas and Images* (Minneapolis: University of Minnesota Press, 1960), 210.

5. Jonathan Arac, "F. O. Matthiessen: Authorizing an American Renaissance," in Walter Benn Michaels and Donald E. Pease, eds., *The American Renaissance Reconsidered* (Baltimore: Johns Hopkins University Press, 1985), 90.

6. F. O. Matthiessen, *American Renaissance: Art and Expression in the Age of Emerson and Whitman* (London: Oxford University Press, 1941), 244–45.

7. W. E. B. Du Bois, *The Souls of Black Folk: Essays and Sketches* (New York: Norton, 1999 ed.), 5.

8. Du Bois, *Souls of Black Folk*, 11.

9. Michael Denning, *The Cultural Front: The Laboring of American Culture in the Twentieth Century* (London: Verso, 1997).

10. John Dos Passos, *U. S. A.* (New York: Library of America, 1996 ed.), 2.

11. Matthiessen, *American Renaissance,* 641.

12. C. L. R. James, *American Civilization* (Cambridge: Blackwell, 1993), 146.

13. Ralph Ellison, *Shadow and Act* (New York, 1964), 311, 316.

14. Fred Moten and Stefano Harney, "The University and the Undercommons: Seven Theses," *Social Text* 79, no. 2 (Summer 2004): 104.

15. Franco Moretti, "The Slaughterhouse of Literature," *Modern Language Quarterly* 61, no. 1 (March 2000): 207–27.

16. Gaynor Pearson, "Nationalism in the College Curriculum," *School and Society* 65 (January 11, 1947): 21.

17. "Major in American Problems," *Bulletin of Sweet Briar College* (Sweet Briar, VA: Sweet Briar College, 1932), 139.

18. Russ Castronovo and Susan Gillman, "Introduction: The Study of American Problems," in Castronovo and Gillman, eds., *States of Emergency: The Object of American Studies* (Chapel Hill: University of North Carolina Press, 2009), 1–16.

19. Vernon Parrington, "Economics and Criticism" (1917), in Vernon Parrington, Jr., ed., "Vernon Parrington's View: Economics and Criticism," *Pacific Northwest Quarterly* 44, no. 3 (July 1953): 98–99.

20. Gene Wise, "'Paradigm Dramas' in American Studies: A Cultural and Institutional History of the Movement," *American Quarterly* 31 (1979): 300 (emphasis in original).

21. Vernon Parrington, "Introduction," in J. Allen Smith, *The Growth and Decadence of Constitutional Government* (Seattle: University of Washington Press, 1972 ed.), ix.

22. J. Allen Smith, *The Spirit of American Government: A Study of the Constitution, Its Origin, Influence and Relation to Democracy* (New York: Macmillan, 1907), 228, and Charles Beard, *An Economic Interpretation of the Constitution of the United States* (New York: Macmillan, 1913), 154.

23. Vernon Parrington, *Main Currents in American Thought: An Interpretation of American Literature from the Beginnings to 1920*, Vol. 3 (New York: Harcourt, Brace, 1930), 69.

24. Leo Marx, "Believing in America: An Intellectual Project and a National Ideal," *Boston Review* 28 (Dec. 2003–Jan. 2004), http://bostonreview.net/BR28.6 /marx.html

25. John Higham, "American Intellectual History: A Critical Appraisal," *American Quarterly* 13 (Summer 1961): 222.

26. Louis Wirth, "The Social Sciences," in Merle Curti, ed., *American Scholarship in the Twentieth Century* (Cambridge, MA: Harvard University Press, 1953), 51.

27. Richard White, "Information, Markets, and Corruption: Transcontinental Railroads in the Gilded Age," *Journal of American History* 90, no. 1 (June 2003): 36.

28. Walter Lippmann, *Public Opinion* (New York: Harcourt, Brace, 1922), 10.

29. John Dewey, *The Public and Its Problems* (New York: Henry Holt, 1927), 111, 148. For Jane Addams's influence on Dewey, see Rosalind Rosenberg, *Beyond Separate Sphere: Intellectual Roots of Modern Feminism* (New Haven, CT: Yale University Press, 1982), 33.

30. Lionel Trilling, "Parrington, Mr. Smith, and Reality," *Partisan Review* 8 (1940): 25.

31. Richard Hofstadter, *The Progressive Historians: Turner, Beard, Parrington* (Chicago: University of Chicago Press, 1968), 395.

32. Sarah Igo, *The Averaged American: Surveys, Citizens, and the Making of a Mass Public* (Cambridge, MA: Harvard University Press, 2008), 1.

33. Michael Denning, *Culture in the Age of Three Worlds* (London: Verso, 2004), 199.

34. Basil Hall, *Travels in North America, in the Years 1827 and 1828* (Edinburgh: Cadell and Co., 1829), 109.

35. Charles Dickens, *American Notes for General Circulation* (New York: Penguin, 2000 ed.), 80.

36. Harriet Martineau, *How to Observe Morals and Manners* (London: Charles Knight, 1838), 53.

37. Martineau, *How to Observe Morals and Manners*, 65.

38. Mark Twain, *The Innocents Abroad, Or, the New Pilgrims' Progress* (New York: Modern Library, 2003 ed.), 49.

39. Twain, *Innocents Abroad*, 164.

40. Yone Noguchi, *The American Diary of a Japanese Girl* (Philadelphia: Temple University Press, 2007 ed.), 8.

41. Margaret Mead, "The Study of National Character," in Daniel Lerner and Harold D. Lasswell, eds., *The Policy Sciences: Recent Developments in Scope and Method* (Stanford, CA: Stanford University Press, 1951), 77.

42. Kathryn Marie Dudley, *Debt and Dispossession: Farm Loss in America's Heartland* (Chicago: University of Chicago Press, 2000), xiii.

43. Bruce Kuklick, "Myth and Symbol in American Studies," *American Quarterly* 24 (October 1972): 435–50.

44. Henry Nash Smith, "Culture," *Southwest Review* 13, no. 2 (Winter 1928): 253–54.

45. Benjamin Botkin, "Paul Bunyan Was OK in His Time," *New Masses* (April 23, 1946): 14.

46. Lissa Wadewitz, *The Nature of Borders: Salmon, Boundaries, and Bandits on the Salish Sea* (Seattle: University of Washington Press, 2012), 122–43.

CHAPTER THREE. AN INSTITUTIONAL HISTORY OF AMERICAN STUDIES

This chapter's epigraph is from the transcript of a workshop discussion, later included in Edwin Bowden, ed., *American Studies: Problems, Promises and Possibilities* (Austin: University of Texas, 1958), 21.

1. Sigmund Skard, "Robert E. Spiller: Bridge Builder and Image Maker," *American Quarterly* 19 (1967): 294.

2. "Bowling Green Course: Riding Roller Coasters," *Pittsburgh Post-Gazette,* April 14, 1978.

3. Roy Harvey Pearce, "American Studies as a Discipline," *College English* 18 (1957): 181–82.

4. Edward Grier, "Programs in American Civilization," *Journal of Higher Education* 25, no. 4 (April 1954): 183.

5. Tremaine McDowell, "An Evaluation of the Minnesota Program in American Studies," May 1, 1953, Box 23, Folder 4, ASA Records, Library of Congress, Washington, DC. See also McDowell, "American Studies and the New Interdepartmentalism," *School and Society* 68 (September 25, 1948): 198.

6. George Rogers Taylor, "Undergraduate Programs in American Studies," *South Atlantic Bulletin* 23 (May 1957): 3.

7. Rachel Mellinger, "American Culture: The High and the Low-Down," *Mademoiselle* 40 (December 1954): 92, 116.

8. Mellinger, "American Culture," 115.

9. "Marvin Felheim Is Michigan's Prof of Pop," *People Magazine,* March 7, 1977. See also "American Culture: Only the Open-Minded Need Apply," *University Record* (Ann Arbor, MI), September 26, 1977.

10. Alan Trachtenberg, "Myth and Symbol," *Massachusetts Review* 25 (1984): 668; and Leo Marx, "Believing in America: An Intellectual Project and a National Ideal," *Boston Review* 28 (December 2003–January 2004), http://bostonreview.net/BR28.6/marx.html

11. Lincoln Steffens, "Sending a State to College: What the University of Wisconsin Is Doing for Its People," *American Magazine* 67 (1908–09): 349.

12. Alexander Olson, " 'You have rescued me from academicism': Selections from the Correspondence of Henry Nash Smith and Mary Hunter Austin," *Southwest Review* 96, no. 1 (Winter 2011): 50–65.

13. Tremaine McDowell to Carl Bode, July 7, 1950, Box 76, Folder 9, ASA Records, Library of Congress, Washington, DC.

14. Taylor, "Undergraduate Programs in American Studies," 2.

15. Robert Walker, *American Studies in the United States: A Survey of College Programs* (Baton Rouge: Louisiana State University Press, 1958).

16. Warren French, "An 'Eye' for America," in Marshall Fishwick, ed., *American Studies in Transition* (Boston: Houghton Mifflin, 1964), 37.

17. Percy Boynton, "American Neglect of American Literature," *Nation* 102 (May 4, 1916): 478.

18. T. J. Baker, "American Literature in the Colleges," *North American Review* 209 (June 1919): 781. Identified as a pseudonym in Crane, *American Literature,* 20 (see note 23).

19. Ferner Nuhn, "Teaching American Literature in American Colleges," *American Mercury* 13 (1928): 328.

20. Ernest Leisy, "The Significance of Recent Scholarship in American Literature," *College English* 2, no. 2 (November 1940): 116–17.

21. Fred Lewis Pattee, "The Old Professor of English: An Autopsy," *Tradition and Jazz* (New York: Century, 1925), 210.

22. Gaynor Pearson, "Nationalism in the College Curriculum," *School and Society* 65 (January 11, 1947): 19.

23. William Crane, *American Literature in the College Curriculum* (Chicago: National Council of Teachers of English, 1948), 13.

24. Tremaine McDowell, *American Studies* (Minneapolis: University of Minnesota Press, 1948), 38–39.

25. Sydney Ahlstrom, "Studying America and American Studies at Yale," *American Quarterly* 22 (1970): 508.

26. Bowden, *American Studies,* 17.

27. Crane, *American Literature,* 47. For the timing of this program, see John Gaus to Carl Bode, September 18, 1951, American Studies Association Records, Box 76, Folder 4, Library of Congress, Washington, DC.

28. Alexander I. Olson and Frank Kelderman, "Ad Hoc American Studies: Michigan and the Hidden History of a Movement," *American Studies* 55, no. 1 (2016): 113.

29. Edwin Rozwenc, "George Taylor and the Discipline of Conscious Choice," *American Quarterly* 17 (1965): 293.

30. Taylor, "Undergraduate Programs in American Studies," 5.

31. Allen Guttmann, "American Studies at Amherst," *American Quarterly* 22 (1970): 435, 444.

32. Crane, *American Literature,* 34.

33. Crane, *American Literature,* 49; "American Calendar," *American Quarterly* 6 (1954): 96.

34. Carl Bode to *Land Economics,* ca. 1952, Box 76, Folder 8, ASA Records, Library of Congress, Washington, DC.

35. Wilcomb Washburn, "Memorandum to Chairman of ASA Committee on New Method of Instruction," 1957, Box 80, Folder 3, ASA Records, Washington, DC.

36. Rubin to Taylor, January 17, 1956, Box 77, Folder 13, ASA Records, Library of Congress, Washington, DC.

37. Rubin to Hirschfeld, December 1, 1954, Box 22, Folder 2, ASA Records, Library of Congress, Washington, DC.

38. McDowell to Bode, April 10, 1950, Box 76, Folder 9, ASA Records, Library of Congress, Washington, DC.

39. McDowell to Bode, April 14, 1950, Box 76, Folder 9, ASA Records, Library of Congress, Washington, DC.

40. McDowell to Bode, April 16, 1951, Box 76, Folder 9, ASA Records, Library of Congress, Washington, DC.

41. McDowell to Bode, July 7, 1950, Box 76, Folder 9, ASA Records, Library of Congress, Washington, DC.

42. "American Calendar," *American Quarterly* 4 (1952): 93.

43. *Newsletter of the American Studies Association of Kentucky and Tennessee*, May 1965, Box 21, Folder 1, ASA Records, Library of Congress, Washington, DC.

44. "A Visit to the Factories and Forests for the Teachers of France," August 7–8, 1956, Box 199, Folder 5, ASA Records, Library of Congress, Washington, DC.

45. Carl Holliday, "A Need in the Study of American Literature," *School and Society* 4 (1916): 221.

46. Mary Turpie, in "American Calendar," *American Quarterly* 4 (1952): 287.

47. "American Calendar," *American Quarterly* 5 (1953): 286.

48. "American Calendar," *American Quarterly* 7 (1955): 103

49. "American Calendar," *American Quarterly* 5 (1953): 94.

50. "American Calendar," *American Quarterly* 17 (1965): 283.

51. See, for example, Inderjeet Parmar, *Foundations of the American Century: The Ford, Carnegie, and Rockefeller Foundations in the Rise of American Power* (New York: Columbia University Press, 2012), 97–123.

52. Robyn Wiegman, *Object Lessons* (Durham, NC: Duke University Press, 2012), 201.

53. Eva Cherniavsky, *Neocitizenship: Political Culture after Democracy* (New York: New York University Press, 2017), 39.

54. Carl Bode to ASA Sponsoring Committee, May 19, 1951, Box 87, Folder 6, ASA Records, Library of Congress, Washington, DC.

55. "Minutes of the ACLS Committee on American Civilization," April 17–18, 1954, Box 71, Folder 22, ASA Records, Library of Congress, Washington, DC.

56. Arthur Bestor, Jr., "The Study of American Civilization: Jingoism or Scholarship?" *William and Mary Quarterly* 3rd series, 9 (January 1952): 4.

57. Anthony Garvan, "The Present State of American Studies," *Revista de Historia de América* 33 (June 1952): 49.

58. *Center for Information on America* (1959), pamphlet, Box 74, Folder 4, ASA Records, Library of Congress, Washington, DC.

59. "American Calendar," *American Quarterly* 8 (1956): 194.

60. "American Calendar," *American Quarterly* 7 (1955): 97.

61. "American Calendar," *American Quarterly* 7 (1955): 93.

62. American Studies Association Executive Council Meeting, December 27, 1958, Box 32, Folder 7, ASA Records, Library of Congress, Washington, DC.

63. Carl Bode to Edward Grier, January 30, 1955, Box 86, Folder 9, ASA Records, Library of Congress, Washington, DC.

64. "American Calendar," *American Quarterly* 7 (1955): 102.

65. Brochure for William Robertson Coe Program in American Studies, University of Wyoming, 1954, Box 26, Folder 11, ASA Records, Library of Congress, Washington, DC. See also "American Calendar," *American Quarterly* 6 (1954): 392.

66. Mary Turpie, "American Studies at the University of Minnesota," *American Quarterly* 22 (1970): 520.

67. Josephine Ober, *History of the American Studies Association* (M.A. thesis, Bryn Mawr College, 1971), 48.

68. *The Campus,* February 2, 1931, Sarah Lawrence College Archives, Bronxville, New York.

69. Sigmund Skard, *American Studies in Europe: Their History and Present Organization* (Philadelphia: University of Pennsylvania Press, 1958), 147.

70. "American Studies in Japan: A Summary Report," 1977, Box 189, Folder 26, ASA Records, Library of Congress, Washington, DC.

71. Skard, *American Studies in Europe,* 218.

72. Skard, *American Studies in Europe,* 371.

73. "Aric Nicolaas Jan den Hollander," http://resources.huygens.knaw.nl/bwn1880–2000/lemmata/bwn2/hollanderanj

74. Christina Heatherton, "University of Radicalism: Ricardo Flores Magón and Leavenworth Penitentiary," *American Quarterly* 66 (2014): 564.

75. Henry Nash Smith, "The Salzburg Seminar," *American Quarterly* 1 (1949): 31, 35.

76. Tony Judt, *Postwar: A History of Europe since 1945* (New York: Penguin, 2005): 27.

77. Smith, "Salzburg Seminar," 31.

78. Robert Merideth to ASA Executive Council, November 3, 1969, Box 42, Folder 1, ASA Records, Library of Congress, Washington, DC.

79. "American Calendar," *American Quarterly* 23 (1971): 753.

80. Betty Chmaj, "Reflections on the Second National ASA Conference," *Radical American Studies* 1 (1969): 10, Box 42, Folder 1, ASA Records, Library of Congress, Washington, DC.

81. "American Calendar," *American Quarterly* 17 (1965): 615.

82. "American Calendar," *American Quarterly* 18 (1966): 573.

83. Robert Scarola, "The Politics of Style, or How Dull It's Been," *Radical Amerikan Studies* 1, no. 3 (1970), Box 42, Folder 1, ASA Records, Library of Congress, Washington, DC.

84. Robert Merideth, ed., "Concentric Circles," 1973, Box 82, Folder 6, ASA Records, Library of Congress, Washington, DC.

85. Drew Fortune, "David Lynch on Why He Hates 'It's a Small World,'" *Slate Magazine,* July 17, 2013, www.avclub.com/article/david-lynch-on-why-he-hates-its-a-small-world-100241

86. Robert Merideth, ed., "Concentric Circles," 1973, Box 82, Folder 6, ASA Records, Library of Congress, Washington, DC.

87. Peter Hartley, "Method and Teaching in American Studies," *Connections* (Fall 1971), Box 42, Folder 1, ASA Records, Library of Congress, Washington, DC.

88. Hartley, "Method and Teaching in American Studies."

89. In 1965, nearly an entire issue was devoted to news from the regional chapters. "American Calendar," *American Quarterly* 17 (1965): 770–76.

90. John Stephens, Memorandum on ASA, April 9, 1983, Box 83, Folder 2, ASA Records, Library of Congress, Washington, DC.

91. John Stephens, Memorandum on ASA, April 9, 1983, Box 83, Folder 2, ASA Records, Library of Congress, Washington, DC.

92. Linda Kerber, "Diversity and the Transformation of American Studies," *American Quarterly* 41 (September 1989): 415–31.

93. Martha Banta, "Working the Levees: Building Them Up or Knocking Them Down?" *American Quarterly* 43 (September 1991): 385–87.

94. Mary Helen Washington, "'Disturbing the Peace: What Happens to American Studies If You Put African American Studies at the Center?': Presidential Address to the American Studies Association, October 29, 1997," *American Quarterly* 50 (March 1998): 1–23.

95. Janice Radway, "What's in a Name? Presidential Address to the American Studies Association," *American Quarterly* 51 (March 1999): 1–32.

96. Richard Pérez-Peña, "Scholars' Group to Disclose Result of Vote on an Academic Boycott of Israel," *New York Times,* December 15, 2013.

97. Robert Lucid, "American Studies: Preface," *American Quarterly* 22 (1970): 431.

98. "American Calendar," *American Quarterly* 14 (1962): 643.

99. George Lipsitz, "What Is American Studies?: An ASA White Paper" (2015), www.theasa.net/sites/default/files/What_is_American_Studies.pdf.

100. ASA Directory, 1956, Box 123, Folder 4, ASA Records, Library of Congress, Washington, DC.

CHAPTER FOUR. METHODS AND METHODOLOGY

1. Arthur Conan Doyle, *Sherlock Holmes: The Complete Stories* (Hertfordshire: Wordsworth Editions, 1989), 67.

2. Kenneth Haltman, "Introduction," in Jules David Prown and Kenneth Haltman, eds., *American Artifacts: Essays in Material Culture* (East Lansing: Michigan State University Press, 2000), 1–10.

CHAPTER FIVE. TEXTS: AN INTERPRETIVE TOOLKIT

1. Robert Pirsig, *Zen and the Art of Motorcycle Maintenance: An Inquiry into Values* (New York: HarperCollins, 1974), 191–92.
2. Clifford Geertz, *The Interpretation of Cultures: Selected Essays* (New York: Basic Books, 1973), 6.
3. Jules David Prown, *Art as Evidence: Writings on Art and Material Culture* (New Haven, CT: Yale University Press, 2001), 53.
4. Thomas Hine, *Populuxe* (New York: Knopf, 1986).

CHAPTER SIX. ARCHIVES: A CURATORIAL TOOLKIT

1. Keith Findley, "'Making a Murderer' Shows That Our Justice System Needs a Healthy Dose of Humility," *Washington Post,* January 15, 2016.
2. Jane Bennett, *Vibrant Matter: A Political Ecology of Things* (Durham, NC: Duke University Press, 2010), 49–51.
3. "What Is the It Gets Better Project?" www.itgetsbetter.org/pages /about-it-gets-better-project/
4. For more on the story behind Lennard's research, see Katherine Lennard, "The Running Stitch," *Journal of American Studies* 52 (2018).
5. "Lin-Manuel Miranda Performs at the White House Poetry Jam," YouTube, posted November 2, 2009, www.youtube.com/watch?v=WNFf7nMIGnE
6. Jeff Chang, *Can't Stop, Won't Stop: A History of the Hip Hop Generation* (New York: Picador, 2005), 111.
7. Lin-Manuel Miranda and Jeremy McCarter, *Hamilton: The Revolution* (New York: Grand Central, 2016), 57.
8. Ludwig Wittgenstein, *Philosophical Investigations,* trans. G. E. M. Anscombe (Oxford: Blackwell, 1953), 48.

CHAPTER SEVEN. GENRES AND FORMATIONS: AN ANALYTICAL TOOLKIT

1. Michael Denning, *Mechanic Accents: Dime Novels and Working-Class Culture in America* (London: Verso, 1987), 21.
2. Alicia Garza, "Black Lives Matter Co-Founder to Beyonce: 'Welcome to the Movement,'" *Rolling Stone,* February 11, 2016, www.rollingstone.com/culture/news /black-lives-matter-co-founder-to-beyonce-welcome-to-the-movement-20160211

CHAPTER EIGHT. POWER: A THEORETICAL TOOLKIT

1. "The Racial Dot Map," Weldon Cooper Center for Public Service, University of Virginia, www.coopercenter.org/demographics/Racial-Dot-Map

2. Michel Foucault, *Discipline and Punish: The Birth of the Prison,* trans. Alan Sheridan (New York: Vintage Books, 1995), 168.

3. Michel Foucault, *The History of Sexuality, Volume 1: An Introduction,* trans. Robert Hurley (New York: Vintage Books, 1990), 22.

4. Foucault, *History of Sexuality, Volume 1,* 104.

5. Louis Althusser, "Ideology and Ideological State Apparatuses (Notes towards an Investigation)," in *Lenin and Philosophy and Other Essays,* trans. Ben Brewster (New York: Monthly Review, 2001), 109.

6. Russ Castronovo and Susan Gillman, "Introduction: The Study of American Problems," in Castronovo and Gillman, eds., *States of Emergency: The Object of American Studies* (Chapel Hill: University of North Carolina Press, 2009), 3.

7. Sven Beckert, *Empire of Cotton: A Global History* (New York: Vintage, 2014).

8. William Cronon, *Nature's Metropolis: Chicago and the Great West* (New York: Norton, 1991).

9. Michael Denning, "'The Special American Conditions': Marxism and American Studies," *American Quarterly* 38 (1986): 356–80.

CHAPTER NINE. A FEW THOUGHTS ON IDEAS AND ARGUMENTS

1. The concept of beats and stepbacks is indebted to a writing workshop that Carlo Rotella ran at the University of Michigan in 2009. For an interview outlining his approach to writing, see "I Am Allergic to Abstraction," *The European,* November 6, 2012, www.theeuropean-magazine.com/646-rotella-carlo/647-the-art-of-storytelling

2. Paul Andrew Hutton, "From Little Big Horn to Little Big Man: The Changing Image of a Western Hero in Popular Culture," in Hutton, ed., *The Custer Reader* (Norman: University of Oklahoma Press, 1992), 404–6; James O. Gump, *The Dust Rose Like Smoke: The Subjugation of the Zulu and the Sioux* (Lincoln: University of Nebraska Press, 1994).

CHAPTER TEN. DISPENSER: A CASE STUDY

1. Kevin Gordon and Rebekah Meredith, *Sueña Despierto* (*Dreams Awake,* 2010), https://vimeo.com/10889695

2. "JRT Jr. ESCORT Jumbo Roll Bathroom Tissue Dispenser with Stub Roll," Kimberly-Clark Professional, January 1, 2017, www.kcprofessional.com

INDEX

Addams, Jane, 54, 58–59
Agamben, Giorgio, 238
Althusser, Louis, 230–232, 236–237
American Council of Learned Societies, 84–85, 89, 94
American exceptionalism, 14–15, 238
American literature: literary canon, 26, 48–51, 132; university curriculum, 49, 86–87; vernacular culture, 48–51
American Quarterly (journal), 85, 90–91, 96, 99, 105–108, 112, 159–161
American Studies Association (ASA): annual meeting, 100, 106–107, 239; collapse of, 104–105, 107; commission on the status of women, 100; committee on international exchange, 96; endorsement of boycott of Israeli academic institutions, 106–107; founding of, 85; funding for, 93–95, 104; membership directory, 108–112; presidential addresses, 105–106; radical caucus, 100–104, 109; regional chapters, 90–94, 104–105, 107
American Studies programs: Amherst College, 88–90; Barnard College, 89; Bowling Green State University, 81; Florida State University, 89; Harvard University, 87; Southern California University, 106; Sweet Briar College, 53–54, 87–88; University of Groningen, 96; University of Iowa, 100–101; University of Michigan, 83, 86–88, 106; University of Minnesota, 82–83, 90–91; University of Pennsylvania, 104; University of

Wisconsin, 86–87; University of Wyoming, 26, 95, 100; Yale University, 87, 95
Anheuser-Busch Brewing Company, 93, 262–263
anthropology, 19, 59–65, 130–134, 162, 168
anti-disciplinarity, 18–19, 45, 83
Anzaldúa, Gloria, 13–14, 66, 69, 74
Arnold, Matthew, 48–49, 55, 208–209
assemblages, 162–163
Associated Press, 58
Atanarjuat: The Fast Runner (film), 255

Bachelor (television series), 175, 178
"Backwater Blues" (song), 67
Banta, Martha, 105
Beadle, Erasmus, 207–208
Beard, Charles, 54, 59
beats and stepbacks, 258–264
Bennett, Jane, 72, 162
biopolitics, 238
Bishop, Bill, 15, 65
bitcoin, 256
blues music, 2, 52, 67, 192–195, 294
Boas, Franz, 130
Bode, Carl, 89–91, 93, 95–97
Boulder, Colo., 142–148
Brokeback Mountain (film), 199–200
Browne, Ray, 81
Bush, George W., 150, 153
Butler, Judith, 218–219, 227–233

camp, 171
canon (literary), 26, 44, 48–51, 119, 132

project archive, 166–174, 185, 187, 201,
    274–275
Prown, Jules David, 122, 153
Puar, Jasbir, 169, 172

queer studies, 3, 67, 171, 229–230, 233–234

Radway, Janice, 47, 53, 106, 108
Rankin, Jeannette, 152–153
Rankine, Claudia, 13–14
rent, 242
research questions, 28, 35–36, 126–127,
    254–257, 264–265
Riis, Jacob, 58, 66, 68
Robinson, James Harvey, 27, 54, 57
Rockefeller Foundation, 93–94
Rotella, Carlo, 73, 267, 310n1
Rourke, Constance, 47, 66–67
Rowe, John Carlos, 71, 108
Rubin, Jr., Louis, 79, 90

safe spaces, 102–104
Salzburg Seminar, 96–99
San Francisco State University, 101
Scarola, Robert, 101
scientific method, 120–123, 136, 235
Scott, James, 37, 165, 238–239
Scott, Joan Wallach, 72, 226
Searching for Sugar Man (film), 80
semiotics, 131, 138, 148–153
settler colonialism, 14, 69, 198, 239–240
Sinclair, Upton, 58
Skard, Sigmund, 81, 96–97
slapstick comedy, 67
Smith, Henry Nash, 44–45, 65–67, 84,
    96–99, 159, 202–204
Smith, J. Allen, 54, 56–57, 59
social, definition of, 10–11
social justice, 3–4, 53, 234–240, 295
Society for American Studies, 90–91
speculation, 140, 146–147
Spiller, Robert, 45–46, 90–91
Star Wars (film), 198–200
state power, 234–240, 247
Stephens, John, 104–105
structuralism, 174–184, 216–217
structures of feeling, 16, 262–263

style, 47, 119, 153–156, 195
surveillance, 222–225

Tarbell, Ida, 54, 58–59
Taylor, George Rogers, 88–89
theory, definitions of, 125, 215–218, 234
thick description, 132–134, 143, 153
Thinking, Fast and Slow (book), 109
Tocqueville, Alexis de, 60, 62, 64
toilet paper dispensers: genres of, 278–281,
    291–292; invisibility of labor, 287–291;
    the janitor's dilemma, 288–289; quanti-
    tative expansion, 281; toilet paper
    narrowcasting, 291–292
toxic masculinity, 197, 219, 227–228
Trachtenberg, Alan, 83
trope, 185, 188–190, 201, 261–264
Trump, Donald, 137, 169, 172–173, 229
Turner, Frederick Jackson, 12
Turpie, Mary, 71, 92, 96
Twain, Mark, 63–64, 77
Twitter, 169, 172–173, 213, 223
Tyler, Moses Coit, 86

undercommons, 52–53, 170
University of California, 101, 159
University of Texas, 43–44
University of Washington, 56, 91
urban crime drama, 198

vanishing Indian, trope of the, 176–184,
    187, 189
Veblen, Thorstein, 54, 57, 243
vernacular, 47–53, 63, 66–67, 74, 132,
    192–193, 204

Warner, Michael, 10–11, 72, 229
Washington, Mary Helen, 106
western (genre), 196–205, 211
White, Deborah Gray, 34, 36–37
White, Richard, 45
Wiegman, Robyn, 4, 93
Williams, Raymond, 16, 243, 262–263
Wise, Gene, 4, 56, 104
WPA slave narratives, 33–34, 36–37,
    164–166
Wright, Richard, 66, 68